★ FIGHTING FOR
RECOGNITION

CW01499230

★ FIGHTING FOR ★
RECOGNITION

IDENTITY, MASCULINITY, AND THE ACT OF VIOLENCE IN PROFESSIONAL WRESTLING

R. TYSON SMITH

Duke University Press   Durham and London   2014

© 2014 Duke University Press
All rights reserved
Printed in the United States of America on acid-free paper ∞
Typeset in Minion Pro by Graphic Composition, Inc.

Library of Congress Cataloging-in-Publication Data
Smith, R. Tyson.
Fighting for recognition : identity, masculinity and the act of
violence in professional wrestling / R. Tyson Smith.
pages   cm
Includes bibliographical references and index.
ISBN 978-0-8223-5709-4 (cloth : alk. paper)
ISBN 978-0-8223-5722-3 (pbk. : alk. paper) 1. Wrestling—Social
aspects—United States.
2. Wrestlers—United States.   I. Title.
GV1196.4.S63S65   2014
796.812—dc23
2014005681

Frontispiece photo copyright Mark Stehle Photography

Cover photo by R. Tyson Smith

I DEDICATE THIS BOOK TO ALL OF THOSE PEOPLE WHO FEEL COMPELLED TO FIGHT FOR RECOGNITION. WHETHER YOU ARE AN INDIE WRESTLER, VETERAN, INCARCERATED PERSON, OR ACADEMIC, MAY YOU FIND IT AS PAINLESSLY AS POSSIBLE.

CONTENTS

ACKNOWLEDGMENTS

First and foremost, I thank all of the wrestlers who shared their lives with me. I am truly grateful for their openness, vitality, and passion. I hope that they appreciate this work despite my critical stance.

After the wrestlers, there is no one I thank more than Justine Stehle. She supported me in countless ways for what felt like a countless number of years. She's one of the sharpest and most focused in the bunch, and her insights were invaluable. Thank you, Justine, for always keeping things in perspective and for reveling in the wrestling world (almost as much as I did).

Michael Schwartz changed my relationship to sociology and, subsequently, life itself. I cannot thank him enough for always believing in me. I have never known anyone as accomplished, influential, and skilled as he is (nor so lacking in the unfortunate pretenses that often accompany these qualities). Thank you, Michael, for being a loving, fatherly friend. I hope one day to be able to offer my students the devotion, wisdom, and love that you give yours.

No one has done as much to help me bring this book through to completion as Javier Auyero. Thank you, Javier, for being so attentive, so thorough, and so damn quick to write back—and for letting me take full advantage of your great mind! You have been the epitome of reliability. You inspired me to do ethnography and always to work harder and go further. I'm very grateful for your mentorship and fantastic energy. If I produce even a quarter of the high-quality scholarship you produce, I will consider myself an academic success. Not sure what you run on (other than maté), but I want some. Thank you, too, to Michael Kimmel for his important political work in this area. He loved the idea of this project, and the time and effort he gave to hypothesis and discussion are deeply appreciated. When I felt overwhelmed, he was great at getting me back on course with ideas, strategies, and enthusiasm.

Thanks, too, to Bernard Stehle, who has read more of this book than anyone, for his love and support. Let's continue to "discuss," Bernard. I feel very grateful to have you in my personal and academic corner—but please resist the urge to read this book for errors! Thank you, Lucia Trimbur, for all your openness and generosity. I appreciate our friendship tremendously, and I have great respect for your mind—one of the sharpest around.

My colleagues Colin Jerolmack and David Grazian played a huge role in this book's development. I am truly grateful for their time and insights. Their close readings and supportive critiques improved the book immensely, and I hope they are pleased with the outcome.

The book also benefited from the close readings of a gang of fellow ethnographers, including Jooyoung Lee, Erin O'Connor, Harel Shapira, and Iddo Tavory. They all know the challenges and wonders of ethnography, and I enjoyed our conversations. I am also grateful to a group of scholars affiliated with the Rutgers University Institute for Health: Owen Whooley, Kenneth MacLeish, Azure Thompson, Igda Martinez, Jason Rodriquez, and Zoe Wool. It was great being IFH fellows together. Wanda Vega, Peg Polanski, Joan Picard, Pat Bremer, and Sharon Worksman all helped me over the past few years in administrative, red-tape-cutting ways. Many thanks to them all. Suzanne Nichols at Russell Sage Foundation has been awesome. Thanks for your help, Suzanne.

I am very grateful for the New Faculty Fellowship from the American Council of Learned Societies. Its generosity gave me the time and resources to finish this book. I also thank *Social Psychology Quarterly*, *Qualitative Sociology*, and *Contexts* for publishing parts of this research, giving permission to publish it here, or both.

Thank you to various colleagues related to Rutgers University: Allan Horwitz, David Mechanic, Debby Carr, Joanna Kempner, Chip Clarke, Arlene Stein, Pat Roos, Karen Cerulo, and Phaedra Daipha. All helped this project in one way or another, and I am very appreciative.

Readings by several other colleagues benefited the book: Matt Gutmann, Phil Brown, Gary Allan Fine, Jack Katz, Michael Kennedy, Don

Levine, Douglas Hartmann, and David Gibson. I'm thankful for their insights and scholarly support.

Several colleagues at Brown lent support: Lundy Braun, Greg Elliot, Margot Jackson, Nitsan Chorev, Josh Pacewicz, Dennis Hogan, Karida Johnson, Kristen Soule, Michael Kennedy, and the Contested Illness Research Group members—Alissa Cordner, Meghan Kallman, Tania Jenkins, Bindu Panikkar, Stephanie Malin, David Ciplet, Mercedes Lyson, and Liz Hoover. They've all been generous, wise, and kind. Working with them has been great fun.

Thanks to Naomi Rosenthal for her feedback, time, ideas, humor—and her oranges and sandwiches, too. Thanks to Valerie Milholland and Miriam Angress; their prompt, thoughtful replies always put me at ease and helped turn pages of text into an attractive book.

A number of wrestlers were especially helpful over the years: Nick Dealy, Mark Rattelle, John Cursie, Luis Campos, Lou Savage, Rob Rampino, and T. J. Sitrin. I appreciate their time and assistance with my research.

In no particular order, I also thank various friends and mentors who have been supportive in one way or another on this journey: Susan Finch, Amy Steinbugler, Diane Barthel-Bouchier, Eran Shor, Anna Sher, Amy Traver, Dick Smith, Barsha Lloyd, Erik Love, Helene Lee, Matt Mahler, Dawn Weist, Mary Hopkins, Staci Newmar, Eva Stehle, Sarah Lipton, Barbara Dundon, Nancy Tomes, Dana Valentine, Shelley Smith, Miles Smith, Todd Sarandos, Jed Melnick, Nicole Pittman, Sam Briger, Gala True, and Doc Hopkins.

Austin Kelley and Brian Schwartz are close friends (and great writers) who know a hell of a lot about sports and culture. I thank them for demonstrating how to strike a healthy balance between sports criticism and fandom. Thanks to Mark Stehle for sharing some of his photos for this book. Mark's photographic skills are first-rate.

Big, loving thanks to Theo and Laszlo. You guys were very patient as I fiddled away at a book that surely had way too many "false finishes." Last, thank you, Mom. More than anyone, you inspired my work in sociology and my commitment to reducing inequality. I am eternally grateful, and I miss you every day.

PROLOGUE

THE MAIN EVENT: FEBRUARY 2004

At about 10 PM a lanky, nondescript white guy in his early twenties, wearing a slightly oversized black suit and tie, makes his way to the center of the ring, holding a microphone in his right hand and a white index card in his left. "Ladies and Gentlemen!" he begins. "The moment you've been waiting for—tonight's main event. The NYWW Interstate Championship . . . introducing, from Hollywood, California . . . weighing in at 225 pounds . . . Tony . . . Lethal!"

As the emcee finishes intoning the last syllable, a loud riff from the heavy metal band Anthrax blares from a tinny PA system. White smoke pours out from behind a thin polyester black curtain that separates the wrestlers' backstage area from the audience. Hearing the first few chords of Lethal's signature music, the wide-eyed eight-year-old boy sitting next to me yelps, "It's Lethal!" Three seconds later, a twenty-two-year-old white male, arms raised, steps out from behind the curtain. Adopting a stance of stoic assurance, he slowly surveys the crowd of about two hundred people. His entrance music drowns out the scattered cheers for him.

At 6'1" and about 225 pounds, Lethal is large but not so imposing that he would turn heads. He has an angular face and short, blonde-spiked hair that was dampened just moments before. He wears a black and dark blue polyester wrestling singlet, black lace-up wrestling boots, and a pair of black kneepads. With a bounce, almost a skip, in his step, he makes his way around the ring counterclockwise, high-fiving the young fans who have extended their arms over the metal railings separating the crowd from the performing space. He reciprocates this show of appreciation with a slight smile that conveys to the fans that he is *their* guy, a face they can appreciate, if they don't already. After completing one circuit of the ring, he slides headfirst under the bottom rope before the emcee begins introducing Southern Bad Boy, Lethal's opponent.

Bad Boy, a twenty-three-year-old white man whose home town is "the South," appears in front of the curtains; he holds his signature torn Confederate flag on a short stick and wears a bandana with the same Dixie pattern. Bad Boy has a soft, round face and wears long cutoff jean shorts, red lace-up boots, and a white T-shirt. He stands about 5′8″ and weighs 180 pounds. He sneers at the crowd while, ironically, the heavy bass of commercial hip-hop plays. Despite his clear disdain for the fans, a few kids still extend their undiscerning arms over the flimsy rails to catch a hand slap from him. As he circles the ring, he waves his Confederate flag and rebuffs the young fans seeking a high five. After tossing the short flagpole into the ring, he hops onto the ring apron that edges the mat, about halfway between the corner ring posts. Placing both his hands on the top rope, he uses the tension to vault into the ring. A few dozen fans boo or hiss as he stomps to one corner post and climbs up. With feet apart on the middle rope, he spreads his arms wide. He nods smugly, slowly scans the audience, and wiggles the tips of his fingers back and forth as if to say, "Who's the man? . . . Look at me!"

A young female spectator cups her hands around her mouth and shouts, "Go back to the South!" Bad Boy replies, "You shut your mouth!" Another woman jumps up and snaps a photograph. He looks at her, flexes his modest biceps, and yells, "Hope you got a wide-angle lens on that camera!" A thirty-five-year-old man, who is sitting with a female companion and a ten-year-old boy, yells, "You suck, Bad Boy!" Bad Boy retorts, "Yeah? Well, you swallow!" A man with a darker complexion, perhaps a Latino, yells, "Who won the war anyway?"

Tonight's main event is the culmination of a wrestling show held in the gym of a former elementary school about an hour outside New York City. I have driven from the city, passing through a handful of lower-middle-class white residential neighborhoods that feature cul-de-sacs, Watch for Children street signs, and common suburban detritus—plastic toys, street hockey nets, and movable basketball stands. As I approach the final turn onto Deforest Avenue, a brightly lit Community Center sign can be seen on the roof of the large, late-1950s-designed building.

The ring sits in the middle of the 100' x 60' gymnasium, dimly lit by four florescent lights on the ceiling. The fans in attendance vary in age and race; nearly a third are female. Many young boys of ten or so have come with a family member. Standing in various places, a dozen spectators with handheld video cameras and phones capture footage of the show. A crowd of two dozen guys in their late teens sit with their girlfriends. Roughly ten younger boy and girl fans thrust upward handmade signs that say things like "Knock him out, Lethal!" in support of their favorite wrestler.

Around seven minutes into the title match between Tony Lethal and Bad Boy, their brawl spills outside the building, and the performers leave the gymnasium altogether. Fifteen eager spectators follow them. The wrestlers and these diehards all awkwardly reenter a minute later through doors on the building's other side. The entire gym is now standing as the mayhem continues.

Soon thereafter, they resume their duel within the ring. Lethal is standing, though his forehead is bleeding from a blow to his head with a fold-up metal chair. Bad Boy, who has just been clotheslined by Lethal, is now lying face down in the center of the ring, next to the dented chair that Bad Boy used to bash Lethal's head. Bad Boy's right leg is twitching slightly, but otherwise he lies motionless. The fans on the far side of the gym start to chant, "Table! . . . Table! . . . Table!" The chant spreads across the gym. With Bad Boy incapacitated, Lethal climbs out of the ring and reaches underneath its near side. He pulls out a brown wooden 3' x 5' fold-up table, yanks its legs down, and sets it on the floor alongside the ring. He then rolls back into the ring beneath the bottom rope. Standing up, he circles the ring while thrusting his arms in the air and stomping his feet to the beat of the thunderous chanting of his name.

Meanwhile, Bad Boy has slowly come back to life and is now on all fours in the center of the ring. He gets to his feet but remains slumped over and drooping. Lethal strides toward Bad Boy and, gripping him like a heavy bag of garbage, hoists him onto his shoulders. The grimace on his face and slight wobble in his legs show he's straining, but he is buoyed by his fans, who are now on their feet. The "Table!" chant has become a deafening roar. Taking a little hop, Lethal repositions Bad Boy's crumpled body so that it is now centered across his back. Pausing for a few seconds before screaming out a "Rah!!" he takes four large steps toward the near side of the ring and flings Bad Boy off his back, over the third rope, and out of the ring. Bad Boy's body drops eight feet and crashes onto the center of the fold-up table, breaking it in half. Bad Boy lies in a fetal position at the feet of the nearside fans. There is a split second of hushed silence before the fans start chanting, "Ho-ly shit! Ho-ly shit! Ho-ly shit!" Looking down on the body of Southern Bad Boy, Lethal thrusts a metal chair in the air amid the wild roar of the crowd chanting his name.

★ INTRODUCTION ★

[I've got a] pinched nerve in my neck, several broken fingers, broken wrist.
I have never seen the doctor about injuries in my knees, but they're wearing down. I use to wear just pads, then went to knee pads, knee braces,
and now it's knee pads and knee braces with the springs in the sides. Eventually I'll be moving up to hinges, I can foresee it already. I limp to work
a lot of days. When it rains, it's hard to get up. And for a young guy, that's
not something you hear. I have arthritis, torn rotator cuffs.
—FISHMAN, TWENTY-EIGHT-YEAR-OLD INDIE WRESTLER

Your life literally does a one-eighty, everything totally and completely
changes, and everything's about wrestling. I mean, *everything*.
—DONNY, TWENTY-THREE-YEAR-OLD INDIE WRESTLER

I would rather be struggling to pay my bills wrestling two or three times
a month on the weekends, few times a week during practice. That's what
makes me happy. You know? That's what it comes down to. There's very
few things that make me feel like I do when I walk out [through] that red
curtain.
TONY, TWENTY-TWO-YEAR-OLD INDIE WRESTLER

Professional wrestling is physical theater where spectators pay to
be entertained by performers who act out a fight. The shows, especially those produced by the most profitable company, World
Wrestling Entertainment Corporation (wwe), have made pro
wrestling among the most watched sports in the United States,
capturing roughly 15 million American television viewers every
week.[1]

This book, instead of analyzing why fans love pro wrestling or how the violent spectacle affects viewers, focuses on the performers who generate the spectacle. It follows independent ("indie") pro wrestlers—young men like Fishman, Donny, and Tony—for whom wrestling has become *everything*. It explains why this violent performance is compelling and what it reveals about how young working-class men understand their relationships, bodies, and identities *as men*.

Independent wrestling is community-based entertainment produced for local crowds at community centers, high school gyms, and similar modest venues.[2] Although a form of show business, these events are low-budget. They involve neither television nor lucrative contracts—most indie wrestlers receive little to no pay for performing. Like its highly profitable and televised WWE counterpart, indie wrestling is a spectacle where performers act out a hyperbolic fight. The shows, typically produced every four to six weeks, are funded by ticket sales and advertising from local businesses.

From the standpoint of the performers, the objective is not winning per se but winning the crowd over with a great story. As with certain other cultural phenomena—obviously theater (including such a refined form as opera) but even certain sports—a contest's outcome is predetermined.[3] As vengeful, virtuous, or ribald characters, wrestlers physically settle the score with other performers. Using age-old narratives involving villainy, jealousy, and justice, the contests embody stereotypes, that connection with simplification we often seek in stories.[4] Despite this connective narrative and the sport's immense popularity, professional wrestling is scorned for its violence, profanity, and most significantly, fakery.

Indeed, fakery is a dominant concern of pro wrestling's analysts and detractors. Throughout this book I address the fakery, but it is my belief that the fakery fixation distracts from other important meanings. Besides, it is hardly unique. Fakery is part of numerous forms of our social life—entertainment, pleasures, cultural events, and everyday interactions. Whether consumed through a medium as ubiquitous as religion or as exotic as opera, stories and encounters that help or allow us to suspend disbelief are what people crave. In opera, knowing the outcome is not central to its interpretation as a cultural phenomenon. Contrary to wrestling, an opera's outcome is never the focus of critics or spectators. I contend that a richer understanding of professional wrestling's representation likewise goes beyond form and content to consider the *effect*: What, if anything, makes the story resonate? How does it transport you out of everyday life?[5]

The fixation on fakeness largely stems from the fact that the show is premised as a competitive sport. Sports compose a highly cherished sphere, with reverence reaching almost epic proportions. In US culture it is perceived as offering character building, authentic talent, and virtuous sacrifice. It is a presumptively meritocratic space, where hard work, talent, and skill allow the best to prevail; any evidence suggesting otherwise threatens the larger national narrative of individualism, hard work, and even upward mobility—the American Dream. Thus, when fraudulence or fakery in sports is uncovered—be it from doping, corrupt officials, rule changes, colluding coaches, point shaving, or very unevenly matched teams—a public outcry usually ensues. Yet how, when, and why we heighten or lessen scrutiny of wrestling (or any other sport) is more important than fakery, as far as I am concerned.

Even despite the fakery, as Fishman's litany of injuries (quoted above) makes clear, this "most lowbrow of activities" is intensely physical and often dangerous.[6] The pursuit batters performers' bodies, strains their personal relationships, jeopardizes their day jobs, subjects them to ridicule, and provides virtually no financial gain. So why do these young men choose to wrestle, and what sustains the appeal in the face of so many costs?

To answer this question, I spent more than two years (2003–2005) conducting participant-observation research among indie pro wrestlers associated with the Rage Professional Wrestling School, located in a New York City suburb.[7] I wove myself into the fabric of the group by attending practices and shows, talking with wrestlers ringside, giving them rides before and after events, running small errands (getting drinks or bringing ice for injuries), taking and distributing photographs, and the like. As they practiced, most of my time was spent in the ringside training space or behind the scenes, in the backstage space. On a show night, I was in the performance space, alongside the other spectators, or backstage in the locker rooms. I also conducted nineteen in-depth interviews.

As the following chapters reveal, the indie wrestling experience presents a set of contradictions.[8] The performance celebrates combat, competition, and antagonism, yet the actual show is scripted and choreographed, making it, as already noted, more akin to theater or dance than to contestation or conflict. The story lines trumpet pain and suffering, yet the wrestlers organize their efforts around avoiding them. Aggressive dominance is the primary narrative, but protection, trust, and respect are the principles that guide the performers' relationships. The show is perceived as hypermasculine and crude, but the backstage training involves learning and practicing maneuvers that may be fairly described as effeminate, homoerotic, and intimate. While wrestlers strive to appear as big, nasty, brutes, real-life success rarely derives from body size or the inducement of terror. Performers thrive on social recognition, but they dwell in an isolated world of derision and ridicule. Finally, although pro wrestling is show business, indie performers receive no significant financial remuneration.

Despite the contradictions within this unpaid or, at best, very poorly compensated world of fraudulence and peril, young men forge, sustain, and affirm new identities. Much of what makes wrestling compelling to participants, even though it is an activity organized around entertaining fans, comes from the endeavor's pain, intimacy, and solidarity—and the recognition of fellow wrestlers as well as fans. Indie wrestling does not offer the uncontested, stable gendered identity that combat soldiers or pro football players acquire.[9] Wrestlers flaunt and flex while "performing" dominance and violence, but their act is fraught with ridicule, injuries, and contentions that they are "gay." Given these challenges and contradictions, why do Fishman, Mike, Donny, Tony, and others like them so deeply immerse themselves in this world?

The literature on the interrelationship of men's bodies, physical labor, and identity has grown considerably in the last two decades.[10] Unlike most such ethnographic investigations, where dignity and virtue tend to derive from discipline and hard work within a bona fide production, this book examines the experience of suburban men, mostly white and working-class, who freely choose a recreational pursuit that exacts tremendous financial, bodily, and often career costs. For the most part, wrestlers do not face bleak life chances; they have not been backed into a corner by stubborn social structures, unemployment, deplorable schools, or racism. While most are not likely to attain the same prosperity and degree of class status their parents achieved, Rage School students and trainers, with few exceptions, come from backgrounds that are not riddled with street violence, homelessness, or the revolving door of the US criminal justice system.[11] All but one of the study participants have some family support, high school degrees, jobs, and a measure of white (and male) privilege. These biographical distinctions, combined with the unique attractions and costs of the wrestling practice itself, distinguish this book from earlier ethnographies of young men campaigning for respect. Indie wrestling captivates, nourishes, and punishes, but it is a voluntarily pursuit.

Primarily this book examines why indie wrestlers are drawn to the pursuit, but its secondary focus is an analysis of masculinity. A behind-the-scenes look at the production, risks, and rewards of wrestling reveals a metaphor for the everyday enactment of contemporary Western masculinity itself. Wrestlers subject themselves to pain, risk, and violence for the rewards of solidarity, intimacy, recognition, and pleasure. Insights gleaned from a backstage look at wrestling can allow us to better understand the dynamics of a variety of male performances—be they behaviors of athletes, soldiers, men colluding while out on the town, or even professors posturing among colleagues.

ORGANIZATION OF THE BOOK

To understand the world of indie wrestling, the book moves from the onstage public performance of the show—which includes an explanation of who indie wrestlers are and how their obscure world operates—to the backstage relations and interactions between wrestlers. As with most of social life, the onstage performance the audience experiences is dependent upon a backstage most cannot see or know. In the case of pro wrestling, there is a literal stage (often in the round) and a literal backstage. In addition to these tangible spaces is a figurative backstage, which is concealed—at least until there is a mistake. In this study, I report on all three spheres of pro wrestling's production. My analysis moves from the stage, the public celebration of pro wrestling, to the less apparent backstage, where relations between wrestlers (and their fans, family, and partners) underpin the entire production.

Chapter 1 explains lesser-known aspects of the world of indie wrestling and who indie wrestlers are. Five individuals are profiled to provide a fuller sense of who wrestles and what brings them to the mat. The participants' intense attraction to wrestling is contextualized by the dearth of meaningful forms of community and recognition their larger social circumstances offer. Despite affluence and a measure of continued opportunity, suburbia's social problems in the first decade of the twenty-first century—alienation, under- or unemployment, ennui, poverty—frequently overwhelmed even the rudiments of the promise of an idyllic existence. Indie participation became a means of redressing some of these short-comings.

Chapter 2 turns to social recognition. Indie wrestlers strive for the thrill of experiencing violence without suffering the injury, trauma, or humiliation that it can readily entail. Recognition is fundamental to the formation of identity and a sense of self. Wrestlers attain it with their bodies. An analysis of the rewards and perils of being on stage and at the mercy of an interactive crowd reveals the tools that help each par-ticipant recast personal narratives in the hoped-for passage from being a nobody to becoming a somebody. Wrestlers are recognized yet simulta-neously ridiculed because, as critics and relatives complain, they partici-pate in unpaid, fraudulent, trashy entertainment. Their quest for recogni-tion comes in different forms; beyond the obvious sources—fans clapping, shouting, yelling, clamoring for autographs—are internal rewards. They find recognition for their technical skills, production acumen, and exper-tise with equipment and props. Some revel less in live cheers than in the more lasting recognition captured by videotape and photography. This chapter shows how, despite its subaltern status, indie wrestling becomes an all-encompassing devotion central to its participants' identity.

Chapter 3 looks at indie wrestlers' actual bodily craft. I show how the men learn and execute what I call "passion work"—jointly performed, highly physical work that amounts to a type of emotional labor. Fake violence, not unlike real violence, is difficult to get right, and success re-quires a significant degree of collusion and communication. The analysis of techniques reveals how wrestlers work collaboratively to elicit a partic-ular feeling from their audience *and* from one another. Most understand-ings of emotional labor dwell on its alienating and negative effects, but I demonstrate that within their high-risk setting, wrestlers' passion work generates a meaningful by-product, one neither tangible nor financial but social. A latent product of this violence, ironically enough, is a feel-ing of mutual trust and solidarity. As the "fight" requires highly skilled coordination and a measure of empathy for and from an opponent, the men develop an unstated intimacy built upon empathy, trust, and protec-tion of each other.

Chapter 4 focuses on what pro wrestling tells about the attractions, ambivalences, and pitfalls of "doing masculinity." Wrestling's pugilistic and athletic associations are what initially draw most participants to it. Once they begin training and practicing, however, participants learn that pro wrestling is riddled with intimate touching, tanning, and ridicule. In pro wrestling's backstage, literally and figuratively, we see the dynamics of masculinity's act. In this space, wrestlers cooperate, primp, and ready themselves to look and act as men. Backstage is rife with what our culture deems effeminate acts—intimate, homoerotic, vain, and choreographed behavior. This chapter shows how acting the part of a burly "man" is, counterintuitively, nuanced, delicate, highly self-conscious, and collaborative. I examine men's simultaneous fear of other men and strong desire for their approval and detail how recasting understandings of their behavior reconciles this paradox. Participants develop an understanding of masculinity through achievements marked by duress, status, dominance, solidarity, and professionalism.

Chapter 5 details how pain is fundamental to indie wrestling even though performers strategically avoid pain and injury and explores how wrestlers' interactions shape the ways they interpret the pain they avoid, inflict, and suffer. Pain is part of both the punishment and the reward for those who devote their lives to this gritty, physically perilous, and poorly understood enterprise. By enduring suffering and making sacrifices for one another, pain acquires an attraction, a substantive meaning encompassing self-realization, status, and solidarity.

I conclude by summarizing the book's connection to masculinity and identity. The contradictory behaviors of wrestlers allow us to see the paradoxical aspects of contemporary masculinity. Wrestlers' behaviors, like many other groups', inherently depend upon a set of backstage relations that contrast with the hypermasculine ideals the more public display flaunts and celebrates. In this respect the interactions examined in this book serve as a metaphor that speaks to dynamics well beyond the squared circle of the ring. Men in a variety of contexts present a facade of strength and invulnerability when in fact collaboration, vanity, self-consciousness, and fear are in operation.

Appendix A explains the origins of my interest in indie wrestling and is an analytical summary of my methodology. The study is based on ethnographic research done from 2003 through 2005. The sources include observations and conversations at more than twenty-five public wrestling events and more than fifty practice sessions, in-depth interviews with fifteen core wrestling participants and three promoters (indie and WWE), and numerous participant observations of stage and backstage interactions among wrestlers at their practice site and public shows. The data were gathered through notes, photographs, e-mails, and audio and video recordings. Appendix B is a list of the study's participants.

CHAPTER 1 ★ THE INDIES

The World Wrestling Entertainment Corporation (WWE) brings pro wrestling into millions of homes in the United States and, increasingly, the world. These highly stylized live productions, which assure the publicly traded company annual revenue in the hundreds of millions, have made professional wrestling one of the most-watched "sporting events."[1]

Indie wrestling, on the other hand, consists of regional wrestling promotions with no central organization and little to no television exposure. These scattered promotions operate in the background of the major league (i.e., WWE) and stay officially unaffiliated with it. Indie promotions can be found in nearly all US states but vary widely in terms of longevity, popularity, and profitability. Despite their independence of each other, the two levels overlap considerably in terms of styles, people, and histories.[2] Modeled on competitive sport, both feature a referee, two or more fighters, a ring, and a declared winner after each match. To excite the crowd, indie wrestlers and WWE performers alike largely draw upon tried-and-true narratives, gimmicks, and stunts from professional wrestling's past.

The shows are outrageous by design. Loud, in-your-face performers turn to bashing each other's heads with steel chairs after a verbal argument. Bikini-clad women escort a wrestler to the ring and then cry when he loses his match. Blaring music, smoke, and nearly naked massive protagonists are part and parcel of the spectacle. There is bashing, bruising, and little subtlety; indeed, pro wrestling has been described by scholars as a "land of mask and monstrosity" (Henricks 1974, 178), "non-ambiguous" (Mazer 1998), and "masculine melodrama" (Jenkins 1997). Widely known is Roland Barthes's early, albeit farseeing, comment on pro wrestling: a "spectacle of excess" (1957).

The entertainment is defined by the live, immediate, unfiltered interaction between fans and performers. Without the spectators there could be no such thing as professional wrestling.[3] Henry Jenkins IV, a cultural critic and avid pro wrestling fan, articulates how crucial this dialog is: "When I buy a ticket to a live show, I'm actually buying a ticket to have a tiny speaking part. . . . Wrestling is not a one-way monologue between the producers and the fans; it's a dialogue" (2005, 326).[4]

The emotional exchange epitomizes what Elias and Dunning see as the function of contemporary sports: a ritual where we can discard self-restraint and revel in the show of strong feelings (1986).[5] Central to the appeal is "collective effervescence"—Emile Durkheim's term (1995) for the energy experienced by individuals when an event creates a feeling of shared identity, emotion, and solidarity. With the story lines' "engaging fantasy," the creativity of the staging and props, the hyperphysicality of the performers, and the predictable yet (usually) fair outcomes, pro wrestling has all the ingredients that make violent entertainment appealing (Goldstein 1998, 223).

Importantly, the WWE dominates the entire American professional wrestling industry. While having one smaller domestic competitor that also televises shows, the WWE has remained the indisputable leader for roughly two decades.[6] Because of this dominance, almost all pro wrestlers who move up to televised productions are at the WWE's mercy. Aside from international venues and the one domestic competitor, the WWE is, for all intents and purposes, *the* platform for professional wrestlers. Yet despite its prominence, the company has only 160 wrestlers under contract (*USA Today* 2007).[7]

In most respects, members of the indie scene—be they fans, wrestlers, or promoters—take some pride in their disaffiliation. While they are undoubtedly envious of the WWE's power and influence, many wrestlers and fans maintain, almost as a moral distinction, that indie wrestling is a superior form of entertainment, one that is more community-based and authentic. Tod Gordon, founder of the indie federation Extreme Championship Wrestling, captured the antagonism for the WWE when he described his federation as "the Little Engine that Could" and noted that the

"WWE [has] billions of dollars. We not only have no money, we're constantly in debt. But we've taken off because we deliver what we promise, without marketing and merchandising and pyrotechnics and all that other bullshit" (quoted in Hackett 2006, 23–24).[8]

Indie promotions have come to have a reputation for "extreme" performances, with more violence and spectacle than the "family friendly" entertainment of earlier eras. The extreme-themed shows target a young male audience and emphasize "exciting, risky, action-packed sports that are culturally coded sites of individual rebellion and creativity" (Messner 2002, 82).[9] Indie promotions commonly incorporate high-risk, dangerous stunts that use barbed wire, tables, ladders, chairs, trash cans, and steel cages as props. It is at least arguable that if such entertainment were exhibited under any other classification (aside from war), it would be perceived as criminal.[10] As Klein found with body building, pro wrestling "combines a variety of cultural forms into something that purists have difficulty categorizing. . . . [It offers] an alternative to traditional athletic events by fusing physical development through training with artistic expression, eroticism, and spectacle" (1993, 44).

Story lines and characters are often derivative, exploiting well-worn, degenerate stereotypes of gender and class (e.g., the effete "pretty boy") and of course race and ethnicity (the southern redneck, the urban black thug). While this book's focus is not on how these portrayals are read and understood by audience members, racialized depictions are undoubtedly harmful in their replication of stereotypes. Nevertheless, I suggest that the depictions are no more harmful than the ordinary fare of the mainstream media that litters the airwaves.[11]

With regard to the behavior of indie wrestlers backstage (during practice and training, in the locker room, etc.), racism exists, but it is a far cry from what certain commentators on working-class, poorly educated white men have characterized as racist. I heard outright, overt racial epithets fewer than a dozen times; in half of the cases, the comment was countered by one from a higher-status white person who addressed the impropriety and sometimes even dressed down the speaker. Furthermore, wrestlers of color are no dupes; they actively draw upon, even exploit, racial stereotypes at times. In the core group of Rage wrestlers was one who was Latino. (Two African American men were participants in the larger promotion, but they more peripheral, not core members.) While none of these men had raced-based characters, there were, for example,

FIGURE 1.1. "Don't make me break my probation." CREDIT: Justine Stehle.

two African American brothers, frequent performers at Rage shows, who played demonic pariahs. One of these "outlaws" always wore a T-shirt that stated, "Don't make me break my probation." In his right eye he sported a contact lens that occluded part of his iris, furthering his menacing look. Curious enough, he also wore a beaded necklace (with white, green, and red beads) that bore a small black piece in the shape of the continent of Africa, pointing to his pride in his African heritage. So despite the fact that his character exploits a racial stereotype of criminal black men, he appears to take some pride in his racial heritage. It is my contention that indie wrestlers are no more racist than people found in most other majority-white spaces in the United States. Whatever racism there is resembles that in other communities in which there is "racism without racists" (Bonilla Silva 2010).[12]

FIGURE 1.2. The Indie scene. CREDIT: Author.

The indies' central institutions are training schools and wrestling promotions. The two are often interwoven, resulting in a single organization with overlapping personnel. Principal players are the training school operator, who typically is a former pro wrestling star; the promoter, an entrepreneur in charge of the business end; and the booker, who is responsible for creating the story lines wrestlers enact in the ring.[13] In most cases, the booker and promoter, working together, jointly oversee everything leading up to and on the night of a show. The promoter usually has the ultimate say, as the production is dependent upon his sponsoring of finances, space, license, and insurance.[14] An extended series of promotions involving the same set of wrestlers, promoters, and bookers is called a *federation*.[15]

Generally speaking, training schools are bare-bones operations with limited resources. Beyond the purchase of a ring (a $4000–$5000 expenditure) and rental of a space, there are relatively few operating expenses. Even when schools and promotions are not merged into a single operation, they are usually closely affiliated because of their symbiotic relationship: shows allow trainers and school owners to showcase their students, and promoters need the wrestlers' talent. Aside from state athletic commissions, which set basic licensing standards for various forms of entertainment, there is no governing body that oversees and regulates the indies. Wrestlers learn of schools through word of mouth, via the Internet, or from information found while attending a local show.

Despite the exposure provided by the 2009 Academy Award–nominated film *The Wrestler*, most of the public remains unaware of the existence of the indies. Unlike WWE stars such as The Rock and Hulk Hogan, a well-respected indie veteran attracts little recognition outside his reference group (detailed in chapter 2). It is not uncommon for neighbors and coworkers of an indie pro, whether veteran or novice, to have no knowledge that their acquaintance moonlights as a wrestler.

The ephemeral, fly-by-night nature of indie wrestling makes the scene's size and scope particularly difficult to determine. Even knowledgeable insiders do not know the exact number of its schools, federations, wrestlers, and promoters. Noting that it was "almost . . . impossible" to make accurate estimates, Dave Meltzer, editor of the *Wrestling Observer Newsletter* and the foremost authority on professional wrestling in the United States, offered a "guess" of "upward of 1,000 to 1,500 [indie] wrestlers and maybe 150–200 promotions" (Meltzer 2008).[16]

While the Rage Wrestling School and its attendant promotion are relatively stable relative to other indie promotions, its financial health has not been consistently secure. Costs—rent for the space, pay for the trainers, and general liability insurance premiums—sometimes run ahead of income from tuition and ticket sales.[17] Many indie promotions prove themselves "shady" businesses—schools suddenly shut down, promoters skip town, and performers receive pay (if any) only after the door proceeds have been counted. Several Rage participants described their experiences with other sketchy training schools. For example, the instructors asked them to pay for training in advance (from a month's to a year's worth, in some cases) and then made the first few days of training excruciatingly bruising—using arduous cardio work and aggressive, painful maneuvers ("stiffs"). Students were quickly intimidated and quit, leaving the instructors to pocket the prepaid tuition. Additional factors that make an estimate of the indies' scope difficult are that a high turnover is endemic to the scene because wrestlers get injured (they also have day jobs) and that promoters sometimes mount only one show with no follow up due to lack of financial success. A number of indie promoters are known for producing only a one-time show and intentionally moving on—a reminder of the entertainment's carnival roots.

ADJUSTED DREAMS

Aspiring indie wrestlers typically begin with the misconception that they can make significant money from performing. Most, though, quickly become reconciled to the reality that the activity provides little, if any, compensation and involves several costs: transportation, food, equipment, medical expenses, and occasionally lodging. Cuss, the primary owner of the Rage Wrestling School, recalls his own entry into indie wrestling:

> I had met some guy who said he was a wrestler, wrestled shows here and there, did matches on WCW. Said he got paid like $300 a match or something. I was telling this to Taz [the big-name star Cuss originally trained with], and he said, "Well, you're not going to make nearly that much money. And if you're doing it for the money, don't even bother." So I pretty much knew there, you had to [already] have money. Most indie wrestlers don't make much at all. Maybe enough to cover expenses. . . . [But] most of us do it for free. We'd do it for free anyway. So anything is nice.

As Cuss notes, younger, less experienced wrestlers are usually satisfied to simply be included in a show, and financial compensation is rarely expected. Some shows extend a small stipend for the night's performers ($25–$75 each), but it is very common for them to receive no pay at all. Compensation occurs at the promoter's discretion, and he is likely to base it on the size of the crowd, the number of performers on the card, and the status of the performer.

For a successful veteran performer, the money earned from indie wrestling might supplement another job, but it is not nearly enough to be a primary source of income. After accounting for expenses, a midlevel indie performer may count himself lucky if he comes out about even. There is no provision for health insurance or compensation for sports medicine support or medical trainers; they often prove quite costly given that injuries are so common. Not surprisingly, all indie wrestlers hold down day jobs.

Almost universally, indie wrestlers entering the scene dream of being offered a contract by the WWE. As they come to understand the subordinate position of the indies vis-à-vis the WWE and the steep uphill road, they adjust their dreams. After a year or two of performing, most wrestlers realize that the indies are where they will remain. Fishman, one of the Rage School wrestlers quoted at the start of this book, captures the realigned dreams of many midlevel indie performers:

> Honestly, I take a look in the mirror and I don't think Vince [McMahon, CEO of the WWE] is going to be calling me up anytime soon. So five years from now, I'd like to be somewhere in wherever the upper arm of indie wrestling is . . . [Wrestlers like me should] take a good long hard look at themselves and say, "I'm not pretty enough. I'm not tall enough. If I'm not in good enough shape, I'm only going to make it this far." Then shoot just past that.

Wrestlers usually accept the reality of never attaining big-time, WWE fame as a function of their own deficiencies. Nonetheless, they take a certain pride in remaining distinct from the almighty WWE and prize the indies as a more authentic, noncorporate production.[18]

Family members ordinarily offer only limited support. Donny, who has been part of the Rage School for three years, sums up the typical concerns of those who are close to pro wrestlers: "A lot of people who come into wrestling say their parents don't support their idea of wanting to become a wrestler because they can get hurt, there's really no money, there's no insurance. You know, no nothing." Several other participants conveyed the outright contempt expressed by their family members. Mike, whose remarks about his father's hatred of pro wrestling are quoted at the beginning of this book, says that although his dad has known for years that his son wanted to be a pro wrestler, this awareness has not lessened his hatred of the activity. His father still "can't stand it."

Tony (a veteran of three-plus years) is more specific about the reasoning behind his father's disapproval. While he was initially supportive of Tony's participation, the more his father learned about the risks and health consequences, the more he disliked his son's choice.

> Ever since we were at the show where Droz [former WWE star Darren Drozdov] got paralyzed, at Nassau Coliseum back in '99 . . . that's when my Dad was like, "Are you sure this is the kind of business you want to get involved in? The guy's in a wheelchair now." Yeah. Big mind-changing thing for him. [Before that accident] he was like, "Oh yeah, my son's going to become a pro wrestler." Now he is kind of like, "He's crazy. I don't understand why he wants to do it." And then my Dad's

also, "You don't want to have a normal life? You don't want to have kids, you don't want to see their first steps, or hear their first words?"

Besides highlighting how indie wrestling threatens a "normal" life (and the fatherly expectations that Tony's father holds for his son), the account shows how pro wrestling's inherent dangers are a primary source of the contempt friends and family often feel for what indies see as their calling. Wrestlers try to avoid injuries, but despite the scripted outcomes they happen all the time. Many of the injuries—to head, neck, joints, and spinal cord—have debilitating long-term cumulative effects. Paralysis and even death are possibilities. Moreover, as recent health research on professional football players has exposed, repercussions of repeated trauma to the head can be catastrophic, albeit invisible.[19] Not surprisingly, it is difficult for those who are close to indie wrestlers to accept, let alone appreciate, the appeal of a lifestyle that involves such high risks and takes such an extensive toll on their loved ones' bodies.

For some family members and partners, one way of coping with the men's neglect of their bodies and health is a withdrawal of social support. Timmy is a veteran and senior trainer at the Rage School. His wife takes a dim view of his pro wrestling career: "Her first experience with pro wrestling I split my lip from here to here [pointing to a half-inch scar below the right side of his lip]. And I could stick my tongue through the hole. So she's wanted nothing to do with it since—and doesn't care." As with many other participants, Timmy now pursues this activity without spousal support.

Other participants say their wives, girlfriends, and parents never attend live shows because they cannot bear even the possibility of witnessing such harm. They consider attendance, despite their love for the performer, tantamount to endorsement. In some instances, the relations watched tapes of the shows only after they were over and their loved ones were out of immediate danger.

Because injuries are frequent, they can have far-reaching effects on participants' jobs, education, or personal development even when they are not "serious." In some cases, wrestlers have dropped out of junior college because of injuries they sustained. Dan describes the fallout from an injury of his:

It was bad. After I landed I knew something was wrong . . . because I couldn't put any pressure on my foot. The next day I went to the doctor.

It was broken, so I dropped out. Well, I didn't drop out. I unofficially withdrew because I didn't do any paperwork. . . . It was kind of over-whelming.

This kind of collateral damage, which contributes to a family's or partner's anxiety, fuels a low regard for indie wrestling.

Of course, not everyone encounters negative feelings from close friends and family. Sometimes their choice is met with either a general lack of interest or begrudging acceptance. Cuss shared his mother's reaction to his participation. "She's kind of like my wife in that she's not a big sports fan. But I think when I first told her that I was going to go to wrestling school, she laughed at me for about five minutes." While the exact basis of her laughter could not be determined, it is safe to say that having a child deliberately risk grave physical harm is a choice that many parents would find preposterous or terrifying; hence it might well elicit a nervous laugh. Moreover, little can be done to stop him from participating in an activity that he is hell-bent on taking up, even if it entails injury and derision.

A few participants report that close relatives relentlessly disparaged their involvement until the sport generated a tangible outcome such as money or public recognition. Cuss's wife, I was told, gradually came to accept his involvement as he grew more accomplished: "Originally, she was able to tolerate that I was doing it, then she grew to hate it. But then, you know, as I started getting a little more recognition. . . . You know there'd be someone from the *New York Times* who would come down and interview me, follow me around taking pictures. BBC TV came down and did something on me. German TV station RTL came down. So then, you know, she started to think it was pretty cool. . . . She'd get to see me on TV every once in a while." Timmy bluntly stated his parents' change of heart: "My parents hated wrestling until I bought them a Cadillac." But Timmy's and Cuss's experiences of gaining wider fame and modest fortune are exceptions to the rule; very few indie wrestlers are able to earn money or recognition outside the scene. So those who love men who love to wrestle usually despise the activity as a dangerous and costly choice.

WHO BECOMES AN INDIE WRESTLER?

While the sport of Olympic (competitive) wrestling is offered in many American schools, pro wrestling has never been an extracurricular activity offered by schools or, for example, a community's Police Athletic

League. Indie wrestlers must find training schools on their own, using their social networks or the Internet. There is no recruitment system (formal or informal) for pro wrestlers comparable to the way teachers, coaches, and family might ready a promising young musician for a conservatory or steer a gifted basketball player towards influential coaches, agents, or schools.[20] Those who elect to pursue a wrestling career do so when most other young men are forgoing participation in organized sports in favor of higher education, careers, and significant relationships. Becoming a pro wrestler is therefore far from a predestined identity. By and large, it is an acquired taste.[21]

Aside from one Latino and two African Americans (the latter two participate in shows but are not part of the *core* group that attend regular training), the group members I examine are all Caucasians. They range in age from eighteen to thirty-eight (most are in their early twenties), and ten of fifteen have working-class to lower-middle-class backgrounds. All but one participant (Al) finished high school; most went to large public high schools. While they might have taken classes at a local college, they did not graduate. The majority work part-time in low-level service jobs in the New York metropolitan area, holding positions such as security guard, drugstore clerk, video store clerk, warehouse distribution worker, and customer service representative for a local newspaper. Five of the men did, however, earn bachelor degrees at a local college, and four of these five are public school teachers. Five participants come from a slightly higher socioeconomic background (lower middle class to middle class), one parent in each case having obtained a college degree. Nine are living with one or both parents; four are married and have children.

The largely white suburbs where most of the Rage wrestlers grew up—and where nearly all still live, work, and train—remain a place of American-dream promise, despite evidence indicating that fewer and fewer economic and social opportunities are available there today.[22] Like other Americans, these young men are less financially secure than their demographic was in previous generations. Their social support, generalized white racial privilege, and a modicum of human capital, however, buffer them from the ravages of poverty, racism, and the criminal justice system, which disproportionately assail young men of color in many urban settings.

Nearly every participant was a childhood fan of televised pro wrestling. This early yearning for the bravado of men fighting one another—

a common-enough penchant among American boys, one I can identify with—is an important factor in their path toward performing. All but one reported that their fathers introduced them to professional wrestling through televised programs in the 1980s or 1990s.[23] A youthful passion for televised WWE wrestling, coupled with a desire for possible fortune and fame, commonly animates the decision to find a school and "give it a shot." This initial inspiration is not, however, what keeps participants immersed in the indie scene. As noted above, dreams of big-time WWE contracts are quickly reassessed and battered bodies become the norm. Indie wrestling, we learn, comes to satisfy deeper needs.

In general, Rage wrestlers tend to perceive middle-class lifestyles and opportunities as fleeting; a theme of inadequacy, even humiliation, is threaded through their personal narratives. Like most low-wage workers in the modern American economy, they contend with financial instability in the form of declining wages, diminished job security, and rising income inequality. Indisputably, their day jobs are *not* the locus of their sense of identity. The intensity of their investment in indie wrestling exemplifies what sociologist Paul Willis identifies as working-class men's "cultural turn towards the body and towards bodily and sensuous expression" (2000, 95).

Tony, for example, chalks much of his struggle up to his looks and his family's socioeconomic status. He was not popular with the girls in high school because, as he sees it, he was overweight. "And a lot of the girls are just rich, stuck-up snobs in this area. So . . . you know, if you don't have anything to offer them in ways of money or model-like looks, as far as they're concerned, [you're nothing]."

Fishman shared that his school experiences from just a few years prior involved being the working-class kid surrounded by what he deemed rich suburbanites. "I was a broke kid who was doing butchering at the fish store. And I was doing side work in construction. So I would always show up . . . smelling like fish, driving a really, really beat-up pickup truck. Much worse than the beat-up truck that I drive now. And I pull into the parking lot and there are kids wearing outfits that cost more than my car." He goes on to mention that he "works with his hands" and makes less money than his college-educated brother. With women, he believes he is forever too short and unattractive—never to be with the girl of his dreams.

This outlook contrasts with the fact that he has a girlfriend, a relatively decent job fixing railroad cars, obvious intelligence, and a physique that garners the attention of some fellow wrestlers. Despite his relative stability and success, he views wrestling as the pursuit that prevents him from sitting "on a roof with a rifle, taking sniper shots at people." Even though hyperbole is common among wrestlers, especially Fishman, the sentiment is nonetheless revealing—he sees wrestling as an activity that keeps him sensible and sane. The soul-saving satisfaction he finds in indie wrestling can be hard for outsiders to understand. The general inability to appreciate the indies, Fishman explains, breeds an insularity among members of the indie community. Nearly all his relationships are tied to the wrestling reference group, and his former friends have changed, he claims. "All my friends from high school moved, and got married, and matured and [they'd say to me] 'I don't understand this whole wrestling thing!'" For the family members, spouses, and significant partners of indie wrestlers, the "understanding" required is more complicated, and moving away from or losing contact with loved ones is rarely a viable option.

RAGE SCHOOL WRESTLERS

The remainder of this chapter looks in depth at the young men who perform the spectacle. The profiles that follow of five Rage wrestlers—Timmy, Cuss, Donny, Mike, and Al—flesh out the circumstances that led them to indie wrestling, the skills and dispositions they brought with them, what has kept them in the scene, and how their families have responded to their deep immersion in this calling.

A closer look at the core group of fifteen men reveals significant variance in terms of age, motivations, temperaments, body types, social support, work opportunities, and very importantly, status within the group's hierarchy. From ethnographic data and personal interviews, we see complexities and differences within a group that might appear homogeneous from the outside.

TIMMY

Timmy is a heavyset, thirty-four-year-old white guy. He is married and the father of a newborn child. In addition to wrestling occasionally and making "spending cash" from training Rage students, Timmy works at a shop that makes signs for small businesses. He stands 5'9", weighs 220 pounds, and has a slight limp from his years of wrestling. When he walks, his body wobbles a bit. His usual street attire (aside from the shirt) is not much different from his performing attire: a pair of blue jeans, running shoes,

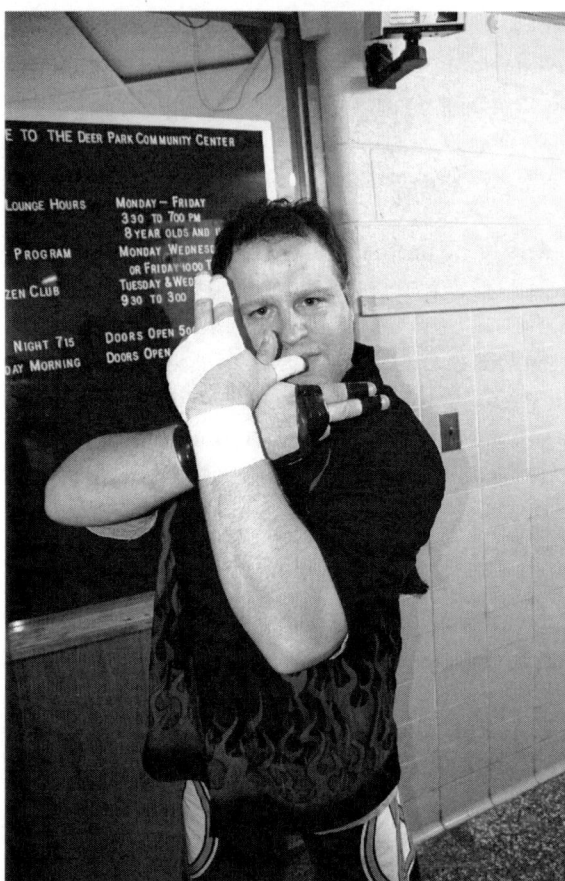

FIGURE. 1.3. Veteran performer and former "extreme" wrestling star. CREDIT: Author

and a T-shirt with Gap or Old Navy printed on the front. He often wears a baseball cap that bears the name of a local business or sports team. When he removes the hat, his light brown hair usually looks frazzled—not in a gelled, spiky way but in an authentically unkempt, have-not-showered-in-several-days way.

He commands the utmost respect among the wrestlers. Having wrestled on television for several years for the Extreme Championship Wrestling (ECW) federation, he is a "known name" in the business, a bona fide star. More than half the wrestlers mentioned Timmy as one of the biggest inspirations for their becoming involved in indie wrestling and, in some cases, for choosing to join the Rage Wrestling School. "I always followed him and watched his stuff. Even on the 'backyard' website when I was in ninth grade, tenth grade," Mike tells me. "So to be able to train with this guy is unbelievable," he continues. "I don't really tell him that; I don't want him to feel weird, but—I don't know, man—it's a pleasure and an honor to train with a guy like that." Five participants mentioned that it was not until they saw Timmy on TV that they realized even smaller guys could become professional wrestlers, let alone achieve star stature.

Timmy is not shy about leveraging his wrestling capital; indeed, he thrives on the measure of intimidation it provides. He is blunt, crude, and utterly uninterested in chitchat, yet when he speaks, everyone listens. If he is suspicious of someone—as, at first, he was of me—he does not directly challenge the person. Instead, he mutters things to other wrestlers, like "Who the fuck is that guy?" He is also quick to seize on opportunities to deliver a put-down. So like everyone else, I found Timmy intimidating. It was only after I interviewed him that he finally showed me more respect. I believe that I represented a threat to Timmy because, as a nonwrestler, I had less need for his approval, and unlike him, I was college educated.

As a teenager, he went to a large high school located in a white working-class/lower-middle-class neighborhood on Long Island. Timmy recalls having missed 130 school days during his senior year despite still managing to graduate. He feels that he never had the aptitude for academics; school was just not for him. "See, I don't understand, when it comes to English, the function of the preposition, the subject, the comma after . . . I can't pick that up. *That* I can't do." Professional wrestling, on the other hand, always came easily. When asked why it was easy for him, he not so modestly responds, "I just had it. I'm a natural at this."

In the late 1990s, while he was still in his twenties, Timmy rose quickly to star status within the ECW. His success brought him money and fame until the federation came to an end in 2001. He was known for performing in amazing matches and executing stunts that epitomized the hard-core, extreme style of pro wrestling that flourished at the time. His character in the ECW (virtually the same as the one he uses today) was a madman "face" who had been part of the ring crew until the booker, Paul Heyman, noticed his skills and asked him to wrestle. Known for being crazy and absorbing punishment, he has retained his ability to enact a vast repertoire of haunting facial expressions that efficiently tell stories to fans. Timmy is charismatic and highly skilled at "psychology," the term wrestlers use for the interaction with fans. Even apart from his household name-level recognition, it is easy to see why he is a fan favorite in the indies.

Having been in the business for many years, Timmy has incurred numerous injuries. Fortunately for his wife and child, he has scaled back his bodily risk considerably. He is in the ring only about once a month, and he now takes a very different approach to performing. As he says, "I can't lift weights because everything pops and cracks. So I try to do cardio, but that's tough too. At this point, I get kind of lazy, where I don't care anymore. I'm only wrestling *here*, I don't want to wrestle anywhere else. . . . Here it's fifteen minutes from my house. I could be home as soon as the show's over." Timmy's current focus is training new wrestlers at the Rage School and putting together creative scripts for the promotion.

CUSS

Cuss is the school's most senior member and its primary financial sponsor. He is also the highest earner in the group. With his stiff gait, "high and tight" Marine haircut, and beefy 5′8″, 205-pound body, Cuss resembles a menacing state trooper. As a performer, though, dressed in black trunks and orange boots, he projects a more benign—and more flamboyantly dressed—face, one whose role usually involves punishing sneaks and cheats. Out of the ring, Cuss wanders around in jeans, running shoes, and a T-shirt with the logo of a popular rock radio station. When not in this casual outfit, he wears high-end suit pants, an oxford shirt, and wingtips— remnants of the attire at the Manhattan financial firm where he works.

Cuss, who is thirty-five, came to pro wrestling much later in life than other wrestlers. When he was in his early thirties, already a well-paid employee of a New York City financial firm and the father of a young daughter, he wanted a change. "I just realized I didn't like what I was doing. I was trying to think about what I would really like to do." Having completed Marine boot camp (as a reservist) eight years prior, he knew he was "strong enough . . . [so] I figured if you can do that, you can do anything." In addition, Cuss and his three brothers—one older and two younger— "always played something" in the nearby middle-class white suburbs where they grew up. He participated in football, basketball, hockey, lacrosse, and wrestling, and since age eighteen he has lifted weights. He considers himself "strong and able to do this stuff."

What kept Cuss from entering pro wrestling earlier was his height. But one night he saw Timmy wrestle on TV. "I used to watch wrestling and all the guys were 6′5″, 300 pounds. So [when] I saw like Timmy [on TV and he was] like my size, I was thinking, why not give it a shot?" He paid $3,000 up front and became the first student at a new school run by wrestlers affiliated with ECW. Both his mother and his wife found this decision ludicrous. "I was thirty-one years old, working in a top investment bank, you know?"

Wrestling has taken its toll on Cuss. Like other veterans, he has sustained an array of injuries. "I've pretty much been injured since '97. My shoulder, my knee, three herniated disks . . . actually both my shoulders, this AC joint over here in my shoulder is three-quarters blown out . . . all from wrestling. It was a tear of the meniscus in my left knee, which I did playing basketball when I was twenty. It got better, but I reinjured it wrestling. And I went to rehab for that for like three months, the herniated disks come and go, sometimes they're okay, sometimes they flair up and it's hard to walk." These injuries, coupled with his accumulated wrestling savvy, have prompted him to change his style of performing. "Now I realize that I don't have to do as much. . . . You can kind of tell what the crowd wants. I don't have to kill myself anymore to get a reaction."

As with Timmy, I initially found Cuss intimidating. He does not volunteer information, and he wastes no time on niceties. He is quick-witted and given to making cracks about people's clothing, girlfriends, or sloppy thinking. Like the rest of the group, he has a decidedly juvenile side that revels in pranks and toilet humor (e.g., asking the group, "Hey, what did the asshole say?" and answering with a fart). At times, his taunts are laced with the homophobia that permeates the interactions at Rage (e.g., addressing the fact that one of the students has been sleeping on the couch at a trainer's house when training runs late into the night, Cuss taunts, "Sounds like Patrick's got a real soft spot for you, Al. . . . It's called his asshole!"). Most of his humor is good-natured ribbing, and almost everyone, including the target, enjoys it. For instance, we all laughed after Louie, a die-hard fan who has cerebral palsy and uses a wheelchair, accidentally bumped it into Cuss's car and Cuss demanded, "You got insurance on that thing, Louie?"

When he is serious, his attitude fluctuates from terse verbal support to harsh reprimands to nonchalant indifference. He might, for example, humiliate a student who is trying his best by commenting, "You have been here nine months and you don't know a hammer lock?" Or after someone fails to properly execute a move, he might ask, "What, you don't want to hurt your vagina?" Overall, Cuss practices a sort of "tough love" paternalism—including maintaining a cold indifference to wrestlers' injuries or struggles.[24] Nor is he averse to pulling rank. If guys are being irresponsible (physically or otherwise), not listening to him, or failing to pay their monthly dues, he throws his weight around.

Yet in private, Cuss seems sympathetic to individual wrestlers' problems and concerns. He is conscious of how much everyone seeks his approval, and even away from the group, he is hesitant to say anything disparaging about group members. Although he is careful to avoid characterizing his school as soft, he does describe it as supportive: "A lot of schools . . . you just go and you pay your money and they beat you up and that's it. We're really like a family, everyone's pretty close, everyone's there to help each other. No one really has an ego. . . . [I'm] not saying make it easier for the guys, but I don't want these guys to have to go through the stuff that I did." Of course, it is also true that when he started the school, he was not in a "position where I could afford to lose a lot of students. You know, if I kicked a guy in the head, he's not coming back. You know, I wasn't subsidized by ECW or a big company, so we needed all the guys to stick around and help pay the bills. . . . We made it tough enough to where guys would appreciate it, but not so tough that guys would quit."

Cuss has mixed feelings about being the primary steward of the school and promotion. At one point during my fieldwork, the school was going beyond his limit of financial responsibility, and Cuss began to make plans to relinquish the operation to others. When I ask what was making the financing so challenging, he told me, "You know, guys stopped coming, guys stopped paying, all these guys lose their jobs." Compounding these concerns is the fact that he bears more of the burden of others' costly mistakes. For instance, the promotion lost money when the group produced a show at a local high school and invited some expensive outside "talent."[25]

Nevertheless, it is apparent that Cuss would have a hard time letting go even if he consistently lost money. He likes performing, he cares about the guys, and they almost always help him. Recalling a point when he was in a jam, Cuss says, "Everyone just wanted to help. They knew I was kind of in a bind. And you know, I've been hurt a lot, so I couldn't do as much physical training as I wanted to. You know, Slaughter had a lot of experience [and] he wanted to help. Donny and Tyler [have] been with me since the first day we opened. So they all want to help."

Although Cuss tries to conceal the fact, you can tell he really wants to be liked and respected. He always sought my opinion of the recent show, and whenever I brought my girlfriend to a promotion, he never failed to ask me afterward what she thought of the show. This concern with how others view him makes Cuss much less graceful at the boasting and bravado that are the scene's common currency. Take the occasion the group went to dinner at a local restaurant after a training session. When a relatively new member asked if the salad the waiter put in front of Cuss was the only thing he was eating, Cuss immediately bristled, retorting, "What, you think all I'm going to eat is a *salad*?" While many actions provide fodder for teasing, that a comment about eating a salad could strike a raw nerve reveals a certain fragility.

DONNY

Donny is an outgoing white twenty-three-year old who has been with the group for nearly three years (more or less since the school opened). He stands around 5′9″ and weighs approximately 170 pounds. With his round face and brown, puppy-dog eyes, he vaguely resembles Scott Baio, the teenage TV heartthrob from the '80s. Although moody at times, he is generally warm—quick to say hello, often as a hug or a gruff (albeit endearingly intoned) "What's up, asshole?" as a greeting.

Donny's background and living situation are like those of many of the other wrestlers. Although he credits his father with initially exposing him to pro wrestling, he does not really know his dad. He lives with his mother and older sister in a lower-middle-class suburban neighborhood an hour outside New York City. This arrangement, he explains, "makes life a hell of a lot easier. I don't have to pay for rent or anything right now. Ya know, it's nice to sit at home right now. Ya know, I think I am at the point of my life where right now, there is only two things in life. It's work and wrestling. Yeah, I do have a girlfriend, ya know; it's a nice relationship, and I love her to death. But I can't think about marriage."

After graduating from a high school in a nearby town, Donny tried college but soon dropped out. "And really what happened was, I wasn't really too hooked on high school, I wasn't the best student in there. So I went to [a] community college and it was just horrendous. I didn't want to be there. I think I gave it a shot just for my mother. I went there, I'm sitting in that class and I'm like, 'What the hell am I doing here? I think I really just need to go to work.'"

Donny works from 5 AM to 1 PM, five or six days a week, loading packages onto UPS trucks headed out for delivery. Most of his coworkers are older than he is. The job gives Donny a sense of adult accomplishment and the attendant pride. He is aware of his good fortune in having a long-term,

FIGURE 1.4. Posing for fans' photographs during the show's intermission.
CREDIT: Justine Stehle.

unionized job that is more secure than most of his friends'. He also appreciates that he has good health insurance through the company's group plan. However, wrestling is his unqualified top priority. Paid employment is simply a means to this end. Although he does not pay rent, the monthly payments on his 2003 Honda Civic Deluxe Edition are high, and beyond his ordinary living expenses, he has additional costs related to wrestling.

He credits the discipline and difficulty of wrestling training for his newly found maturation as a young adult. As with eight or nine others in the group, Donny was not a jock in high school. He never considered himself physically gifted, and he felt anxious about his body image and athletic ability: "Yeah, I was smaller and I was very nonathletic. I've never done any athletics in my life. Well, I played a bit of street hockey . . . but other than that [and] street basketball, I really don't think I played anything that qualifies as athletics or [as my being] someone who used to play sports. So me, I walked in [to Rage], talking twenty years old, never ever had any athletic ability." He gained a sense of accomplishment by persevering through the grueling training, thereby gaining the respect of the Rage School veterans.

Donny is in the middle stratum of the group's often fluctuating status hierarchy. Like most of the lower-status wrestlers, he pays close attention to the opinions and advice of the veteran performers. He is not as naturally gifted (dramaturgically or physically) as most of the other young men in the scene; that is, compared to those who have as much experience as he does, he is a "lesser." However, he works hard, is not afraid to ask for help and advice, and is very keen to improve. When Donny is around the veterans, he makes a lot of self-deprecating remarks, seeking to establish himself as an eager subordinate in pursuit of mastery. In front of younger, newer wrestlers with even less status, however, he does not want to appear inferior. This may account for his sometimes moody behavior; he wants to assert authority, but it comes out often coupled with bravado and an anger that masks—or reveals, depending on one's perspective—a deeper insecurity about his abilities. In private conversations with me, he expressed his fear of certain moves and matches. Since such candor is taboo within the group, I found these admissions rather refreshing.

Despite being a decent performer, Donny is unlikely to advance much (if at all) beyond this indie federation. He seems a bit lost as a character, and this undermines his crowd appeal. He has never found the perfect fit as a character fans either love or love to hate. Initially he was encouraged by a big name to perform as a gay wrestler, with a provocative name that included a not-so-coded reference to male anatomy. This minstrel-like parody, which included hot pink outfits, boas, and over-the-top effeminacy got him lots of cheers and laughs, but after a year and half or so, he came to feel that this role was "not serious enough." He first switched to being a straight wrestler who nevertheless wore pink and had highlights in his hair; then he became a brooding, bulked-up, long-haired tough guy who kept his bottom lip jutted out (presumably to look more scary, although arguably more chimplike, too). Neither of these changes really resonated with fans—or, it seems, with Donny. He continues to long for the old days when the house went crazy over his flaming gay minstrel character.

Like his fellow wrestlers, Donny identifies as heterosexual. For about half of the time I was in the field he had a girlfriend (they later broke up). Donny's numerous acts of affection toward other wrestlers, like an arm wrapped around a friend's waist for half a minute, suggest genuine affection and maybe even greater comfort with his feelings of love for the other wrestlers. When such moments exceed *others'* comfort level and Donny is brushed aside, he looks as though he has suddenly been reminded of the norms against tender, outside-the-ring affection. On several such occasions I heard him blurt out "Now I want to fuck you more!" Comments like these are not usually remarked upon since such brusque sexual language is commonplace—part of the larger milieu of gestures and dialogue that blend sexual language and dominance. But Donny's statements have a different exuberance than others' do.

MIKE

Mike is a handsome white eighteen-year-old with short brown hair; he stands about 5′11″, weighs 180 pounds, and is very fit. Although quiet, he has a warm, humble demeanor. Of all the group members, Mike has a body type that most closely resembles the ideal of an Olympic wrestler: not a chiseled muscularity but a marbled look of strength and toughness. When we first met, Mike had been a member of the group for nine months. A North Carolina native, he relocated to Long Island to enroll in the Rage School.

He now lives with his father in Riverhead, a town about an hour away from the school. Mike grew up living with his mother and does not get along well with his father. Still, he describes the transition to living with his dad as going better than he had expected. He says he did not expect much because his father, an auto mechanic, is "the angriest man I have ever met in my life." Despite the strained relationship, Mike respects his father enough to describe him as amazingly good with cars and able to fix anything. However, since Mike has no interest in cars and his father has no interest in wrestling (as noted above, he hates it), the two men have little in common. For companionship, they sometimes drink beer together.

Mike works at a retail store that sells outdoor sheds and has a big gift shop. He says, "They pay $10 an hour and I don't do anything all day, nothing at all!" He got the job after walking in and saying that he was from North Carolina and looking for a job. "They [were] like, 'Oh, you go to school?' And I was like, 'No.' You know, I can't tell them I like wrestling, [so] I was like, 'I want to be a cop.' They were like, 'Oh, okay. You're hired.'"

He finished high school in North Carolina early (having taken several liberal arts classes that he received credit for) but has no plans for college. No one in his family has ever gone to college. One of the most intellectually sharp people in the group, Mike is insightful about life both inside and outside wrestling. He seems very wise for his age, and it's easy for me to imagine him thriving in the educational environment of a liberal arts college if he were ever so inclined.

Mike's desire to attend the Rage School was not the only reason he moved to New York. In North Carolina, there were few opportunities of any kind, and his life was spiraling downward. He drank and did lots of drugs with his "boys."[26] "There is nothing down there," he explains. "[Taking drugs is] all you do. . . . I had to get away from all that. I had to step away from the party. And once you do step outside and look back, you feel sorry for them. They're your best friends, but they're two, three years older than me, doing the same stuff. It's like, 'Who are you going to be, man? Where are you going to go?'" Being thankful that he left does not keep Mike from missing his old friends. He mentions them appreciatively numerous times. His longing for these buddies is heightened, I suspect, by the fact that he is still somewhat new to the wrestling group and has not yet been entirely woven into the fraternal fabric.

Mike has always been a wrestling fan. He started doing backyard wrestling with a trampoline when he was in sixth grade.[27] Then in ninth grade, he and his friends built a ring. "It wasn't a good ring, but you know, off the ground about three and a half feet, twelve by twelve. It was more than any other backyard fed had!" Mike became known for high-flying stunts and wrestling prowess. Many of his ideas came from watching the ECW shows on TV. "We were watching hardcore stuff at the time," he tells me. "You see Timmy come out with the flaming baseball bat that week on TNN, [you can bet] you were gonna be out there on Sunday with a bat that was on fire." The backyard stunts were taped, passed around school, and posted online. "We always taped it. The fun part was watching it later, you know?" By his sophomore year, Mike had quite a reputation. "Everyone sees it, and that kind of gives you some respect to begin with because these guys think you're crazy. So I never got picked on or nothing like that. . . . Everyone was cool with me. The whole football team was like, 'Oh, this guy is crazy!' They'd break me limb from limb, but when they see this, they think this guy is crazy. So, okay, I won't deny it."

By the end of his junior year, however, Mike and his buddies had stopped doing backyard wrestling because they were getting hurt too much. Later, shortly before leaving North Carolina, Mike witnessed a kid sustain a serious, life-altering wrestling injury. Even though he and this boy were not well acquainted, Mike joined him in the ambulance, racing to the nearest ER, which was almost fifty miles away. He was the first to see the boy's mother as she walked in, bawling, "not knowing if the kid was going to live or not." The boy survived, but he no longer wrestles and is a "little slow and has vision problems."

I witnessed many moments of stark humility on Mike's part. He is new enough to the group to still experience a mild state of shock when he finds himself in the ring with men who were the wrestling stars he used to watch endlessly on TV. On the night he met Mick Foley, a pro wrestling legend, Mike confided to me that he "could not believe it." He was suiting up in the same locker room with a legendary wrestler and getting to perform in the same shows. He was starstruck. Later that night he told me that he had planned on "asking him [Foley] to sign a painting I did of him in tenth grade, but I knew the guys would give me too much shit, so I didn't." When he talks about the satisfaction of wrestling, it is not the fans' recognition he emphasizes; rather, he speaks of his interest in getting the recognition and attention of the veterans and older members of the group.

AL

Al is a nineteen-year-old white wrestler who has been with the group for just over a year. He has short, spiked hair and an innocent-looking face, but when necessary he can look tough. His strong, chiseled physique is impressive. The fact that he is only "five feet, and three and half inches," however, makes him the target of endless ribbing from the group. Al maintains a good attitude through it all. There is a radiant, youthful energy about him.

I sometimes give Al a ride to the train station because this cuts his commute time in half. He travels three times a week from Staten Island to the training gym, using public transportation. His journey begins with a bus ride to the Staten Island ferry terminal; next, he takes a ferry to Manhattan, followed by an uptown subway to Penn Station, where he catches a

FIGURE. 1.5.
Standing strong
backstage. CREDIT:
Author.

train to Long Island. Then he walks the final 1.5 miles from the train station to the gym. The three-hour journey each way is bad enough, but since
the train is running infrequently by the time he finishes at the school, his
return trip can take as long as five hours. He often stays overnight at fellow
Rage member Patrick's place, sleeping on the couch.

Among the group members, Al has faced—and continues to face—the
greatest personal hardship. He has the smallest network of social support; the only family member he knows is his grandmother. His mother's
house was so run-down that the state deemed her unfit to keep him. A
social worker and a police officer appeared at the door of his first-grade
classroom one morning. They entered the room and took him away. "My
mother did not want to take care of me," he explains. "She was a complete
bitch." More or less raised on the streets of New York City, he was shuffled

in and out of numerous foster care homes and institutions. He says he hated the "diagnostic centers" because they were "like a jail." From eleven to sixteen, he was fortunate enough to remain with the same supportive foster care family. In the three years since then, however, Al has been in more than fifteen different living situations all over New York City. Many were in neighborhoods with lots of violence; he has been robbed, jumped, and beaten. Not surprisingly, he is the least educated of the group and seems to have the least amount of money (or access to it). He did not finish high school but is interested in earning a GED.

Al believes that being the only white kid in an all-black neighborhood explains why he got into a lot of fights. Unlike most of the other guys at the Rage School, he has long experience with true random street violence and has proved himself tough. Although he "does not like to see them," he has witnessed "a lot of brutal fights." He showed me scars from his own fights. One sizable mark on his right-hand knuckles (still visible when he makes a fist) is from a tooth that he dislodged from another boy's mouth as they fought in an orphanage cafeteria. Echoing the old adage, he tells me that although he did not start that fight, he did *finish* it. He does not like seeing people getting beaten up. There is "no need for that."

Since he was seven years old, Al has dreamed not only of being a pro wrestler but of being a victor, holding the WWE championship belt above his head. He remains a faithful fan of the televised WWE shows. I often heard him and some of the other young wrestlers exchanging news about recent episodes. He would love to be a sufficiently popular WWE champion that people would "have my action figure." He wants to "have a name for myself" and "wants people to recognize me." Elaborating on these desires, he says,

> I don't want to be the guy who sits behind the desk. Right now, I am waitering as a barback at a restaurant. I don't wanna do that shit! I don't wanna serve people! Fuck 'em! I wanna be a wrestler. I wanna entertain. My goal since I was little was to be somebody. Someone who stands out, who's special. Not to be above people—that's not the case. I just wanna be *somebody*! Since I had nothing as a kid, I wanna have stuff as an adult. I guess that's what I like about it.

Al is very low in the group's hierarchy. In addition to being short, a lead trainer thinks he's slow to pick up on things. Because of this status, Al is assigned many lowbrow gimmicks and stunts when he is performing in the ring; since he is eager to be a wrestler, he cannot afford to refuse such assignments. The bookers exploit his size to create further spectacle. One night Timmy told Al to repeatedly "hump people and the corner posts" whenever he was in the ring. While he was running around like a dog, humping people's legs, Al came up with the line, "C'mon, everybody's doin' it—it's cool!" He reports that the guys loved it, and that night he garnered lots of laughs (and attention). But it is clear that he had mixed feelings about generating recognition from this kind of disparagement. He loved the attention, but since he wants to be "taken seriously," this minstrel role was, at best, a mixed blessing.

Like Mike, Al is amazed that he now communes with former big-name WWE stars. On the night he met Marty Janetty, a former star who was one of the legendary Rockers (with Shawn Michaels), I half-jokingly suggested that Al tell Janetty that he had dressed up as him for Halloween just a few years earlier—a detail Al had mentioned during our interview. "Are you kidding?" he quickly retorted. "No way!"

The Rage wrestlers share a working-class background but range widely on various personal and social measures, including income, marital status, body size, athletic experience, and self-esteem. Cuss works in a well-paid corporate finance job, Al has been orphaned and gets by working as a barback, Cobra is a gifted athlete, the Latino excels at embroidery, and Brickman is handsome, athletic, married, and stably employed as a high school teacher. The variety disrupts any propensity to categorize this as a strictly working-class white phenomenon.

Having said that, the overall socioeconomic status and white racial privilege of most, while modest, extend a modicum of opportunities that slightly buffer the ravages of modern inequality. Unlike the dangerous violence surrounding many young impoverished men, pro wrestling is not a last resort, a back-to-the-wall option. Indie wrestling is a voluntary activity—opting out is possible at almost any time—in which men *elect* to subject themselves to the hardships, pain, and sacrifices that this activity entails. Electing to suffer from concussions and herniated disks (for little to no pay) demonstrates the truth of this contention, above and beyond the immense gratification and pull of the pursuit. Any generalizations to be made would need to include steadfast commitment to craftsmanship within a recreational pursuit that consumes a huge part of life. There is, furthermore, the spectacle of young men striving for a solidarity they are unable or unwilling to find in any of life's other social realms.

These portraits also show how indie wrestlers might have ended up doing something completely different with their time, energy, and bodies. "One of the most significant facts about us," Clifford Geertz notes, may be that "we all begin with the natural equipment to live a thousand kinds of life but end up in the end having lived only one" (1973, 45). In due time (and with due commitment), wrestlers' lives, bodies, and mentalities come to look as if they were predestined for pro wrestling when, in fact, this social world could have ensnared entirely different individuals.

In this regard, the indie wrestling, like other all-encompassing, intensive pursuits, makes its veterans appear a natural, predestined species of their habitat, whereas the skills, bodies, limps, and devotion they exhibit largely derive from intensive training, commitment to the craft, and some combination of body-disciplining regimens. Contrary to the stereotype of professional wrestlers as monstrous, intimidating men who draw upon inherently aggressive instincts, indie wrestlers have ordinary dispositions, average physical talents, and, at least initially, standard body sizes.[28]

CHAPTER 2 ★ FIGHTING FOR A POP

WRESTLER RECOGNITION

No act is so private it does not seek applause.
—JOHN UPDIKE 1996

Professional wrestling contests are among the most watched sporting events yet also among the most reviled. As millions watch weekly and politicians court their fan base, events are routinely ridiculed by various media commentators.[1] In the midst of this noisy adoration and scorn lies a personal validation that motivates the sport's participants, especially indie performers who pursue it for reasons that have little to do with money or profit.

Choosing to leap off ladders, occasionally shatter vertebrae, and receive scorn for doing so—all for little-to-no pay—makes little sense until we grasp the various rewards that spring from the experience. This chapter explores pro wrestling's recognition—moving from the larger, cultural understandings of pro wrestling to the personal, everyday deterrents, including financial and bodily costs and derision from friends, family, and coworkers. I discuss the centrality of recognition to identity before turning to an explanation of the participants' deep immersion and the inescapable hold that the indie world has on their lives. This discussion is followed by an analysis of the various forms of recognition found within the indies.

PUBLIC DEPICTIONS AND UNDERSTANDINGS

Pro wrestling blends sport and drama into a campy extravaganza of physicality and emotions. As Susan Sontag says, "the essence of Camp is its love of the unnatural: of artifice and exaggeration," and pro wrestling's camp is certainly part of its charm.[2] Yet the entertainment's hybridism animates the ridicule and disparagement wrestling faces. Since it is not a "true" sport, it is derided for its fakery, drama, and pageantry. Because it is not conventional theater, it is lambasted for its violence, lack of subtlety, and over-the-top characters. It occupies a cultural position far below the exalted status of traditional sports, a status sometimes associated with "religion" (Deford 1976, Burstyn 1999, Price 2001). A *USA Today* columnist, for example, vilifies wrestling because "it wasn't sport. It was carnival-barking at its loudest, a seedy diversion at its tawdry worst" (Saraceno 2007).[3]

Notably vociferous criticism typically comes from men with a strong social investment in sports.[4] Pro wrestling strikes a sensitive nerve with those who cherish what they see as the authenticity and meritocratic values of "real" sports. We read that pro wrestling is "the id run wild, a virtual overflow of primary-process [primitive-level thinking], where sex and violence rule and where steel chairs are the most effective problem-solving device. It teaches the exact opposite of the message of sports and is, in many respects, the antithesis of sports, or 'The Anti-Sport'" (Waxmonsky and Beresin 2001). Another outraged polemicist condemns pro wrestling and its followers as "the epitome of violence, sadomasochism, and sleaze," nothing but "trash TV" for its followers, whom he labels "ugly Americans" (Rueter 2000). Representations of the entertainment in media other than television and advertising campaigns harp on the pageantry, costumes, and fakery.[5] Men who fake-fight while wearing tights warrant suspicion in a culture obsessed with the proof of one's manhood (Kimmel 1996). It is sometimes called "male soap opera"—an oxymoron in many people's estimation.

While the disgust expressed almost always concerns the well-known televised WWE productions, indie wrestlers are hardly immune from this scathing disparagement, since the indies have almost all the same features, lacking only the commercial success. Being performed in small, obscure venues—vets halls, community centers, middle-school gyms— the indies have nowhere near the WWE's influence, televised exposure, or profitability.[6] The fan base of "odd, lost souls" is composed mainly of friends, family, and a set of hard-core devotees, many of whom revel in the marginalization and obscurity.[7] In an era of Comedy Central, the *Onion*, and ubiquitous "snark," the scene represents comedic fodder: a shirtless variation of the community theater parodied in Christopher Guest's *Waiting for Guffman*.[8] The physical slapstick, often accompanied by tables, ladders, chairs, and barbed wire, can resemble a Kafkaesque blend of *Jerry Springer* and *Jackass*. This marginality can be hard to reconcile with a celebrity-obsessed era, in whose new social media (YouTube, Facebook, Twitter) fame is positioned as imminently possible.[9] Neil Genzlinger, in a *New York Times* review of Hackett's *Slaphappy*, one of only a few books about indie wrestling, manages to praise the book while slurring members of the indie community. He states that *Slaphappy* "shed[s] light on this most lowbrow of activities" and concludes that pro wrestling is "unredeemable garbage after all" (Genzlinger 2006).

Indie wrestlers often experience the revulsion personally. Patrick, a veteran and booker for the federation, explained this common disdain:

> People have some stupid outlook at professional wrestling. That it's a bunch of idiots. "They don't know what they are doing." "A bunch of idiots jumping around in the ring." And "untrained." "They are not athletes." "They are a joke." And "white trash." It's such a stigmatism that goes with professional wrestling. And to sit there and explain to ignorant people that already have their mind made up that it's fake? They have their mind made up! "They are not athletes." People that are not wrestling fans go to wrestling shows to prove that it's fake. They sit there and go, "Look, look—it's fake." Well, no shit it's fake! We know it's fake! We are never telling you it's not! They associate people [like us] with white trash people, heavyset people, and fat people, like, low people in society. It's wrong.

Only a small proportion of the general population has, in fact, even heard of *independent* pro wrestling. I asked Donny what his coworkers think of his wrestling, and he stated that most do not even know about the indies. "Oh, I take a lot of, a lot of shit for it. . . . Most of the time, people just can't believe it. 'There's pro wrestling other than WWF?'[10] People don't know about independents. So when you say that you wrestle, 'Oh, it's backyard wrestling!' *No! It's not!* . . . people just don't know about independent wrestling."

The obscurity and vulgarity of the entertainment prevent many participants from revealing their very identity as a wrestler. Some painstakingly deny their identity even though participation is the center of their existence. In these cases it is usually not until they are injured so badly that they limp to work or consume all their sick or personal days that participants reveal they are indie wrestlers.[11] Because of this they must manage the stigma. For example, Mike told me that to get his recent job at an outdoor furniture store, he lied in the interview about wanting to be a police officer. "I can't tell them I like wrestling. I was like, 'I am [a wrestler] but I want go to school to be a cop,' [and then] they were like, 'Oh, OK. That's really good. You are hired!' So I was, like, OK."

Tony, like Mike, got a disdainful response when he told his coworkers he was attending a pro wrestling school. "I was like, 'Yeah, I'm gonna be a wrestler.' They were like, '*Wrestling*?' You know, they bash it like everyone else. 'That's stupid. You gonna wear a costume?' . . . I have been hearing it all my life. Like, 'Oh, wrestling is stupid'—wrestling is this, wrestling is that. I don't really care what they think. I have been wanting to do this for, like, ten years."

Patrick, a teacher in a middle school, explained his teaching colleagues' reaction after I asked what they knew about his wrestling.

> P: Some of them know . . . It's got out, but no one makes a big deal about it. If someone asks, I don't make a big deal about it: 'Oh it's going great. Yeah, I still do it. Not so much anymore.'
>
> T: So you don't want to talk about it?
>
> P: No. You know, I wanna be looked at in a professional way there. And then a professional way here. I don't want to cross. . . . I couldn't have a principal knowing I go out there in pretty much underwear. Black panties, in a pair of boots and kneepads. . . . I am in that [newspaper article featuring the Rage promotion]. There is a picture of me. But I have my back to the photographer. I would never dare go [newspaper in hand] and say 'Look it's me!' There are a bunch of young teachers who wanna see me in a show and I'm like, 'Oh, that would be great. That would be awesome.' But then I die the subject down. . . . I am respected in the school and taken very seriously. I am looked at in a different level. The assistant superintendent knows who I am, and he's seen my work. . . . And I would never want the wrestling to mess me up there. You know, you never know. You don't want some bad press coming out about the district.

Professionals like Patrick feel the need to obscure their wrestling identity on a daily basis. Indie wrestling is a threat to their socially approved, *other* lives as professionals.

Most participants enter pro wrestling holding the misconception that they can make money from performing, but almost immediately they learn how unlikely this is. All indie wrestlers have day jobs, and as there is no labor contract from the promoters, younger wrestlers adjust their expectations accordingly. Any money paid for a performance depends on the integrity of a given promoter and the attendance. Unless one performs internationally, the WWE is the sole (if steeply uphill) avenue to greater wrestling exposure, fame, and fortune. Opportunities for upward mobility as an indie performer are small, unless you consider the move made from wrestler to trainer—a slight change in status but a financially insignificant one. Promotion to the WWE is extremely difficult, so indie wrestlers sooner or later come to terms with having to pay their own way for transit, food, lodging, equipment, and routine health issues. Lastly, even though performances are scripted and wrestlers try to avoid injuries, they happen all the time (more on injuries in chapter 5). Much of the damage is invisible, but there are long-term cumulative effects, and paralysis and even death are everyday possibilities.

RECOGNITION AND IDENTITY

Two hundred years ago G. W. F. Hegel explored the human "struggle for recognition," identifying recognition by others as a primary human need. In his view, the "struggle" was understood to take the form of a hostile conflict. Following Hegel, understandings of recognition have emerged from the fields of philosophy, psychoanalysis, and political theory.

French sociologist Pierre Bourdieu insists that an indisputable, anthropological fact is that "man is . . . haunted by the need for justification, legitimation, recognition" (2000, 239). Jessica Benjamin, feminist psychoanalyst, suggests that recognition is the very sustenance of life, the energy humans depend on as social beings. She analogizes recognition as functioning like the "essential element in photosynthesis, sunlight, which provides the energy for the plant's constant transformation of substance" (Benjamin 1988, 22).[12] In the immediate, concrete sense, recognition equates to acknowledging something as valid, true, or entitled to consideration.[13] Despite recognition's significance in shaping identity, the concept remains vague; some definitions consider only *favorable* notice integral to the process of being recognized. According to Jessica Benjamin, to recognize is to "affirm, validate, acknowledge, know, accept, understand, empathize, take in, tolerate, appreciate, see, identify with, find familiar . . . love" (1988, 16).[14]

Leaving aside definitional differences, scholars agree that recognition is fundamental to the formation of identity and a sense of self. Bourdieu contends it is "via the judgment of others that we are granted the legitimacy of our existence" (2000, 237). Kelly Oliver argues that we have a "fundamental dependence on each other. Subjectivity . . . is the result of a process of witnessing that connects us through the tissues of language and gestures" (2001, 223). Charles Taylor approaches its necessity by analyzing the absence of recognition; misrecognition is the basis of domination and suffering (1992).

Given that recognition is universally needed to sustain identity, it is logical that it is sought in endless forms and settings, with differing audiences and to varying degrees.[15] Outlets for securing it are as varied as the interactive contexts within the social world itself. Few empirical studies, however, explore how it is attained, much less how to attain it using one's physicality.[16] In pro wrestling, performers make and sustain their identities dialogically with fellow wrestlers and in the iconic call-and-response exchange with their fans.[17]

IMMERSION

Indie wrestling constructs a nearly impermeable "enclave of experience" (Schutz 1976) that alters participants' way of being in the world. Functioning as a nearly complete immersion, wrestling takes over performers' daily routines and dictates most aspects of their everyday existence, bleeding into nearly every corner of life. Like an addiction, it taxes relationships and almost all other realms of the self. As Dan states, "It's very difficult to be normal and wrestle at the same time. Wrestling gets in the way of *everything*. . . . As Timmy warned me (I think in my second week), 'Wrestling will get you fired from jobs.' 'Wrestling will make you lose your girlfriend.' And *it does!*"

Basic necessities of life—eating, sleeping, earning money—are usually the only reasons wrestlers do not invest even more time, money, and energy in wrestling. Wrestlers train *as a group* for about twelve to fifteen hours a week, but this time together is only a small fraction of a week devoted to wrestling development. The various other activities and mental states include going to a weight/workout gym to train their bodies, watching wrestling videotapes, working on promos, traveling and performing in other indie shows, traveling to and watching other wrestling shows; reading and viewing wrestling magazines and websites, and when all else is accounted for, making their way through life's routines preoccupied with wrestling thoughts.

Nearly all of the members spoke of the profound effect this immersion has on their lives. Time previously spent on the mundane distractions and doldrums of school, work, and suburban consumption now teem with ideas about pro wrestling moves, looks, gimmicks, entrances, and potential pops from the crowd. Alternative interests and passions are forfeited as wrestling takes over. Donny articulates this life-altering transition.

> When you're in the wrestling business, wrestling is 24/7. There's never a time when you're not thinking about wrestling. Your life changes dramatically. . . . Your life is wrestling. When you're out at [your day job], every minute that you have to yourself, you find yourself thinking about wrestling. Anybody in that school will tell you, you are constantly thinking about something to do, a new story line, something new to say when you get into the ring. Anything! Anything that will help jump-start the character or story line; you're always thinking about it. . . . So your life literally does a one-eighty, everything totally and completely changes, and everything's about wrestling. I mean, *everything*.

While this preoccupation can be difficult to quantify, it is a total focus that saturates the mind—even in the midst of other activities, such as paid work.

Indie wrestlers commit to several types of investments of time, energy, and body work. I will describe their development—their "acquired, socially constituted dispositions" (Bourdieu 1990, 12–13)—in the order of time allocation. First and foremost is the investment in physical training—with other trainers, veterans, and wrestlers at the gym.[18] The group meets three times a week for three to five hours (often followed by a meal at a nearby restaurant). If the members are able to stick around for eating and carousing afterward—most try, but because of transportation needs, money, or early work the next day, some cannot—the average training time per week, as a group, exceeds fifteen hours. Group training focuses on learning and improving the physical techniques of the craft. Even though participants may spend as little as thirty minutes of their four hours being physical in the ring, the remainder is filled with exchanging advice, sharing wrestling lore, and listening in on coaching directed at other students.

During each practice at the training space, a sizable group (at least ten guys) stands on or below the ring apron and watches the action in the ring. The rest loiter nearby, exchanging tips, talking about moves, critiquing those in the ring, and telling stories about wrestling experiences or recently viewed "classic" matches. This gym culture stands in contrast to the disciplining space of a boxing gym, where individuals spend extensive time outside the ring hitting the bag, jumping rope, doing push-ups and pull-ups, and sparring (Wacquant 2004, Trimbur 2013). Unlike boxers, the wrestlers at Rage are rarely encouraged to work out individually outside the ring area itself, even though such exercises could hone many theatrical skills.[19]

Since participants live throughout the greater metropolitan New York area and some rely on public transit, about a quarter of the participants travel more than an hour to get to the training space; a few travel much farther. As noted, Al travels from Staten Island by bus, ferry, and then train—a journey that can take as long as five hours each way if connections are not synched.

Second to the fifteen hours per week of training time at the gym is the work that goes into improving the look and image of each wrestler's "character." Depending on a range of personal situations—financial resources, work schedule, self-esteem, physical size, experience—wrestlers do self-work for as many hours as they devote to in-gym training, if not more. This "look" enhancement takes place at a local weight gym, in a tanning salon, at home with weights, or simply in front of any mirror one happens upon. Wrestlers do this work on their own time, and as Donny states, the time is hard to tabulate since it saturates every day.

> Now that I know I'm very serious into it, I'm in the gym at least five days a week. I just started that recently. Five days, 'cause I'm really small. I need to get bigger to enhance my look in the ring. . . . Sometimes people catch themselves in front of the mirror and sometimes they talk to the mirror, start to promo themselves to see if, you know, to enhance your mic skills and see the way that you walk and the way that you talk. So I mean, as far as devoting time outside the training facility, seriously, people could just go to the bathroom and start to wash their hands and just cut a promo right in front of the mirror.

The third major investment is the commitment to improving wrestling psychology. This cultural capital is developed from talking with other veterans, watching other matches, and most commonly, through studying videotapes of performances from the last five decades of televised pro wrestling. These videos, dating back to the first popularity spike in the 1950s, are the subculture's recorded history. A knowledgeable, innovative pro wrestler scrutinizes these tapes as the veritable textbooks of the trade. Just as a conventional stage actor might have old copies of playbills or posters of Eugene O'Neill and Arthur Miller throughout the home, wrestlers have piles of taped matches from Hulk Hogan, Ric Flair, and Terry Funk. Viewing these classic bouts, wrestlers learn the history of the business, the moves, the gimmicks, the spectacle—and the legendary characters upon whose style they seek to build their own.

Fishman's account illustrates just how seriously participants take the study of tapes. "I have like 150 tapes in my house. [When] I started collecting them, I'd watch them, 'Oh, let me watch this one from a couple years ago.' But now, it's like homework, you know. You know why they do [that gimmick], when to look for it." Since viewing tapes can be done while conducting other activities, the videos, as Tony explains, run nearly round the clock:

> I get home from work at about three o'clock because I have to be up [in the morning] at five. So a wrestling tape goes in, food goes on the George Foreman grill, and I'll watch wrestling waiting for my dinner. Eat and watch wrestling, and then if something comes on I want to watch, put wrestling on pause. But you know, I watch wrestling every time there's not something on TV that I want to watch [or any time] I have a free second and I'm not in the gym and I'm not in training.

In terms of the amount of time per week, tape viewing often comes right after training and working out in the gym. Tony takes partial inventory of his week: "Eight to twelve hours just training. I spend two hours in the weight room, usually between four and six days a week. And that's another eight to twelve hours. And I watch tapes. [When] I'm working out at my house, the tapes are on. If I'm doing nothing at the house, the tapes are on. If I'm doing laundry, ironing, the tapes are on. The tapes are always on. I really don't watch much else."

This preoccupation, unsurprisingly, impinges on the social sphere of wrestlers' lives. The first sacrifices include relationships outside the wrestling scene. Longer-term relationships with women are tentative because time not devoted to wrestling is limited, and partners, not surprisingly, have difficulty appreciating the wrestling life.[20] Donny explained the limits of his relationship with his girlfriend, Clara, in the following way.

> I think I'm at the point now where there's only two things I really want, work and wrestling. . . . I can't think about marriage because I'm very stuck in the wrestling, and life is easier to live without throwing a monkey wrench in and trying to get married right now, 'cause I've already told her, you know, 'I'm not ready for it right now.' It's really not time. It's really time to concentrate on the wrestling. And when the wrestling dies down, maybe we'll talk about that stuff.

Of course, if everything did go Donny's way, the wrestling would never "die down," and so the dream envisions no long-term commitment to any partner at all. In Al's case, he tells me he turns down invites to parties "with college girls" because he needs his sleep and energy for work, going to the gym, and wrestling.

An additional by-product of the immersion is the forfeiture of investment in such conventional expressions of human capital as education, work experience, and job training. As participants become more invested, they simultaneously divest themselves of other social spheres. Tony recounted the conversation he had with his girlfriend about how his passion for wrestling conflicted with other goals, one of which was educational. "She says 'You know, you put so much time and so much effort into becoming a great wrestler . . . you could be putting that toward anything else. Anything!' But I'm not motivated to do it with anything else, anywhere else. You know? [But] if I apply myself half as much at college as I do now [to wrestling], I'd be finished by now."

About six members of the core group have stable, full-time jobs with good benefits and long-term prospects, although even these are usually interpreted as a means to an end. As Matt states, "You will find a lot [of school teachers] . . . it's the perfect thing for what we do. One: Weekends and summers off. Two: Insurance."

Donny spoke of wrestling's sacrifice almost as though it were beyond his control.

> I had the opportunity to work for the Regional Railroad and because it would be a damper on my wrestling schedule, I didn't do it. Like

Tyler just got accepted into a police academy. If they take him, he's got to stop wrestling for at least two years. I wouldn't be able to do that. I would rather be struggling to pay my bills wrestling two or three times a month on the weekends, few times a week during practice. That's what makes me happy, you know? That's what it comes down to. There's very few things that make me feel like I do when I walk out [through] that red curtain.

While the number of hours per day can vary, the state of mind is constant. For most participants, mental devotion is nearly total. As Donny states:

Between watching tapes, training, going to the gym, working on my appearance, thoughts that roll through my head, there are some days that it can be 90 percent of my day. But the fact is that, again, it's a passion. . . . So sometimes it can consume my whole day. I don't think a day goes by where I don't think or do something directly or indirectly related to an upcoming show or to wrestling. . . . I'm in the gym about an hour and a half when I go. And I go between four and six days a week. If I'm not there, I'm in the wrestling gym training two times a week. And I'm doing shows two times, sometimes three times, a week. There's very rarely a day—though there should be—where I just, you know, go slow.

When I asked Donny's girlfriend, Clara, about his obsession, she said with dismay that there was nothing she could do because he loved it so much. "This is his whole life. He wakes up thinking about it and he dreams about it. He is constantly thinking about it or watching it, going to websites, and watching tapes."

GETTING THE POP

The grip of the indie pursuit should become more evident to outsiders once they understand both the wrestlers' intensive immersion and the ongoing sacrifices they routinely ignore, deny, and contest. This continual labor of repelling, overcoming, and denying detractors and deterrents shows how intense the gratification they get from the indies is. Indeed, wrestling redefines daily habits and interactions; it transforms everyday glances in the mirror and routine household chores into character development and leisure time with friends or family into image work at the gym. Moreover, jobs are threatened (in some cases passed up), relationships are sidetracked, and chronic pain is endured.

The following vignette—derived from an amalgam of field notes taken on two nights of shows I attended in my first few months of fieldwork—shows the look, feel, and sound of the dialogue wrestlers and fans exchange. The crowd response, or "pop" as wrestlers call it, is at the heart of the professional wrestler's experience.

I get out of my car and walk over to join the roughly thirty eager fans waiting to get into the community center. We stand below the low-hanging orange sodium lights fixed underneath the metal awning. I say hello to a clearly devoted fan in his early twenties who appears to have a mild mental disability. He blurts out, "It's freezing out here!" Despite his frustration with the cold, he shares with pride that he talks to Cuss just about every day and might go to a bar with the wrestlers after the show.

At 6:30 the doors open and we file in, stopping at a fold-up table to pay the eight-dollar admission to two new wrestlers who collect tickets. The halls have all the generic trappings of a public school designed in the 1950s: bulletin boards, low-to-the-ground porcelain water fountains, glass-covered trophy cases, aluminum lights encased in flimsy clear plastic, four-foot-high skinny metal lockers lining the walls, and bluish-green-speckled linoleum flooring.

In the middle of the gym where the show is performed is the ring, surrounded by four-foot-high gates that, along with dozens of blue padded mats, create a five-foot-wide buffer zone between fans and performers. Two large white men in their fifties wearing orange nylon coats with Event Security emblazoned on the back stand near the gates. The show begins, going from match to match about every ten minutes. At one point after a really heavy, not well known wrestler enters the ring, someone yells something about ordering another pizza, and other fans high-five each other upon hearing the taunt. One match comes to a draw, and the two wrestlers embrace with a mild, stiff hug after the ref raises the hands of both in the air. When they hug, the same gang of spectators yells out "Homo!"

As is common, the devoted fan, Louie, and another young disabled man in his early twenties sit side by side in their electric wheelchairs, near where the wrestlers enter the space from behind the curtains. The friend clutches a foot-wide piece of a fold-up table that must have been handed to him after being shattered by a wrestler's body in an earlier match. Louie's friend awkwardly raises the broken table piece into the air as he cheers for Fishman. The father of one of the young men sits directly behind them, occasionally checking on his son's needs.

Before the intermission at 9 PM, the emcee encourages fans to get wrestlers' autographs in the room across the hall from the performance space. Four or five wrestlers sit in this room at fold-up cafeteria tables either signing autographs or waiting to be asked for an autograph by the two dozen fans who linger about. It is unclear who is an eager fan in search of an autograph, who is a friend, and who might be a girlfriend or family member. On this night, at the far end of the room is a former WWF midget wrestler offering autographs for three dollars. Wearing suspenders and a baseball cap, the forty-something former wrestler sits alone at the end of the long table, looking forlorn. I see a wrestler signing a piece of the broken table that a fan recovered from the ground near the ring.

In a later match, Scud is struggling to get up after being flung out of the ring and onto the ground in the peripheral space below the ring but inside the gates. Fishman yells, "Man overboard!" and barrels across the ring, grabbing the top rope with both hands as he approaches it, and springs over and out of the ring. He lands on the writhing Scud, who is several feet below on the thin blue mats that lie between the ring and the gates. It looks really painful. Out of some need to determine my own threshold for pain, I glance around for reactions and see that a few other veteran wrestlers are also grimacing. It had to hurt.

In the front row sit the son and father I often see at shows. The father is always vocal, yelling taunts and epithets—"Get a suit" or "You pencil-neck geek!"—to the Prince character, who does a short interlude between matches. The Prince character is a very thin white guy who never wrestles but works an aristocratic gimmick designed to insult the parochial crowd. At one point the Prince taunts the fans, calling them pencil-neck geeks. The father fan yells back to him, "Hey, you stole my line!"

As the two wrestlers perform, the overweight man taunts Bad Boy: "Are you Mr. Ed? Because you look like a real jackass!" The father turns around and congratulates him, "I like that one, I'm gonna use that one."

Matt stands in the hallway just outside the space, giving autographs to a few fans and posing for photos. As Matt flexes the sizable biceps on his

FIGURE 2.1. A referee signs the night's card for a young fan. CREDIT: ©2006 Mark Stehle Photography.

right arm, a nine-year old boy comes up to him and, without asking, gleefully slides both hands up and down Matt's upper arm. Matt, says to the excited boy, "Hey now, that's what girls do."

During the Saturday night shows, performers revel in their heroism as they walk down the halls before and after matches. Spectators say hello, ask for autographs, or simply stare at them. Having already seen the wrestlers in the squared circle (or on the promotional flyers and websites), young kids are eager to take their photographs or get a high five. During the intermission, some wrestlers sit in the adjacent room and sign posters and flyers for young fans.

If the fan is lucky, he or she gets to stand next to a favorite wrestler as

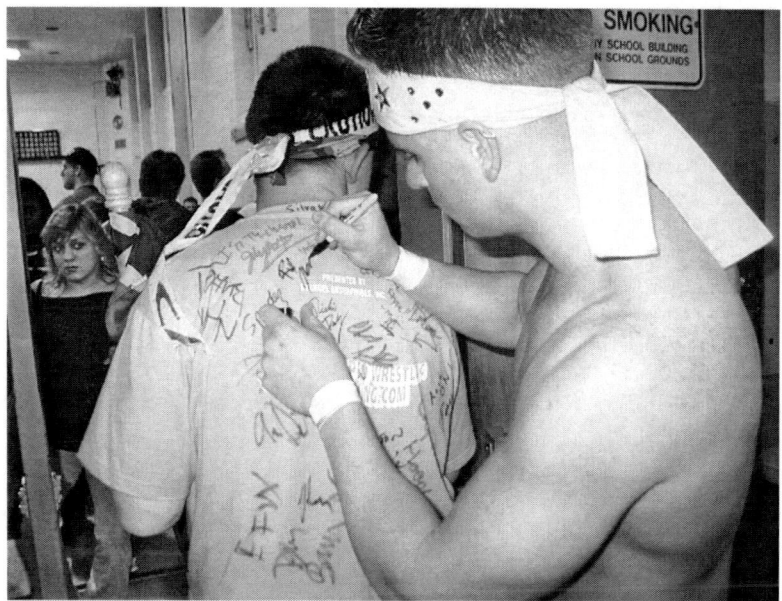

FIGURE 2.2. Autographing a fan's T-shirt. CREDIT: Author.

friends or parents snap photos. Wrestlers are more than happy to autograph the event's promotional flyer, a poster, a T-shirt worn by a fan, or even an album of autographs collected from the wrestlers in the show.

The shows feature a merchandise table selling T-shirts, programs, posters, DVDs, and other items featuring some of the night's more entrepreneurial performers. These sit alongside books and DVDs of the big-name formerly televised wrestlers.

Several indie wrestlers have created their own homemade brands of T-shirts, videos, and autographed photos of themselves in character. All are available at this table and on the Web.

While the shows offer abundant opportunities for gaining recognition, certain instances nevertheless stand out. The following example of Al's epiphany is from a field note.

At a Saturday night show I speak with Al just after he is in the ring performing. Al has been with the group for just over a year now. On this night, I see him backstage after his second stage appearance. Overflowing with energy, he immediately asks what I thought of him. So eager is he to know my opinion, I feel ashamed to admit that I missed him the

FIGURE 2.3. Wrestling action figures sold at a merchandise table. CREDIT: Justine Stehle.

first time he was in the ring (I was backstage talking to others). Fortunately, I managed to catch him the second time, so I tell him he looked great (I didn't have a clear memory of his every move, of course, but I knew his overall performance was smooth). Having heard some people yell out "Oscar" (his stage name), I tell him I noticed that he was getting some fan attention. As he radiantly beams, he states with immense satisfaction, "Now, I *am* somebody!"

The elation at having the self affirmed is rarely stated so starkly, but Al is an eager, sincere kid who wears his heart on his sleeve.

In Donny's case he believes wrestling has led to material rewards, including his first romance.

I had two matches that night. She watched me in the first. The second one she got vocal. Started yelling at me from the crowd. And I looked down and, to be honest with you, I didn't even see who the hell was yelling [but] I knew I had a girl yelling at me and really, the whole oh, twenty [some] years I'd been alive, I'd never dated anybody and it was really never nothing I ever wanted to do. And all of a sudden, I was reaping the benefits of wrestling—I had this person yelling at me.

Donny's performance places him in a spotlight, a spotlight missing from the doldrums of his everyday life; from his perspective he would never have been noticed had it not been for his wrestling. Finding a girlfriend through wrestling is very unusual (the girl in question was the sister of a wrestler), but his recollection suggests that it was more than just establishing a new romance. Wrestling meant people were "yelling" at him, affirming his sense of self, his identity.

Tamara spoke of indie wrestling as a vehicle to fame and recognition. For her, local indie wrestling is a stepping stone to that desired status.

> One day I was just watching it and I said, "I want to do this, I want to be famous like this. I want to do autograph signings and have fans line up for me. . . . No matter what, I want to be famous, because I can't live an average, everyday life." You know what I mean? I can't be them [*pointing to the women at the next table in the diner*]. . . . I just want everyone to know my name.

Tamara views indie participation as a means for people to "know her name."

The pop, the roar from the crowd, is the almighty prize that Tony lives for. "I love getting popped. Love it! The 'Holy shit!' chant, that's what I live for. If I can get a 'Holy shit!' chant, I'll do anything. . . . The best one, I think, was when I was wrestling Johnny Cola and he did a dive over the top rope, and I got him and power-slammed him in the aisle—and that got one. That was the first one that I got. Awesome! Live and die for it!" It is not difficult to see why the wrestling immersion masks the numerous deterrents that participants face. Aside from wrestling, what in these men's lives can match the sensation of such loud and immediate recognition?

DOCUMENTED RECOGNITION

As a spectacle, pro wrestling lends itself to visual documentation. Wrestlers' accounts testify that tape and video recordings are a primary vehicle for exchanging history, culture, and tricks of the trade. In this digital age almost nothing goes undocumented.[21] Fans with handheld devices—digital cameras, video cameras, and cell phone cameras—are seen throughout the space detailing the men's acts.

Recordings are typically added to a catalog of videotaped matches that diehard fans and participants collect, watch, and archive. Nowadays footage is posted on a promotion's own website, on YouTube, and on the indi-

FIGURE 2.4. Indie performer soaking up the appreciation. CREDIT: Author.

vidual's own website or social network page. One function of the recordings is the perfection of the craft. As with game tapes football or basketball coaches use, tapes allow wrestlers to find areas for self improvement. A secondary, related purpose is the provision of recognition.[22]

Mike's obsession with tapes conveys the desire to have each match and move recorded and catalogued. "The greatest joy that I get from it is watching it on tape. . . . I wanna have two or three spots in every match [where] you're gonna say, 'Oh, rewind! We wanna see that again.' I wanna have something like that. . . . What I love the most is sitting back and watching it. I watch my matches a hundred times." Recordings provide tangible evidence of glory, eternalizing the amazing move or the thrilling stunt, even if it is solely for the performer's own gratification. Such footage provides a secondary proof. Footage allows a wrestler to repeatedly relive the fantastic moments of recognition.

The desire to relive and confirm oneself through footage is common to many onstage performers, whether amateur or professional, rookie or veteran. Even some veteran professional actors cop to the gratification of

FIGURE 2.5. Digital documentation during shows. CREDIT: Author.

owning footage that eternalizes a successful act.[23] Since performers can be shot down and humiliated whenever they step in front of a live audience—especially an interactive audience such as pro wrestling fans—wrestlers expose themselves to this inherent risk. The interactive exchange ups the ante and makes every match all the more unique. While winning is predetermined, one never knows how the crowd will respond. Tapes provide proof of excellence, much as stats sheets do for baseball and basketball players.

Most footage consists of in-ring fighting, but a portion comes from the participants' entrances and promos—the brief, contrived interviews shot at close distance. The Brick, a 6′3″ wrestler with two years of experience, likes to showcase his large, chiseled physique and his ire to fans and their cameras. His wife, a spouse unusually supportive of wrestling, often videos him with a handheld device while supporting their infant daughter in a Baby Björn pouch. At one point during most shows, the Brick will stop, grit his teeth, scowl, and flex his biceps while staring at his wife and child. Such posing looks bizarre, as if it is his wife and baby he is threatening. (His wife does not usually respond in kind with a yell or whoop; she just smiles.) It reveals the presence of an invisible audience—future at-home viewers.

One Saturday night, when I had to leave a show early, I learned the hard way about another function of the tapes. I had brought my girlfriend and two other friends along with me. We stayed for just about the entire night but had to leave before the end of the final match, the main event between Donny and Maniac.[24] When I attended the next training session two days later, Donny immediately confronted me. Instead of asking his usual "What did you think of the show?" he stated, "*You left before it was over!*"[25] I defended myself, explaining that we had been there. I even had a photograph of his match (taken moments before leaving) that I gave to him. He said, "I saw you leave!" I couldn't believe he knew this, since he was performing in the ring the moment we exited. Donny followed up, "I saw it on the tape!" I felt compelled to explain how we came with friends in one car and they needed to get back to the city.

Donny knew of our early departure only because he carefully inspected the *spectators* in the tapes. While I knew I had offended him, I wasn't aware how deeply until much later. As Donny was rummaging in his car for tapes to lend some new students, I asked which one he was going to lend them. He said, "The June show; you know, the one you weren't there for."

The tapes' function as a means of audience surveillance underscores the yearning to reexperience the acknowledgments. For one performer tapes capture an amazing physical feat; for another, a sea of faces all focused on the performer—a collective legitimation.

Of course, detailed documentation that allows someone to retroactively analyze a past moment comes with some measure of risk, because the reaction sought may not be the one received. As Benjamin notes, recognition is "reflexive; it includes not only the other's confirming response, but also how we find ourselves in that response" (1988, 21). Donny's frustration with my early exit stemmed from my failure to provide a "confirming response."

Scrutinizing this recording also reveals indies fans' sheer proximity. The hyperstylized WWE productions staged at large sports arenas seat the thousands of fans far from the action, but indie wrestling lets fans interact much more closely with performers. It is common to have a performer give a fan a high five or fall at their feet. On occasion, I heard young fans exclaim exuberantly that "I was the kid who the Brick yelled back to!" Moreover, manipulating the crowd's response takes greater effort and ingenuity than it does in televised WWE productions, where producers are known to pipe in canned applause and cheers from the audience.

Video also provides the means for legitimating the entire promotion.

FIGURE 2.6. Indie recognition. CREDIT: ©2006 Mark Stehle Photography.

I observed this collective quest when the group held small Sunday night shows in the converted garage that also served, during my initial fieldwork, as their original training space. Halfway through the matches, a fan holding a video camera yelled to the small crowd of about twenty-five people, "We are taping this whole thing, so in ten seconds, make some noise for thirty seconds. Let's get this on cable-access TV." He counted down from ten, expecting everyone to enthuse on cue, but he got only a tepid response. I was leaning against the metal garage door with another guy, so we banged the door with our fists, adding deep loud thuds. Others caught on and joined in. The fan to my left, thinking about cable-access TV presumably, began yelling, "Pay per view! . . . Pay per view!" repeating the phrase until nearly all forty attendees chanted communally.

For some guys this is the first time they have been stopped and asked for a photograph. Donny gave me his take on the experience. "Your girlfriend was taking pictures one day at the [show]. She had taken a lot already but stopped me for one. It was probably the first time I had been stopped [because someone] wanted pictures of me." Donny understands the portrait as a moment that might never have happened had he not become a wrestler. There surely are other photos taken of him during his life, but only now is he selected by a virtual stranger. Indeed, I was occasionally chastised for failing to take and provide photos of certain more cocksure veterans. Patrick, for example, frequently pestered me for pictures of him performing. Until I could finally provide some, I avoided him; his disappointment in me had turned to outright contempt (a methodological puzzle I address in appendix A). I often heard performers say, "*This* should be the cover of your book!" or something similar when I looked over photographs of wrestlers with them.

RECOGNITION FROM FELLOW WRESTLERS

Even though the production is organized around fan appreciation, fellow wrestlers can bestow equally compelling intragroup recognition. Backstage relationships between lower-status wrestlers and veteran wrestlers is a paramount concern for many wrestlers. Vets wield tremendous influence and play a powerful role. As Mike attests, this is the greatest reward.[26]

> To get to have the fans like you—that would be one thing, that'd be alright. But it's not something I need. You know, the fans' appreciation would be one thing . . . but to have the boys really like you—to have them say, "Hey Mike, you know it was a good match"—that would be the top. That would be the best.

Being assigned a match with a "big gun" is a powerful experience in and of itself. Donny nervously spoke of his upcoming match with Timmy. "That's a big gun. That's something you work for. That's like one of your goals. It's like . . . oh, I want to get in the ring with one of these guys—see how I do, see how I feel—with a guy who was on television, with a guy who at one time [was] pretty much a household name."

Tony shared his appreciation for how veterans "straight-shoot." "That's the best part about it because you know the guys in the back room are straightforward about it. Straight-shoot you. If it looked fine and you got away with it, people would say, 'You know, it looked good . . . it was fine. There is nothing wrong with it.' But [if not, vets will] let you know."

Donny speaks of fans as though they are almost nonexistent. In his experience the greatest concern is the respect and recognition from other wrestlers.

> So you can be walking down the hall and everyone's congratulating you. The fans, people who just watch it, "Oh great match!" "You did fantastic!" . . . [but] when the workers come to you, "Yo, it was a pretty good match [pause] except that one thing . . ."—that one thing that you

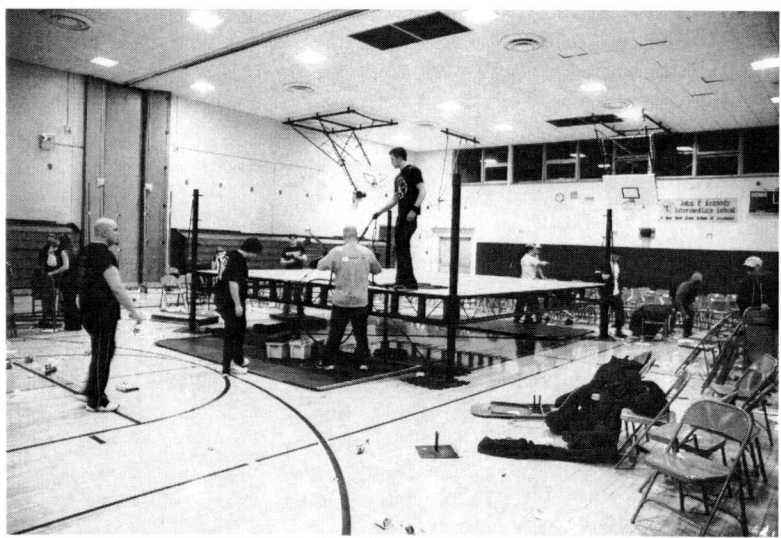

FIGURE 2.7. Striking the ring after a show. CREDIT: Author.

know stuck out and they're telling you, "Yeah, it stuck out. And it was a problem." And you go back in the locker room and you just turn off to everybody.... You know, it turns your great day into a shit day.

Some wrestlers allude to performing for an imagined spectator, one not even in attendance. In Matt's case, it is his father's affirmation that is most prized, despite his father's never coming to shows. Here is his account of having the first opportunity (in another federation) to wrestle a "legend" at a big show.

I went to the locker room, put a towel over my head. [I was] crying into that towel like a baby. Like a baby. At twenty-eight-years old, you know? The first thing I did when I got home the next day was pick up the phone and call my Dad. Told him [about this big match]. And even now I realize that even though I don't get the response I want from him that the inner child in me is looking for, it's still kind of cool. I mean, he's got things going on in his life. But every now and again he'll just turn to me and say, "So who'd you wrestle this weekend?"

Considerable skill and labor go into producing a Saturday night wrestling show. In addition to being wrestling performers, participants in essence also work for a local production company.

FIGURE 2.8. Setting up the ring before a show. CREDIT: Author.

Wrestlers are expected to have (or develop) facility with the following trades: setting up and moving the ring, set design, lighting, acoustics (speakers, microphones, and wiring), video setup (cameras and live footage for simultaneous backstage viewing), makeup and wardrobe design, concessions, merchandising, ticket sales, striking the ring, and lastly, cleaning up at the end of the night.

Some tasks are straightforward, like setting up chairs, tables, and gates (between fans and performers), while other assignments require higher-level skills. The various behind-the-scenes tasks provide a forum for intragroup recognition. Cobra, a soft-spoken twenty-one-year-old Latino member of the group, has acquired many specialized behind-the-scene technical skills. For one, he adjusts the ropes of the ring, tightening them so that they have just enough give. If they are too loose, wrestlers cannot easily bounce off them; if they are too tight, they cannot bounce at all and consequently experience pain (because in actuality, the "ropes" are metal cables wrapped in tape). Additionally, Cobra does the makeup and wardrobe design for almost all the performers.

During the preshow in the locker room, Cobra painted a design using acrylics on Scud's face. It was a triangular "nuclear" icon, in yellow outlined by green, with a red flame coming up and out of it. This week

I sat and watched as he meticulously painted Scud's face for close to forty-five minutes. Being very delicate, it looked as good as I had ever seen it. Scud said, "He's the best!"

SUMMARY

In this chapter we have seen how indie pro wrestlers receive loud, immediate, and live recognition from fans and fellow wrestlers. Within this social world, performers have the chance to earn pops, high-fives, cheers, taunts, and "Holy shit!" chants. We see individuals finding recognition by different means, even as members in the same distinct subculture. Above and beyond the obvious forms apparent to casual observers—fans clapping, shouting, yelling, and clamoring for autographs—is recognition from fellow wrestlers. For some participants recognition comes less from the stage than from backstage interactions related to their technical, equipment, or production acumen. Some of the men revel more in the documented recognition of digital recordings than the live, immediate, yet fleeting cheers from fans on the night of a show. Although indie wrestling affords little mainstream respect, sometimes even taking its practitioners down a dangerous financial path, the pursuit nevertheless offers a powerful enclave of legitimation, adoration, and confirmation of self—a "bootstrapping of motivations" that binds wrestlers to the pursuit.[27]

In chapter 3, I turn to an explanation of the craft itself. The recognition and emotions wrestlers fight for can be achieved only through the cooperative craft of passion work. How wrestlers evoke emotional responses from fans demonstrates the danger and difficulty of pro wrestling as well as its intrinsic, often unseen, rewards.

CHAPTER 3 ★ PASSION WORK

THE COORDINATED PRODUCTION OF EMOTIONAL LABOR

FIELD NOTE

It is a hot, August night, and instead of driving to the school, I take the commuter train out from the city. After walking past the hundreds of cars waiting for returning rail commuters, I make my way south on a divided four-lane street lined with small businesses: a pet store, Indian restaurant, sporting goods store, and several standard middle-class suburban businesses (nail salons, pizza shops, fast-food outlets). The walk feels treacherous, and people in their cars look out at me, the lone pedestrian, as if something might be wrong. As I speed up to make the flashing walk sign at an intersection, I take care to look for one of the darting cars that carelessly exit the numerous fast-food drive-throughs.

I walk through the back of the Pep Boys Auto Parts parking lot and cut diagonally toward the school, a nondescript building tucked away in the back corner of a worn-down strip mall. The former auto body shop is an independent structure situated next to an alley and behind a large commercial supermarket. At the front of the building are three large metal roll-up garage doors opening onto an alley. On this night, the garage door on the far right is up because it is nearly 80 degrees outside and even warmer inside. As I walk in, an eight-car commuter train rumbles by behind the building and drowns out the incessant thuds as a student performs "bumps" on the mat of the wrestling ring, located in the center of the 50′ x 30′ garage.

The 18′ x 18′ ring takes up most of the space in the former auto body shop. The remaining five-foot-wide perimeter is littered with two dozen or so brown metal fold-up chairs, all of them dented from head bashing. The floor, a concrete slab with old oil stains, has interspersed pieces of hard matting and carpet scraps. The three windowless cinder-block sidewalls are light blue. One corner of the garage space looks like a graveyard for a wrestling ring that has been salvaged. What remains are several metal posts, plywood boards, and a few beat-up gym mats. A drywall partition divides the garage area. A mural with the school's initials has been spray-painted on one side of the partition. The smaller of the two spaces, a makeshift backstage office, has a fold-up table, TV, VCR, small refrigerator, posters of previous wrestling events, and a few chairs.

Five new students in their late teens and early twenties who arrived early are milling about. As more novice students arrive, they timidly enter the main area, remove layers until they are wearing only a T-shirt and gym shorts, then take a seat on one of the fold-up chairs. They slip on their knee pads and elbow pads, lace up their boots, slap some Icy Hot pain-relief gel on their lower backs, and climb onto the apron of the ring. They wipe their boots off on the apron, then quietly stand alongside one another waiting to be called into the ring by Cuss.

Cuss is standing in the center of the ring in orange wrestling boots and a white Z100 FM T-shirt that hangs down over his short trunks. The eight new students, who by now have grouped themselves on the apron of the ring, are about to learn the lock-up move, the initial embrace in most matches. Cuss has called Mike into the ring; he is a nineteen-year-old white male wearing a high school wrestling shirt that proclaims State Champs on the front and lists team members on the back. Mike is having trouble staying loose during the lock-up. Instinctually, he gets tense and braces for conflict. "It's just like a basketball shot," Cuss says, in his usual terse, instructive voice, raising both his arms in the air and dropping them softly onto Mike's shoulders. Cuss then instructs Junior, another new student, to practice the lock-up with Mike. The two grasp each other by their shoulders and lock up. They move within the ring over to the far corner while staying embraced. Like dancers choreographing a tango, the two men try to move in a fluid motion, each mirroring the other's steps. As Junior's right foot moves forward, Mike simultaneously moves his left foot backward. Mike is looking down at his feet as the two of them slowly step in sync. Another experienced veteran who provides instruction, Slaughter, barks out, "Don't look down! You never want to look down because no one can see your face! You have to look up at each other or at the audience. Remember, *you have to tell a story*!" A moment later, Slaughter notes the resemblance to dancers and says, "It's just like Fred Astaire!" Unlike the recognition ordinarily granted to Slaughter's asides, no one responds to this one.

On break from the nearby Indian buffet restaurant, a short, dark-skinned man, wearing a touristy Florida T-shirt and a white apron with curry stains, stands at the garage's open metal door. He remains there for nearly ten minutes, silently watching the in-ring training, a look of bemused fascination on his face. Unlike many of the onlooking wrestlers, who observe with intensity, he seems to be enjoying it all.

A student named Drew then gets in the ring with Junior. They begin practicing the hip toss as Slaughter watches from the near corner of the ring. Drew's face is intense, and his body movements are sharp and fast. With his head down, he whips his right hand around to his opponent's back, quickly applying pressure. "Hey! What the hell are you doing? It's fake!" Slaughter snaps. Frustrated with Drew's continued intensity, Slaughter yells at him again: "Relax! Relax! What did I tell you last time you were here? What was lesson number one? It's *fake*! . . . Lesson number two? It's *fake*! . . ." Drew and Junior resume their positions while Slaughter goes to the corner post, slowly shaking his head.

A few minutes pass before Cuss, sensing that students do not understand what he meant by "loose," yells "Stop!" and quickly rolls his body underneath the ropes and back into the ring. "Junior, come here." Cuss extends his right forearm outward at waist level. It is rigid and his fist is clenched. "Try to move it," he says to Junior. Junior moves Cuss's arm slightly from side to side, but there is great resistance. "Okay, *now* try it," Cuss says, placing his forearm in the same position but staying loose. Junior grabs Cuss's forearm and with no effort instantly swings it up to Cuss's head. "See!" Cuss says, "It's that simple."

While Cuss is demonstrating the difference between loose and firm, Slaughter undercuts this teaching moment with whispered sexual banter: "Oh yeah . . . no, a little lower . . . now touch me here." Most students who hear him laugh. But Slaughter, singling out Junior, gently reprimands him for laughing while still in the ring wrestling. "Don't break kayfabe, Junior!" he says, loud enough for all to hear ("kayfabe" is explained later in the chapter).

Cuss informs the students that they will now practice a basic bump. One by one, students pull apart the middle and top ropes, step into the ring while bending down beneath the top rope, and attempt this fundamental move. Cuss explains that a good bump is done by falling straight backward onto your back while slapping the mat with both arms and slightly raising your butt in the air at the moment you make contact. All of the students successfully execute the bump except Bobby, a heavyset white eighteen-year-old.

Bobby tries repeatedly. He stands in the middle of the ring and slowly leans backward, but each time he breaks his fall with his butt instead of having his shoulder blades and arms make the initial contact with the mat. "Fuck the sky!" Slaughter exclaims—his phrase for the pelvic thrust required at the moment one simultaneously strikes the mat. Cuss advises Bobby to jam his chin into his own chest and hold it. Attempting to provide an easier, intermediary step, Donny, another veteran, hops into the ring and shows Bobby how to do it from a squatting position. "Keep your back straight and your knees bent like you're taking a shit—then just fall back." But Bobby cannot unlearn the instinct to safeguard his body. More wrestlers chime in with advice. "Bobby, fall back and keep your back straight! It's like you slipped on a banana peel." Bobby squats and very slowly falls backward, but again he breaks the fall with his butt. Bobby's face is flushed, and perspiration is forming on his forehead. After three minutes or so of increasingly aggressive goading, Donny goes to the far corner of the garage and drags into the ring a foot-thick blue foam gym mat and places it behind Bobby. "Yeah, use the mat so Bobby doesn't hurt his *vagina!*" Slaughter teases. Even with the extra cushioning, however, Bobby is still reluctant to fall. He finally manages to do one fall without the mat there, but again he breaks the fall incorrectly. Bobby lowers his head and retreats to the apron of the ring.

There is no plumbing in the garage, so Mike wanders out and leans against the dumpster behind the school to urinate. As Mike reenters the building, Jimmy, a veteran indie wrestler who also helps train new students, approaches the school from an adjacent parking lot. At the same time, an 18-wheeler thunders down the alley toward the supermarket. Jimmy rolls a black carry on luggage bag behind him. Upon entering the garage, he immediately lets go of his suitcase and circles the ring, reaching his hand up and greeting each of the wrestlers standing on the mat's apron. Their customary exchange is not a firm handshake or slap but rather a very loose grasp of each other's slightly closed hand. After he makes his way around the ring, he strolls toward the veterans, who are casually standing by a corner of the ring. Donny is the first one he greets. "What's up, asshole?" he says, extending his right hand as he curls his left arm around Donny's shoulder.

"THE IMAGE OF PASSION, NOT PASSION ITSELF"

The scene I describe above was an evening training session at the school. The field note highlights the main challenges of learning the craft; most moves that novices must master are counterintuitive. Learning to "fight" while moving slowly, relaxing, and being trustful: this requires a bodily adaptation that is nothing like the brusque hyperbole of violence that pro wrestling showcases. Second, although the triumphant wrestler is a timeless icon of strength, domination, and individual perseverance, the backstage construction of this symbol, as the vignette suggests, demands cooperation and coordination. Wrestlers appear to be opponents when in fact they are entirely interdependent. Finally, as Mike's and Bobby's time in the ring shows, becoming a pro wrestler is a trial of uncertainty, both painful and rewarding; most of all, it is a trial filled with counterintuitive adaptations that the novice must manage, if not fully master. This chapter elaborates on these techniques of the craft.

Through interaction with an opponent, a pro wrestler tells a story that strives to evoke passionate feelings in audience members through physical acts of punishment and retribution. The more emotionally invested the audience becomes in seeing the triumph (or defeat) of the "wounded storyteller" (Frank 1995), the more successful the match. Roland Barthes (1957) presciently noted this passion more than half a century ago:

> The most socially inspired nuances of passion (conceit, rightfulness, refined cruelty, a sense of "paying one's debts") always felicitously find the clearest sign which can receive them, express them, and triumphantly carry them to the confines of the hall. It is obvious that at such a pitch, it no longer matters whether the passion is genuine or not. What the public wants is the image of passion, not passion itself.

To get a strong reaction, positive or negative, from the audience, performers must establish who their characters are, what each character represents (some version of babyface or heel), and why there is something at stake in the particular fight. Babyface (often shortened to face) is the guy supported by the crowd, whereas the heel is the despised character whom fans (ideally) detest. In this symbiotic relationship between wrestlers and fans, performers strive to manipulate the audience through an unfiltered emotional display. Creating the passionate response from an audience means executing crucial (albeit unseen) backstage emotional labor with an "opponent." It is a high-stakes endeavor because performers are completely at the crowd's mercy. When done well, wrestlers have the audience in the palm of their hands, captivated by their every move and utterance. When done poorly, wrestlers receive dead silence or soul-destructive chants of "Boring! boring!" or perhaps worse, "You fucked up! You fucked up!"

In her 1983 groundbreaking book, *The Managed Heart*, Arlie Hochschild introduces the concept of "emotional labor," defining it as the work required "to induce or suppress feeling in order to sustain the outward countenance that produces the proper state of mind in others" (1983, 7). Her research on airline employees and bill collectors argues that the management of emotions is a common aspect of many occupations and a social process contingent on ideology and social context. Studies on a wide variety of workers have flourished since *The Managed Heart*, but the bulk of research has focused on women who do service work and use "face-to-face or voice-to-voice contact" in an occupation.[1] In these contexts, behavior is primarily organized around the structure of the market and its effects on individuals selling their labor for profit. In general, the research has focused on the negative effects of emotion work, effects that have developed as a result of the transition to a more service- and information-based economy.[2]

This chapter extends research on emotions in three ways. First, professional wrestlers at the indie level are not performing for their immediate livelihood, so their work is not driven by financial incentives. This *voluntary* emotional labor—work that is an aspect of the business of entertainment though not directly imposed by profit-driven schema—allows us to examine emotional labor within a dangerous physical activity. Second, unlike traditional emotional labor, which is intended to produce a "sense of being cared for in a convivial and safe place" (Hochschild 1983, 7)— work that produces warm emotions traditionally coded as feminine—pro wrestling means to create passionate feelings of contempt, indignation, and suspense among the audience. While positive feelings such as adoration and appreciation are also summoned, their expression occurs only in conjunction with a more "evil" emotion worker. The craft that goes into these "surface acts" of hostility and aggression—acts that have received less attention in the literature—are closely examined in this chapter.

Most important, this chapter complements understanding of emotional labor by scrutinizing professional wrestling as an instance of the *joint* performance of emotional labor conducted with the body.[3] Pro wrestling enacts a duel between two or more fighters who are, in actuality, colluding with each other. Unlike other emotional work (where, for example, an individual worker serves customers or an individual professor teaches students), pro wrestlers do joint emotional labor with one or more opponents. Indeed, the passionate onstage interaction with fans is impossible unless this elaborate, skilled backstage social relationship develops between two or more wrestlers.

The emotional labor wrestlers conduct is the reverse of the more studied emotional labor: instead of females serving customers with a smile, men work together to serve an audience a performance of pain, suffering, and antagonism. For these performers, hostility is almost always *displayed*, although empathic feelings of cooperation, protection, and trust are often actually *felt*. Furthermore, within this high-risk setting—where participation is generally voluntary and motivations are less likely to be driven by financial incentives—wrestlers enact intimate emotional labor together. I suggest that the attraction to indie wrestling is due in part to the social product their craft generates with one another.

ONSTAGE EMOTION WORK

I go for cover on Joey. Then people are like, "Oh, that's it. One, two, kick-out." They go, "Oooh!" False finish. Then you bump the referee. And then when you bump the referee, people are like, okay, bad guy's going to win. They think that. Then we stall a little more. Playing with people's emotions is really what we do. —TIMMY

Yelling, cheering, and verbal taunts (exchanged between the wrestlers and spectators), along with grunts, moans, music, lights, and smoke, set the emotional mood on the night of a show. There is typically very little subtlety; indeed, some contend that pro wrestling's enactment is widely adored because it allows male spectators to express emotion overtly (Jenkins 1997).

Performers follow rules similar to the rules of magicians: make your "move" appear as real as possible without it actually being real. Participants refer to this illusion of realness as "kayfabe" (pronounced *kā-fāb*).[4] Keeping kayfabe requires three essential qualities: charisma, psychology, and physicality. *Charisma* refers to the spirit and dramaturgical skills of the wrestling character, *psychology* describes the interaction with the spectators, and *physicality* refers to the kinesthetic moves and motions conducted while interacting with one's "opponent." All three skills require extensive facility with emotional management because the wrestler is simultaneously managing two separate relationships, each with its distinct "feeling rules":[5] the onstage relationship with the audience, which attempts to elicit passionate emotions such as awe, fear, and anger, and the backstage relationship with his partner, which demands skilled coordination, control, trust, and empathy. Kayfabe derives from the successful management of these simultaneous interactions.

Performing with kayfabe means negotiating a demanding—and often contradictory—terrain in which the feeling rules that govern backstage conflict with those governing the stage. The crux of the contradiction is that agony and the infliction of pain are enthusiastically celebrated on the stage at the same time they are skillfully avoided backstage.

All manner of gimmicks and props are woven into the story lines to enhance the sights and sounds of the spectacle. All of the following props and scenarios have been used by wrestlers in various shows: ladders, tables, chairs, barbed wire, hay bales, trap doors, trashcans, razors, forks, pumpkins, Christmas wreathes, cigars, "wet floor" signs, large plastic candy canes, flags, belts, leather whips, yellow plastic "caution" tape, large metal bells, foam fingers, wine bottles and glasses, duct tape, haircuts, Hooters girls, smoke, dogs, fights that spill into the crowd, fights that spill out of the building, fights involving cars in parking lot, an ambulance with swirling lights removing a wrestler, a "fan" being provoked to the point of jumping in the ring and fighting, former superstars doing cameos, and doctors from backstage being called forth in panic. While the onstage fight is designed to appear out of control—run amok with rage, mayhem, and destruction—the performers are (at least ideally) in complete control. It turns out that receiving passionate indignation (or adoration) from fans requires trust, protection, and empathy within the backstage relationship.

THE BACKSTAGE

Even though performers of violence are often considered to be naturally predisposed to handling a higher threshold of pain, for most of the participants a "natural" acceptance of pain did not in fact exist. Emotional labor is utilized to assuage the initial transition, which is evident when

FIGURE 3.1. High spot. CREDIT: Author.

new students learn the most fundamental pro wrestling move, a bump. The initial test is whether one can manage his own emotions, beginning with fear. Surely some new students start off with less fear than others, but even for them, there is an instinct they have to resist. Fishman gives an account of this instinct and the need to psych oneself up. "No one falls down on purpose except pro wrestlers. And so, it's something you need to train your body not to react to. And it's something you need to psych yourself up to do. It's probably something you shouldn't be doing." In one respect, this conditioning resembles the adaptation necessary for any type of fighter (e.g., a boxer or mixed martial arts fighter), but it also represents a central tenet of the emotion work on the self: the need to take an "active stance vis-à-vis feeling" (Hochschild 1979, 561).

As in the culture at large, being able to endure pain is a source of pride. For wrestlers, admissions of distress are sanctioned, and feelings of vulnerability or pain are routinely policed by those with higher status. As I explain in chapter 5, when a wrestler experiences pain in the backstage, he must work hard to deny, overcome, and control his response to it. Participants suppress their feelings of vulnerability, and confessions are seldom heard. Yet because of wrestling's extensive bruising and battering, it is impossible for every response to hurting to be silenced. In the rare moments when wrestlers' actually confess their pain or vulnerability, we can see the most influential ideals shaping the interaction. The "ideal formations" in this context are virtually synonymous with gender ideals: stoicism and invulnerability.[6]

The primary physical technique for wrestling with kayfabe is the development of a loose and light body. When both performers are malleable, pliable, and relaxed, moving as a synchronized couple is easier. The adjustment to the pro wrestling praxis demands emotion work because it is antithetical to the ordinary, hard body of an athlete, especially one in contact sports. As the sports sociologist Michael Messner contends, if an athlete is to be successful, he must "develop a highly goal-oriented personality that encourages him to view his body as a tool, a machine, or even a weapon utilized to defeat an objectified opponent" (1987, 323). This traditional understanding must be deconstructed by new participants. This has proved to be counterintuitive since being hard and firm is so valued by men, especially athletes, in almost every other context.

Adjusting to the need for a more flexible, malleable, and loose body is also difficult because it is difficult to remain calm when something usually seen as a threat, such as someone running at you with an outstretched fist or jumping on you from a height of five feet, happens. Those who develop skills more quickly learn to release their inhibitions and "submit." Fishman, a quick learner, referred to himself as a "meat puppet":

> You get to be what I nicknamed a "meat puppet." . . . I was easy to put into submission moves. I went up light, I came down fine, no matter what people did. So if somebody wanted to try and create a move or invent a move, or see if they could do something on someone my size, [they'd] drag me into the ring and see what happened.

Wrestlers are also encouraged to use "light touches," soft grasps of the opponent that help performers lead or manipulate each other. This looseness enables the opponent to move his partner's body in the necessary motion or direction. Donny explained a light touch when describing Hammer, a wrestler with excellent skills.

> [Hammer's] a great worker. When I wrestled him at a practice, I wasn't sure when to sell because he was so light. But if you look at him, he looks like he's wrenching and wrenching and wrenching, but he had me in an armlock and I didn't feel anything. That's the kind of worker for the wwe. They want you to be as light as you possibly can be.

While illustrating prototypical emotion work, this example also shows the distinction from traditional gendered types (in which warm cheerfulness is displayed). Hammer displays gritty toughness and bruising strength to the audience when, in actuality, he is employing delicate, nuanced, and respectful "body work."

Hammer himself supported this essential, albeit rarely stated, guideline when asked about his experience in the wwe:

> Because [pro wrestlers are] on the road [together] four or five days a week, they're not going to kill each other. There's a difference if I grab your arm and flex my muscles and it looks like I'm squeezing you. It's a trick. As opposed to doing this [*yanking my arm forcefully behind my back*]. So yes, I would think "the touch," as you put it, is certainly more advanced. . . . Without a doubt.

Besides revealing the importance of the light touch for playing a trick on the audience, Hammer's words demonstrate even more how being "light" functions to maintain good relations with one's fellow wrestlers.

SHARED UNDERSTANDINGS

Performers share understandings about what to expect from each other; this information is conveyed in three main ways. First, the wrestlers talk in the locker room before the match. The booker has already decided who will be "going over" (winning), but performers still need to know the general plan for the match. The more veteran wrestler typically dictates the proceedings with a discussion that varies in precision depending on a variety of factors, such as the two performers' familiarity with each other, the larger story line (i.e., who is heel and face), and the appropriate excitement level. In general, the show builds toward the main event; matches prior to the main event should never upstage the final fight.

On the whole, performers establish a basic framework with an established beginning, ending (i.e., "finishing move"), and a few moves in between. Wrestlers often clarify the framework by referring to a former star wrestler and his signature move (e.g. "You know, like Ricky Steamboat"), references that help calibrate their understanding of each other. They then lightly demonstrate what they mean physically with one another (e.g., "OK, so then we bump and you go through, and then a drop"). The framework helps wrestlers know that they need to be in certain positions at given moments, but as in a jazz performance, there is ample room for improvisation. As Timmy put it, "The heel normally calls the match, the pacing of the match. But it's up to the babyface to know when to fire up and get the people into it."

The second means of conveying expectations is through brief directives issued during the match itself. Wrestlers whisper instructions to one another when they are closely embraced in a corner of the ring (or positioned in a "submission move" on the mat). These exchanges with one another, hopefully inaudible to the audience, clarify or confirm an upcoming move (e.g., "tackle," "drop-down," "leapfrog," "dropkick"), verify that a partner is OK (i.e., not in fact injured), and sometimes express apology. Empathy was rarely revealed explicitly, but it was almost always operating. Take the following example from when we are all in the backroom watching the video of a previous night's match. On the TV screen is Dan, standing several steps up a ten-foot metal ladder stationed in the corner of the ring, embracing a guy from another promotion whom most of us don't know. Dan relays to us the conversation he had with his opponent in the midst of setting up his finishing move. "He said, 'Do you have me?' and I told him I had him. I said, 'It's all right . . . put your arm here.' . . . He needed to move his leg [for the move to succeed] so I told him to move his leg." The two performers then fly into the air from several feet up the ladder and do a flip while embracing (see figure 3.2).

They land safely on the mat nearly ten feet below, and the crowd roars its appreciation. This move, one of the most spectacular and (seemingly) painful of the match, demonstrates in crystallized form the importance of cooperatively working to manage the emotions of the audience. It lends insight into the backstage emotion management (of anxiety, in this case), since the whispered interchange on the ladder was essential to avoiding the slight mismatch of action that could have produced a serious injury to one or both wrestlers.

FIGURE 3.2. Ten-foot stepladder used as a prop. CREDIT. Author.

The third type of shared understanding is the ideal: performers use their intuitive sense of one another, anticipating the other's position unguided by any audible exchange. A forthcoming swing or kick is sensed by reading the partner's bodily and expressive cues. As with professional dancers, this type of synchronicity develops only when two wrestlers are well acquainted and have previously worked together in tandem. Hammer, a veteran, explained this phenomenon:

> You're sitting up, for instance. I might say, "Just stay." And you don't know what I'm doing, but I might just—boom [*stamps his foot*]. I'll do this, you come up again. And if you're smart, you'll just stay there [seated] because the people will be popping. But you have to really have this [sense] with somebody, because what if—boom! He puts his knee up. "Oh, fuck!" You know?

Because Hammer has confidence that his partner will not lift his knee at the crucial moment, he can execute a spectacular maneuver that makes the crowd pop. Such intuition allows performers to seamlessly move and coordinate with one another. In such cases, the movements flow from their synergy and trust in one another.

TECHNIQUES OF THE COORDINATED WORK

In nearly every match, wrestlers create a contrast in which one wrestler represents good, the other bad.[7] As Fishman explains, it is crucial to establish this "bond" as enemies. "If you don't take the time to establish that bond, like I'm the good guy, you're the bad guy, I need you to clap for me, I need you to make fun of him here, we hate each other because *why*—[then] why does the match even matter?"

Before the show begins, the booker determines which of the two performers in the match will be winning, or "going over." Wrestlers are designated as characters—usually by some trainer or booker they meet early in their wrestling career—but they require a secondary designation as a heel or babyface. (In some cases the character is automatically a heel, as he represents disgust by definition; e.g., "southern bad boy.") The heel or face designation tends to stick either for many months (if not forever) or until there is a "heel turn" or "face turn," a moment when the character completes a moral makeover, going from hero to corrupt villain or villain to humble hero who makes amends.

The creativity of gimmicks and story lines comes from a mashup of old and new, tried and tested ideas; other material comes from recently conceived capricious schemes. Sometimes they are even inspired by dreams, as Timmy explained: "I'll dream ideas and spots. I'll dream matches in my head—wake up at four in the morning and I'll write them down. . . . I'll be driving to work in the morning and be like, 'Oh, wait a minute,' and say 'I got to pull over and write this down.' It just pops in my head. A lot of story lines are just rehashed, [they are] old story lines, just with different twists and different people. . . . [Last night's gimmick] was old stuff from Memphis, they've been doing that spot for forty years."

The following techniques are used to jointly work the collaborative illusion. Most fundamentally, wrestlers must *sell their moves*. When a wrestler grips the body of an opponent, both must make a convincing facial expression of agony, pain, or distress. At the same time, loud grunts and groans are made to convey the physical duress. Selling the move demonstrates to the audience the strength, will, and ferociousness of your partner.

In order for the story to have logic, wrestlers must *sequence and build* so that moves sensibly follow one another. To maintain suspense the fight, like any good story, must make sense. For example, if one performer is (supposedly) more invulnerable than the other, this superiority must emerge after an initial period of give and take. As Timmy, the veteran, says, "You can't *start* the match with a double arm-flippin' crazy DDT, and then do an arm bar.[8] Who wants to see that? You have to *build*." Performers need to keep track of what has already occurred in the match. If a performer has wrenched his opponent's arm and (supposedly) inflicted harm, it would not make sense for the opponent to later use this "damaged" arm with great ease or force.

As the chapter's opening field note shows, wrestlers often need to slow down to achieve proper timing. The following example also demonstrates the importance of timing and other fundamentals.

> Dan and Pete are working each other. Cuss gives some basic pointers about being a heel. He says, "Remember, when you are the heel, think of it like you are being paid by the hour." I am not sure what he means, so I ask Fishman for clarification. He says, "Take your time," as he raises both his arms up and slowly walks around while grinning, gesturing toward an imaginary crowd. He says, "You go slow and milk everything."

This illustrates an overarching, though more tacit, rule of thumb—skilled performers can typically do more entertaining with less dangerous physicality. Getting fans invested in a good story does not necessarily require high risk and danger; it requires *convincing* acts of retribution, injustice, and vengeance at the right moment. Telling a physical story, like comedy, requires perfect delivery and timing. Physical drama needs the blow to the back (or head) delivered at the peak of sensible suspense. Performers must read and accommodate the crowd's emotions. It is, after all, show business, and the intention is to make money through the manipulation of fans' emotions.

Wrestlers are trained to *avoid the harder, bony parts of the body*. Performers want to make contact with the more fleshy parts of the body, so they usually avoid closed fists. Open fists soften the blows and make the contact noise more audible. If they exchange blows while standing, they usually use the outside forearm to make a more fleshy strike. When a prop such as a metal fold-up chair is used as a weapon to crush the top of the opponent's head, performers surreptitiously place a hand above their

FIGURE 3.3. Two opponents bounce off each other. CREDIT: ©2006 Mark Stehle Photography.

forehead to bear the brunt of the blow, sparing the skull from a more painful strike.

Wrestlers typically "work the left side." This means grabbing your opponent's left arm or leg so that he knows which limb you expect to grab and which of the two to give you. It is not always possible to do this, but this shared understanding cuts down on misunderstandings and poor timing.

Performers, like stage actors and many athletes, must develop *proper footwork*. Footwork is crucial: it establishes the foundation for success with the entire body. Before executing a move, a participant should move toward the center of the ring, where his opponent, who often cannot see clearly, will expect to find him. Lazy or poor footwork gets wrestlers out of position and in dangerous situations, such as being tangled in the ropes. Being quick on your feet also lets you bounce backward from a blow more promptly; this might lessen any impact.

Jumping is another technique that must be acquired. At the exact moment your opponent lifts you in the air, a wrestler should jump up. Instead of straining to hoist a two-hundred-pound man in the air unaided, your opponent will actually be lifting a much lighter person because you are simultaneously rising. When executed correctly, fans will not notice that one wrestler is assisting the other with the heavy lifting. If poorly timed, a wrestler is obviously leaping upward on top of his opponent and the collusion between the two fighters is made obvious, thereby breaking the kayfabe.

JOINT LABOR

As in all forms of work, wrestlers improve with experience. Veterans' emotional labor skills tend to be smoother and (apparently) more effortless than those of novice wrestlers. In general, "green" (less experienced) wrestlers progress from a performance heavily reliant on physicality to one more reliant on charisma and psychology—the dramaturgical skills and the interaction with the audience. New wrestlers first master the bump, a fundamental move constantly emphasized during training because the loud thuds it produces add to the audible dimension so important to theatricality. But physicality and bumps are not essential for "drawing heat"—getting the crowd fired up. As Fishman states, "You need to stop, take your time, and make things matter. A lot of times in that first match, you're just trying [so hard] to show people how good you are physically that you miss that whole other huge thing that makes the match."

Veterans learn to limit the number of bumps in their performance. Cuss explained this acquired knowledge during my interview with him.

> I don't have to kill myself anymore to get a reaction. Back in '99, I wrestled this guy almost every week in some kind of three-way match (or four guys, whatever). And, you know, I go to the locker room after the match, and I was always the smallest guy there. I'd hear him say, "I only bumped once." And this other guy, he says, "I didn't bump at all." The other guy, "I only bumped once." Meanwhile, I bumped twenty or thirty times. Oh my God, Jesus! Maybe I shouldn't be doing this. These guys are walking around like nothing, and I'm half dead.

Instead of repeatedly battering the body for pops, performers learn to assist one another by selling their painful agony (to the audience) with convincing expressions of pure suffering. The shared, implicit reality is that convincing portrayals of hatred, agony, and domination matter as much as, if not indeed more than, hard contact.

Timmy explains his knack for using joint emotion work to reduce drastically the hard physicality while still creating passionate emotions for the audience.

I seem to have a knack, thankfully, of controlling people's emotions, which a lot of guys don't have. . . . When you turn around, I poke you in the back of the head and poke you in the eye. Which is designed to make you [the fan] pissed off. "Now why'd you do that? You didn't need to do that!" And I beat up on your favorite [guy] for a little while. I do the simplest things—the other night with Patrick I stood on his hand while talking trash to the crowd. And people were into it. So I say, "Okay, why get away from that and take several falls on my back and run around when, if I stand on your hand, I'm going to get the kind of reaction I want." Smart way of working.

Even though he describes such emotional labor as doing "the simplest things," it in fact involves significant skills in coordinated emotional labor: the opponent is in position, the gimmick makes sense in terms of the sequence and timing of the story, the partner is selling the agony, Timmy steps on his opponent with only a light touch, and he is trash-talking to the crowd—all at the same time. This illustrates the collaborative creation of indignation.

It is important to note that being *too* light can be a problem. But if the format of the WWE production is an indication of proper performance techniques, we can infer that well-performed emotion work utilizes less physicality. The WWE format benefits from extensively crafted scripts taking place outside the ring in hallways, interviews, and the locker room. Additionally, color commentators narrate the drama and help convey the story to television viewers. In fact, in two hours of programming, viewers likely see no more than thirty-six minutes of in-ring physical wrestling; the rest is an "elaborate, soap-opera-style story line detailing a host of feuds, rivalries, grudges, and byzantine subplots" (Rosellini 1999, 1).

This ability to work the crowd with titillating psychology becomes a source of pride among the more experienced performers. The following passage from an interview with Timmy describes exactly how a skilled wrestler might work jointly with an opponent to get a reaction from the crowd without relying on more risky physical stunts.

Some guys feel . . . they have to do eighty flips to get a reaction from the people. But they don't interact with the people! It's move, move, move, move, move. I'll do moves, stop, and look at somebody. The best [fans] are kids and old ladies . . . you try to look for them. So you do a move and you do something right, and I'll see Hammer creep out of the thing on the side—I'll stop and stare at him. And I'll go and play to him. Maybe I'll come back this way, and I'll tell the little kid, "Let me know if he comes back and tries to get me!" I'll work [it], so I'll say [to the opponent], "Hey, give me a minute, then come get me." I'll go up to Hammer, stop right in front of that kid. Then I'll walk past him just a bit and as he's coming from behind; the kid will say, "Timmy, he's coming! He's coming!" Then the rest of the kids say, "Timmy, he's coming! He's coming!" And I'll go "Ooh!"—turn around—and he'll back off.

Their backstage relationship with one another generates a heightened suspense, less attainable from emotional labor done as an individual. Good performers therefore manage several simultaneous relationships: with the fans, with the other character, and with the other person playing the character. Not unlike those in other professions, wrestlers take increasing pride in these emotional labor skills as they advance.[9]

LATENT EMPATHY

Each performer, despite the outward display of hatred and domination, is responsible for his opponent's welfare (further explained in chapter 5). The two main manifestations of empathy are protection and trust. Rarely are these expectations stated explicitly, but when something goes wrong in the social script—a "disruption" according to Erving Goffman—the rules that govern our behavior are revealed.[10]

One example is the following admonishment by Tyler (posted on the group's Web message board) on the day after I witnessed him sustain an injury during training.

> I want to say thanks to those who called and e-mailed me about my injuries sustained Thursday night at the school. Doctors told me I have severe spinal and neck wear-'n'-tear for my age, and that it's time to hang up the boots. It's not something any wrestler wants to hear, but it's something that time will decide. I will be out for the next 2–3 weeks and hope that I will be in good condition by the next show. I am grateful because things could be much worse. With that said, I leave all of you with one thought: This is a serious business and we all MUST look out for each other, and PROTECT each other. Accidents happen, yes; but if you are not comfortable taking a move, giving a move, and/or don't know what a move is, you don't have to take it, and you shouldn't give

it. I will be bored as hell these next few weeks SO SOMEBODY PLEASE BRING ME SOME [wrestling video] TAPES!!!!!!

Instead of singling out Fishman, his partner in the ring at the time he was injured, Tyler channels his frustration into a strong edict that stresses the collective need for protection. Tyler, 28, took a couple of weeks off, but he did not "hang up the boots," as his doctor had recommended.

Another example of the protective dimension of empathy work is the intense teamwork needed when jumping, falling, and landing. These moves require a partner to catch or slow down a flying body. Tony explained: "I did a diamond clothesline to the outside, and Vinny didn't catch me. So I landed on my knee. If you watch the tape, you'll see me limp. I get up and I limp because I'm like, 'I have to catch Fishman.' And once Fishman did [his jump], I just laid down. Oh, that was the worst pain!" Here, the feeling of pain is actively suppressed on behalf of his opponent's (and the entire performance's) welfare. Despite the splitting pain when he landed on his knee, Tony had to get in the proper position for the next move. If he had not moved into the proper position, his opponent would likely have suffered an injury far more severe than a wrecked knee.

A corollary of the importance of protection is the need for trust. Wrestlers must suspend any fear and entrust their body to their in-ring opponent. Even among the self-selected group of people who choose to become professional wrestlers, staying relaxed when a person swings a fist at your face or holds you upside down as you and your partner leap off a ladder together is not natural. Suspending this instinct is a significant challenge for participants. Hammer explains how pro wrestling's elaborate coordination is embedded within a relationship of mutual trust:

> You're allowing me to put my hand behind your head. You're allowing me to hold your arm—which can easily be turned into a very compromising position. There's a difference between holding your arm like this, and holding your arm like that. It's very simple. And a lot of these guys know I can take the bony part of my arm [and drill it] into your shoulders, into your rotator cuff, into your elbows, underneath your neck.

To remain a participating performer, one must learn to rely on the precision of the opponent's movements. In essence, wrestlers develop and depend on feelings of trust in order to maintain a surface act of passionate anger, agony, or subordination.

An excerpt from an interview with Timmy illustrates the (ordinarily tacit) faith that performers must have in one another:

> When it comes to the big move and he picks you up over his head, if he's blown up and can't breathe, he drops you. You're at risk for being injured. He's out of shape. And people won't trust you. . . . [Essentially], you aren't going to lie to me. I'm saying, "I trust you, I'm going to give you my body. You're going to take care of me."

The imminent danger and risk of pro wrestling is managed with a backstage understanding that each wrestler will safeguard his opponent throughout the routine.

Occasionally, this reciprocal empathy breaks down. Timmy explained why he stopped putting himself in a position where he had to trust his opponent.

> [For the most part] I stopped doing crazy things. If I'm doing really crazy things, everything I do I make sure I can control myself, or if something does go down it's my fault. I'm not trusting somebody else, you know. Like Warrior, it's not that I didn't trust Warrior, but I don't want to take a chance of an "oops" happening. If an "oops" happened, I did it to myself. So I don't put myself in positions where I depend on someone else.

Timmy, who made his name doing "extreme" gimmicks with flips, ladders, tables, and pile drivers, no longer does such moves. Not all wrestlers, however, have enough status or seniority to choose to minimize the number of these risky acts. Wrestlers must be amenable to the booker's plans if they want to be booked in future shows. Rarely can a low-status wrestler simply choose to skip the personal risk. Nevertheless, this exception further demonstrates the (often implicit) negotiation that members must always operate within: follow the rules of mutual trust and protection, or you will not remain a pro wrestler.

BREAKDOWNS IN PASSION WORK

Every so often, the coordinated emotional labor between performers breaks down. While these breakdowns are rare, they are exceptions that

FIGURE 3.4. A veteran's fierce grip on a manager who fails to "sell" it. CREDIT: Justine Stehle.

prove the rule and allow us to refine the limits of passion work. A disruption typically occurs for one of three reasons: (1) a performer's labor is poorly executed or a signal is misread; (2) a wrestler feels disrespected to such an extent that the collaboration is called into question (often because he feels his opponent did not help to "sell" his moves); (3) a perceived threat to the group's hierarchy is so great that coordination is replaced with actual antagonism.

The most common reason is that someone's work is not being executed well, causing signals to be misread. In some of these instances, props such as baseball bats, chairs, ladders, barbed wire, and broomsticks are involved. Such gimmicks raise the stakes by providing more spectacular violence, along with greater risk of injury and mistakes. If a prop such as a broomstick is to be whacked on a wrestler's head (or back) but is not correctly notched (i.e., in the middle so it can crack more easily on contact) or the performer errs with the strike (missing the breaking point), the impact of the strike will be drastically different. Take, for example, Tony's explanation of a broomstick gimmick gone awry despite careful preparation:

> I told him I had a broom under the ring [that] I had sawed down about half way. [I was] thinking, "Oh, this thing is going to break real

easy" . . . but I pulled him over the apron and instead of just hitting him in that one area [of the broom], I hit him with the whole broom—and all you heard was "smack!" And I looked down and the broom didn't break, and I was like, "Oh, shit!" So what I did was I took the broom and broke it over my knee. It had broken, it just didn't break [in half]. It was at the maximum breaking point. So I must have looked like a he-man. I whacked him with this broomstick as hard as I could and it didn't break, then I broke it over my own knee. But from the top of his shoulder here, diagonally down across his back, it looked like he was caned . . . I felt bad about that.

Tony was lucky in this instance, because while the passionate hatred and agony were sold to the audience, his opponent suffered no serious injury.

Nevertheless, as Tony's account shows, he appears to be a powerful he-man, impervious to feeling pain, even though he actually "feels bad" at this very moment. He thus exhibits a form of dissonance, feeling guilt and sympathy while displaying anger and stoicism—one of many instances where we see the inverse of prototypical emotion work. Instead of an error causing feelings of anger and frustration (veiled by a display of ease and nonchalance), we see an error causing concern (veiled with anger and intent). Many analogous moments arise in which emotions of rage and anger are displayed when, in fact, sympathy and concern are felt.

The second form of disruption—what wrestlers call "big timing"—occurs when a match is underway and a wrestler is too pompous to sell his opponent's moves. Tony describes the arrogance this way: "Yeah, like I'm too big to bump for you, too good to sell for you. I'm somebody, you're nobody. Why am I going to put you over at all?"[11] As big-timing makes your opponent's moves appear as if they have *not* caused any pain or harm, it is deemed a breach in respect for your opponent.

The third type of disruption is a "shoot." In any match, either in the preparatory training or performance space, there is the possibility of a shoot: a true fight where the implicit coordination is suspended and painful "stiffs" are exchanged until order or some type of symbiosis is restored. One type of shoot (from prior to the match) is premeditated; the other begins when someone accidentally stiffs an opponent one too many times during the match, triggering an exchange of stiffs.

The aim of premeditated, intentional shoots is typically to maintain

FIGURE 3.5. Smashing another performer in the midst of the audience. CREDIT: Author.

respect for the group's hierarchy. A participant who is "not liked" or someone seen as getting "too bigheaded" often has no warning; it is not until he
is in the ring that he finds out what he's in for. Shoots can be frightening
because the taken-for-granted rules (i.e., the "loose," "relaxed" protocol)
have been abandoned by one member, thereby making his opponent virtually defenseless. Expecting a softer, looser grip or contact but, instead,
having a firm arm thrust at you creates extreme vulnerability because one
has no time to tense up or flinch in anticipation of the strike.

An accidental stiff that triggers an escalated exchange "happens all the
time," according to Timmy, because it is easy to unintentionally stiff an
opponent. Since the two partners are simulating a real fight with each
other, performers come extremely close to drilling an opponent's cheek or
choking his neck. As Slaughter states, "Sometimes you just can't help it."

For a seasoned wrestler, the standard response in such accidental instances is to send a firm shot back (known as a "receipt"). Timmy described what occurs:

> T: [If] the mistake happens repeatedly, you receipt the guy, give it back
> to him.
> TS: Doesn't that escalate?

T.: A lot of guys get it. "Ooh, sorry." [But] I mean, you only say you're sorry so many times before a guy's like, "Look, dude, you're killing me here." Then you give it back to him. [Some guys] will work as stiff as they can until you give it back to them. See how far they can push you. See if you're a pansy or not.

TS: So you get respect from pushing back?

T: [Yeah,] otherwise they'll just walk all over you. Like the first time I worked with Gary. He was killing me with his kicks. He hit me right in the back of the hamstrings, and I punched him right in the face. And everything was fine after that.

The receipts demonstrate several core, albeit implicit, rules of the game. Opponents must get synched with one another to keep kayfabe and put on a good show, but rules can be negotiated with the body. Information is exchanged through your movements and handling of each other—how hard, how light, where, and for how long express crucial elements of any relationship—like intent, trust, competency, and sympathy. At the same time, fighters all have different thresholds for what is too stiff or uncomfortable, and receipts allow them to adjust accordingly. Nevertheless, each exchange is precarious, because although receipts are an acceptable assertion of self-respect, something interpreted as unwarranted retaliation can be a provocation.

The intensity of the negotiation is heightened by the fact that at public shows adrenaline is flowing, the crowd is cheering, and wrestlers draw on "emotional memory" in which character and self are often blurred identities (Stanislavsky 1967). I have witnessed wrestlers take a lost match to heart as though it was *not* an outcome predetermined by the booker. These moments of frustration demonstrate the entanglement of the wrestling character and the person playing that character.

It is worth noting that disruptions can cause a match to lack a degree of kayfabe, potentially destroying the show's story line or causing an injury. A wrestler who repeatedly disrespects the rules and causes disruptions is pressured to leave the organization. However, these breakdowns in craft are all typically backstage, invisible to the spectators. On the stage—notwithstanding the big-time type of disruption—the spectators are likely to witness the infliction of suffering, hatred, and physical confrontation, just as they would if the performers were selling it rather than (in these disrupted moments) truly experiencing it.

SUMMARY

While the stage celebrates "natural man"—a brusque, uncivilized, and primitive being animated by basic needs of survival—a closer look reveals that the actual performing is relational and intimate, a fusion of the physical, cerebral, and emotional. Successful matches require strength and physicality, but even more, they require intuition, planning, and empathy for one's partner. Although the overtly emotional exchange with the audience is what the overall performance is known for, the backstage emotion teamwork—which takes place within the self and with other performers—sustains the show. This coordinated emotion work not only contradicts popular ideas about fighting, it also challenges conventional understandings of emotional labor and men's intimacy.

Instead of inducing a comfortable, relaxed state, as most studied forms of emotional work strive for, wrestling opponents use facial expressions (snarls, scowls, grimaces), sounds (grunts, moans), physical moves (lock-ups, bumps), and gimmicks (ladders, folding chairs, bottles) to stir fans to a state of agitation, indignation, or reverence. The repertoire, heightened by risk and coordinated actions with a partner, is more expansive than the traditional, individually crafted emotional labor. Performers jointly produce this passion by evoking positive feelings of association from the audience largely by engineering powerful negative feelings toward their seemingly dastardly partner. While this corroborates research finding that men excel at emotional labor that calls for the suppression of positive emotional displays and the presentation of negative emotions (Erickson and Ritter 2001), it also demonstrates how the coordinated performance allows for the sort of emotional breadth that is difficult to achieve in solo emotional work.

Emotional labor is usually analyzed as having negative mental health outcomes, particularly as a threat to one's sense of authentic selfhood.[12] Yet pro wrestlers demonstrate a contrary effect. Intimate, physical work with each other within a high-risk, dangerous context has the potential to generate something satisfying—a product that is neither tangible nor financial but social. Rather than cause them to experience emotional labor as harmful or alienating, their craft, because of its inherent empathy built upon mutual trust and protection, has the capacity to be connective, intimate, and a means for solidarity. Wrestling provides a forum in which men who closely adhere to normative masculine ideals—and shun outright expression of affection and care—actually find a degree of intimacy with other men. It stays undiscussed, and though the intimacy inhabits a quiet space within the broader framework of loud violence, it is nevertheless one of the craft's rewards.

The dynamics of passion work can be found within other staged (or ritualized) performances organized around audience appreciation or impact. Two stage actors on Broadway acting out a passionate display of vengeance perform similar surface acts of hostility while simultaneously coordinating technically precise movements that place a particular premium on cooperation and trust. In fact, a range of physical performances, not necessarily those set on stage, exhibit a certain degree of collaborative passion work in which workers deploy surface feelings that evoke feelings of uncertainty, suspicion, anger, or fear while simultaneously drawing on "deep feelings" of protection, care, respect, and trust for each other. These include, among other things, stunt men, magicians (e.g., knife throwers), figure skaters, tall tower-building gymnasts (e.g., Los Castells of Catalonia), pornography (or sex) workers, circus performers, dancers (e.g., break-dancers), TV talk show hosts and their guests (Grindstaff 2002), and street performers. Other examples include how prisoners of war (and by extension other incarcerated people) potentially develop relationships with sympathetic captors. In such an instance a guard must feign hostility and dominance while possibly experiencing empathy and connection with an individual prisoner.[13]

In fact, many displays of violence and bravado rely on a similar shared (backstage) understanding about the rules or structure of their interactions.[14] Consider the implicit agreement between professional hockey players who go to fisticuffs during games. Despite the brutality and significant corporeal consequences, players usually cooperate and abide by certain rules, such as unbuckling each other's helmets and waiting until gloves are off and bodies are squared (Branch 2011).[15] Like indie wrestlers, these performers work collaboratively to induce a particular feeling in their subject, and for the overall interaction to succeed, they must rely on skilled coordination, respect, and a certain degree of empathy for their partner.

WRESTLERS MANAGING THE MALE GAZE

BACKSTAGE IN THE LOCKER ROOM

Wrestlers arrive at the community center where they produce their Saturday night shows anywhere from two to six hours before the opening bell at 7 PM. After they pass through a set of cheap black curtains that more or less separate the back hallway from the opening portico, they walk about a hundred feet down to an old beat-up room. The long, narrow room (about 40′ x 15′), likely the teachers' lounge before the middle school closed and became a community center, appears to be undergoing an identity crisis. Its walls enclose three ugly couches, a beat-up pool table, some scattered student desks, an enormous metal desk moved toward a corner, two toilets within small closets, a sink, and in the near corner close to the first door, a makeshift kitchen with a coffeemaker and hot plate. Along the far wall of the room is a bank of translucent windows running the entire forty-foot length of the room.

While the room vaguely resembles a faculty lounge, it gives the appearance of also having served as some type of recreation and rumpus room for children. In addition to the pool table, there are several low shelves strewn with worn-out board games like Sorry and Boggle and a few thick gym mats piled into one of the corners. On a blackboard at the end of the room two sentences declare, in cursive, "No name calling" and "Clean up after yourself." A cinder block wall bears an awkwardly phrased dictum: "Feelings go both ways—yours get hurt so does mine."

Tonight, this room serves as the wrestlers' locker room. Looking around from the door that everyone uses to access the room, I see as many as twenty different men doing their own preperformance rituals. Small groups of them huddle here and there, the veterans generally closer to the door and the younger, less experienced wrestlers farther down to the right, near the ratty pool table. Standard-issue small-wheeled flight-attendant-like luggage bags lay helter-skelter among the puny student chairs and grungy couches.

Not everyone is huddled: I see Cuss, having taken off his T-shirt, stepping out of his khaki pants, CU and SS emblazoned in bright orange on the rear of his black Speedo-like trunks; Al, sitting on a miniature orange plastic chair designed for grade-school students, is lacing up his shiny boots to just below the knee; Brickman, wearing nothing more than black spandex shorts bearing his character's name stitched down their left upper thigh, is standing alongside Donny, the two of them working out plans for their match; Epic, standing alone with one shoulder strap of his blue spandex singlet hanging down, is methodically applying Pam cooking spray to his whole body to create the wet, glistening look of light sweat (being careful not to get any on his hands because he doesn't want the grip of his opponents to easily slip).

Fishman enters the room, rolling the requisite suitcase behind him; Tony is generously applying Axe aerosol body spray to nearly every area of his body, saturating the entire room with the smell of cheap cologne; the doctor, a sixty-year-old bearded white man with a stethoscope around his neck, sits near the windows at the massive metal desk, pumping a blood pressure cuff tightly around Matt's arm. Cuss has now begun to help Patrick apply tanning lotion to his arms. Two other guys are vigorously brushing their teeth at the corner sink, making loud guttural noises as they spit out toothpaste and saliva.

Taped to the wall next to the main door to the room is an 11″ x 17″ piece of white paper listing tonight's card, with the sequence of matches and the booker's plans for how many minutes each of the seven preliminary matches should last: 8, 8, 12, 10, 8, 12, and 12, respectively. Below that appears, in larger print, 18–20 for the main event. One of the two referee names is written next to each time allotment. At the very bottom of the sheet, the wrestlers are addressed as follows: "Do not leave locker room once the show starts. All times are from bell to bell. Stick to them! No mic times unless stated. Any questions about your match, ask Tyler. Be safe and have fun!"

At one point I see Tyler, the booker who created these guidelines, going over tonight's card with Nick, the emcee for the show. I listen as he gives instructions: "Announce next month's show, announce that guys will do autographs during intermission . . . remind them about T-shirts at the intermission. We have them in different colors. . . ." Nick scribbles the instructions on an index card, which he then places in his breast pocket. Guys keep walking up and inspecting the sheet of paper with tonight's card as though it were constantly changing, but it rarely does.

After getting dressed in their outfits, wrestlers each spend a couple of minutes taping up their wrists and fingers. They wrap the tape around their wrists about three or four times, some choosing white athletic tape, others choosing shiny black electrical tape. Taping up is pretty effortless as most guys have shaved their arms and wrists.

Brickman flexes his biceps as he speaks with Hammer; a few minutes later I notice that Matt is doing the same. A couple of guys in the hallway are stretching their hamstring, quadriceps, and back muscles. About four different guys take turns using a short rubber tension cord with handles on the end of it to get the blood flowing and "get more puffed out." Just outside the room, I see Dan doing push-ups on the hallway floor.

Meanwhile, Cobra is painting a design, in acrylics, on Scud's face. It is an iconic yellow nuclear warning sign, bordered in green with red flames coming out of it. Someone comes up and jokes, "Dude, he's painting a big fucking cock on your head!" Cobra completes it after about forty-five minutes. His delicate brushstrokes make a bold, arresting insignia that defines Scud's character. "He's the best," Scud says of Cobra's artistry.

Around 6:15, roughly forty-five minutes before the show begins, Patrick pops a new "Best of Rage" highlights videotape into the TV. A dozen guys rush over and huddle below the screen that hangs from the ceiling above the pool table. Music and lighting are professionally mixed to feature several thrilling acrobatic, high-flying moves. The well-edited clips of the promotion's previous shows and matches are impressive. Fishman, noting the nicely edited, stylized depiction on the screen, exclaims, "Tyler looks so sexy in those pants. He has the best ass!"

Andrew, a chiseled, tan twenty-two-year-old white guy, walks around wearing a flowing red cape trimmed with red feathers and a three-inch-high headband with "Star" stitched on it. He acts sober and brooding whenever I see him, so it is hard for me to contain my amusement with his Liberace-like outfit.

Wayne at one point wanders around inquiring about a "beater," a beat-up old car, to see if he can drum one up for the show. My car is a run-of-the-mill ten-year-old Honda sedan—and I try to contribute to the group in any way I can—so I start to volunteer it. But I renege after realizing the gimmick—two wrestlers would be slammed onto the hood as their fight spills into the adjacent parking lot, and the car would be majorly dented.

Just when it seems to me that the odor of the Axe body spray cannot be any more oppressive, I witness Tony spraying the aerosol can (for fifteen straight seconds) on both socks and on the front of his trunks. Only then do I consider how the alternative—a heinous, several-days-old acrid body stench—would be much worse for someone like his opponent. As I watch, he looks over at me and says that he is wrestling the Assassins and that he "expects it to be physical . . . I mean, I'm not sweatin' it, but I think it'll be physical."

Just before the opening bell, someone who had looked out at the main performance space returns to the locker room and triumphantly states, "There's *a lot* of people out there!" Timmy returns a few minutes after this proclamation and says loudly to the entire room, "This crowd is *easy*!"

A palpable energy always permeates the group during the Saturday night shows. Nowhere is this more evident than backstage during preperformance rituals just before the opening bell. Performers are excited but also very anxious about how they will perform and how the crowd will respond. The tension manifests itself in disparate ways: some men exude intensity as they go about their preparations with quiet focus, while others are outright silly and distractible, teasing and carousing with jokes and fake punches—a gesture of gruff affection that reminds me of my seventh-grade days at an all-boys school.

The men's energy is marked by the self-consciousness of preparing themselves to play the part of strong, intimidating men.[1] Enhancing the look of one's individual character—identities they are only partially "in" while backstage before the show—is disconcerting because it forces everyone to confront the absurdity of the collective farce. In this locker room we see men completely preoccupied with preparing to be men they are generally not. It is men prepping to play the part of intimidating, invulnerable men—men who, if they actually were intimidating and invulnerable, wouldn't have *any* concern with how they look.

Despite being regular, routine preperformance behaviors of wrestlers, the acts are nonetheless an exercise in ambivalence. Regardless of your status or years in the business, getting yourself "puffed out"—looking good and ready for a fake fight—remains unsettling. Primping in the mirror and plucking body hairs with tweezers enhances your character's look (and shows a degree of professional respect), but these are behaviors that men ordinarily do only in private, if at all. For these men, who in everyday life strive for "cool, calm and collected" indifference, rehearsing a look of anguish or shock to coincide with coordinated intimate movements does not come easily. Moreover, in the locker room there is no screaming audience to defuse or absorb the awkward tension associated with playing the role of a man who, for the most part, you actually are not.

With particular focus on the backstage training and preparations of wrestlers, this chapter analyzes the complexity of "doing" acts of intimate, self-conscious masculinity.[2]

MASCULINE SPECTACLE

Masculinity is popularly portrayed as a derivative of some inherent, inescapable hardwiring. "Boys will be boys" remains a common explanation for men's and boys' behaviors, particularly the negative ones that stubbornly persist. Despite the prevailing pull of this biologically based rationalization, gender scholars have demonstrated that masculinity and femininity are largely acts that we learn and sustain through everyday interactions with one another. Scholars challenge the explanations by demonstrating that masculinity tremendously varies across time and space.[3] Our gendered behavior appears natural because our actions often adhere to the set of gendered myths the culture upholds.[4] "Masculinity," as Segal declares, "as any type of inner essence, is a fiction, or set of fictions—however real, perhaps disastrously real, men's attempt to live out these fictions may be" (1993, 630).

Pro wrestling's show of loud disgruntled men solving their disputes through physical violence is usually characterized as masculine. The critiques, especially those coming from scholars, critique wrestling's intersection of the masculinity with violence. Messner and his colleagues identify pro wrestling as part of the "Televised Sports Manhood Formula," a "commercialized version of hegemonic masculinity [that is] constructed partly in relation to images of men who don't measure up" (2000, 392). Other analysts characterize pro wrestling as "hypermasculine" (*Worcester Telegram* 2000) and misogynist (Ricard 1999, Trujillo et al. 2000, Hardin and Hardin 2000, Smith 2004). Jackson Katz and Sut Jhally, for example, were so concerned about the messages within televised pro wrestling that they produced an educational film about its dangers. Pro wrestling is harmful because it teaches viewers that "taunting, ridiculing, and bullying are what defines masculinity" (Katz and Jhally 2000). One study found direct causal evidence regarding the viewing of professional wrestling and violent behavior (DuRant et al. 2006).[5]

Performers themselves are likened to the bawdy characters they play within the ring: caricatures of working-class masculinity, like other media depictions of white working-class males as immature and irresponsible "buffoons" (Butsch 2003). Given the class associations with physicality and the long-term decline in overall wages, there is presumed correlation between the loss of masculine capital (and financial capital for that matter) and the interest in performing (or "doing") masculinity. The assumption by both lay and academic commentators is that participants who play the part of muscular pugilistic men are drawn to wrestling because they long to possess the very traits they can no longer achieve in everyday life. These ideas emanate from the popular "compensation" theory; since the ideal of Western masculinity is hard to achieve, especially for subordinate groups of men, males modify their "manhood acts" when they are "unable or unwilling to enact the hegemonic ideal" (Schrock and Schwalbe 2009). Pro wrestling participation represents a reclamation project in which men enact a version of manhood that they have lost or never successfully found in other realms of life. With these acts of bravado, violence, and dominance, participants salve the wounds of perceived loss inflicted by depressed wages, economic uncertainty, or women's rise in the labor force.

Take, for example, the *New York Times* characterization of an indie wrestler who, having lost his day job, "finds his revenge" in the ring. This was anything but the case, since he had been gainfully employed as a schoolteacher and lost his job as a result of his commitment to wrestling—he took sick days in order to do wrestling shows. He certainly did not "find" wrestling as a means to get "revenge" after being laid off.

There is *some* truth in the compensation characterization: all of the Rage wrestlers identify as heterosexual, most are working-class, and wres-

Matthew Kaye, a k a Matt Striker, puts his opponent in a headlock. Until April, Mr. Kaye led a double life — as a teacher and a pro wrestler.

Robert Payes/Stiff Store Photography

Truant Teacher Who Lost Job Finds His Revenge in the Ring

By SUSAN SAULNY

He might have lost his job as a teacher, but Matthew Kaye is on his way to becoming a wrestling star. And his real-life story has become part of the melodrama in the ring.

Mr. Kaye, a former social studies teacher at Benjamin N. Cardozo High School in Queens, lost his job after he was caught taking sick time to go on a pro wrestling tour. Now, he says, he has signed a contract with World Wrestling Entertainment, which produces televised wrestling shows.

"I'm on Cloud 9; I've been numb for weeks," said Mr. Kaye, a chiseled muscleman who is known as Matt

on a wrestling tour in Japan. Faced with disciplinary action, Mr. Kaye chose to quit.

Investigators from the office of Richard J. Condon, the special commissioner of investigation for the city schools, said that in December a woman who identified herself as Mr. Kaye's mother called Cardozo and said that her son was out because of

A thrilling change of scene, from classroom to 'SmackDown!'

FIGURE 4.1. "Finding revenge." SOURCE: *New York Times.*

tling offers the rugged physicality and symbolic domination that have had a sustained appeal for them since childhood.[6] Pro wrestling is an "alchemy of theatrics and competitive testosterone" (Weber 2005) in which, as Sharon Mazer found, "what is presented, affirmed, and critiqued is nothing so much as the idea(l) of masculinity itself" (1998, 5). In addition, physicality is indisputably central to the identity of most of these men. As Linda McDowell found in her study of working-class men, "Embodiment is a crucial part of their masculinity, both in the workplace and in leisure arenas, as the disembodied rationality of idealized hegemonic masculinity is contrasted to the strength, agility or sporting prowess that are advantages of subordinate masculinities" (2003, 13).[7] As Fishman said to me, wrestling appeals to his "guy" sensibilities. "It's wrestling . . . it's like the ultimate guy thing. I mean it's soap opera, it's gigantic, larger-than-life characters. It's physical—there's blood, there's violence. There are ridiculously attractive women that no man in his right mind could ever think he had a shot with."

However, the esteemed notion of being a "badass"—often combed from years of being sons, peers, and players on fields and teams—is nearly the reverse of what they must do to become a pro wrestler.[8] The vanity, pageantry, and choreography of pro wrestling, plus its kinesthesia of intimacy and homoeroticism, flout the ideals of hard masculinity. To be a successful pro wrestler, performers must unlearn the rugged, individualistic habitus they have spent their lives being groomed into. While they may have been drawn to pro wrestling because of its masculine symbolism, these young men end up in a pursuit in which doing masculinity can be self-conscious, soft, and counterintuitive (not to mention painful). To address this conundrum, they cast the interpretation of their acts within a new system of meanings. The pages that follow contain an analysis of the gendered puzzles and alternative interpretations of their behavior.

HARD MASCULINITY

Western culture continues to venerate the man who elides a concern with image and appearance.[9] While capitalism has done its best to ensnare male consumers (e.g., "metrosexuals") and an increasing proportion of men are exposed to the body-shaming and image-conscious constraints that women have long been subject to, it is still a maxim that men should overcome image consciousness and dismiss any concern with appearance.[10] Dominance has no need for self-consciousness; moreover, the male gaze is traditionally directed at women. "One might simplify this by saying," as John Berger does in his book *Ways of Seeing*, "men act and women appear. Men look at women. Women watch themselves being looked at" (1972, 47). Susan Bordo further clarifies. "'Do you like what you see?' . . . [Men, in contrast to women,] must never seem as though they are asking this question, and may display their beauty only if it is an unavoidable side effect of other 'business'" (1999, 199).

In professional wrestling, of course, men act *and* men appear. Appearance, image, and presentation of self—the look—generate the meanings of what is, after all, a *show*. Wrestlers heavily invest in their look because being a pro wrestler "means cultivating and displaying a wrestler's body, living as the embodiment of a particular kind of physical power" (Levi 2008, 14). Pageantry and vanity are normalized more than most any other activity, although as we learn, it does not necessarily come with great ease.

FIGURE 4.2. Vanity. CREDIT: Justine Stehle.

A wrestler's outfit is a fundamental part of his in-ring character. Wrestlers carefully select accoutrements like boots, leggings, hairstyle, and knee pads. Most at Rage design their own outfits with the assistance of Cobra, a regular member of the group who handles many of the design details. On the night of a show, the accoutrements include any or all of the following: an outfit and boots, a spare outfit in case of a wardrobe problem, body spray or deodorant, baby oil or spray on cooking oil, tape, hair bands, hair gel, makeup, mouthwash, tweezers, tanning lotion, toothbrush and toothpaste, hairbrush, water bottle for misting/wetting hair, and rubber exercise tension cords for puffing up muscles. Handheld mirrors are never around despite their potential utility; performers instead opt to use the small mirror on the wall above the sink in the closet bathroom.

Participants exchange opinions and tips about exactly where on their body they would like to see an increase in bulk or firmness.[11] Tips are traded on how to gain more weight (e.g., "set an alarm and wake up every two hours and force yourself to eat a full meal"; "take androstene"), remove body hair (e.g., "use an electric razor, *then* a disposable for difficult spots"), and how to avoid looking pale (e.g., "go to a tanning salon"). About three-quarters of the participants remove body hair from their entire upper body, and nearly half of them patronize tanning salons right before a show.

The greatest scrutiny is usually reserved for one's own body. In an effort to gain recognition for his efforts in the weight room, a wrestler might ask another wrestler (or me), "Do I look bigger to you?" Yet everyone, aside from those with the highest status, is subject to being judged. Remarks are heard about a guy's "six pack" (or "cubes"), biceps, pectorals, buttocks, and leg size. An occasional wrestler wants to shed weight, but most are interested in gaining bulk to look larger or be more "fit," their term for muscularity. Guys discuss their increase (or decrease) in size from week to week; unsolicited comments, even ridicule, can occur at nearly any moment. One night at training, for example, Chris, a referee, remarked on Johnny's slim but wiry body to folks alongside the ring. "Johnny has a good body," he said. Slaughter, Johnny's opponent, retorted incredulously, "Good body? What, by Gumby's standards?" On another night at training, after I handed Dan a photo of him and Johnny performing a complicated high-spot, Donny leaned in, looked at the photo closely, and said to Dan, "Looking at your and Johnny's legs doesn't make me feel so bad about *my* legs."

No part of the anatomy is spared, including penis size. The following example illustrates a moment where the concern for the size of that organ actually interrupts the training.

Hammer was in the ring with Fishman showing a move to the rest of the wrestlers. He used Fishman as a partner to demonstrate where the hands need to be placed in order to execute the back drop. Fishman was wearing some tight gray shorts. As he holds his hands around Fishman's waist, Hammer stops halfway through the demonstration and exclaims, "Jesus, Fishman!" (referring to the bulge in Fishman's spandex pants). Fishman stops and calmly states, "Yeah, I've always thought about being a stripper, if I weren't so fat." Donny, standing outside the ring, watching, chimes in: "It's not that you're fat, you just have a fat cock!"

This illustrates the body consciousness as well as the intrinsic intimacy. Wrestling requires close physical contact with opponents—on every part of the body. Men must place their hands in strategic positions to make moves easier to execute. This is complicated because homophobia, as Michael Kimmel contends, is "the animating condition of the dominant definition of masculinity in America" (1994, 282). A "German suplex," for example, requires one man to stand behind and lift his opponent into the air. At the exact time he places his hands around his opponent's waist, his opponent jumps (so that he does not have to lift his opponent's entire body weight). In the process, the one lifting, who often has the side of his face pressed to his opponent's buttocks, inevitably ends up touching the opponent's legs, waist, groin, and torso. Obviously the lack of clothing compounds this physical intimacy—often wrestlers are wearing only shorts and boots.

Trainers try to explain, sometimes even apologize for, having to repeatedly touch another half-dressed man's body in sensitive areas. The following example demonstrates this constant repudiation.

Tyler yells at six new students like a drill sergeant as he leads them through push-ups, squats, and spins. When you fall from "up" to "drop," you are to hit the mat with your arms above your head so that the slap makes a thud. After the squats, Tyler shows everyone how to do a spin—an exercise where one man spins on top of another wrestler with his chest pressed to his partner's back while the partner is positioned on all fours. While demonstrating this Tyler states, "You gotta really grope him! I know it looks kinda gay, but you gotta grab him."

Of course, these apologies are an exercise in futility as the intimate groping is neverending. In fact, avoidance of it would produce a terrible match that no one would want to see. In other words, if *that* looks gay, then most *everything* they do looks gay.

It is no wonder that Tyler states this, given the perception many have of pro wrestling as being gay. It is easy to find cultural artifacts that sexualize wrestling, and various treatments celebrate the association of wrestling

FIGURE 4.3. The inherent intimacy. CREDIT: ©2006 Mark Stehle Photography.

with homosexuality. In Brian Pronger's research on masculinity, for example, a research subject states that "wrestling and sex to me are the same thing; there's no difference" (1990, 186).[12]

Even the entertainment itself flirts with this association. Characters with an ambiguous sexual orientation have been part of pro wrestling story lines for more than fifty years. The Rage promotion was no exception, as Donny played the part of a gay wrestler—he entered the ring with a rainbow flag and hot pink pants—for nearly two years (he is profiled in chapter 1).[13]

It was just after I entered the field that I encountered an acknowledgement of this symbolic frame. My exchange with the veterans Timmy and

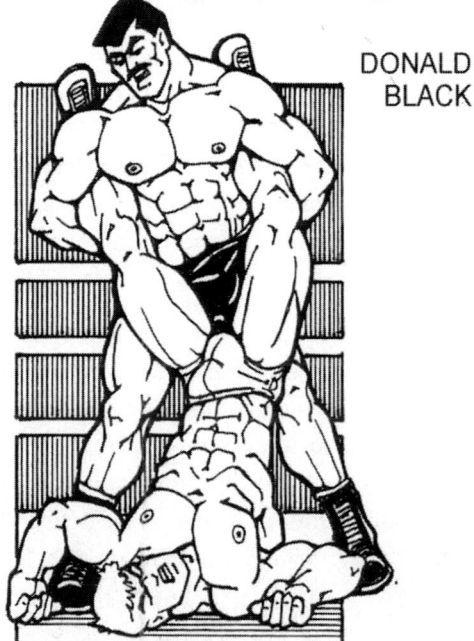

WRESTLING
FOR
GAY GUYS

DONALD
BLACK

POWER
BOOKS

FIGURE 4.4. The cover of Donald Black's 1995 manual *Wrestling for Gay Guys: Overcoming Problems, Fears, and Hangups*. This how-to manual considers wrestling as a type of fetish within certain gay subcultures. Although wrestlers would prefer not to, they must contend with this persistent sexual association. Reactions range from confusion to anger to lighthearted amusement. SOURCE: *Wrestling for Gay Guys*.

Patrick witnesses to their consciousness of the connection between pro wrestling and homosexuality:

> PATRICK: So you're a professor?
> TS: No [trying to downplay it], I only have, like a master's. I'm working on a Ph.D.
> TIMMY: *Only* a master's? Phew . . . I barely have a high school diploma. Ph.D., master's . . . does it make a difference?

PATRICK: You gotta write like a 400-page book to get the Ph.D.

TIMMY: So are you interested in how wrestlers have a lot of gay tendencies?

Since we were interrupted before I had a chance to respond, I asked Timmy what he had meant by wrestlers having "gay tendencies" in a later interview. He answered:

> I think it's because we touch men and things like that. It's just a way we joke about it. "Hey, just joking." I don't know exactly how to put it, just fucking around. It's hard to explain. . . . None of my friends outside of the business can understand it. You're wrestling around with men half-naked. Grabbing them by the crotch and body and things like that, so you just kind of joke around about it. Kind of makes us feel better, I guess. I don't know. . . . I can't explain it. It just happens. It's weird.

I expected more from a fourteen-year veteran than this hesitant, vague explanation, but it is a thorny topic, especially given how much is at stake. What is clear is that joking about the intrinsic homoeroticism functions as a relief valve for the pursuit's incessant tension. Label it, joke about it, and then file it away so no one truly confronts it. More than anything, Timmy's response demonstrates the anxiety of performing with other men within a contrived act that requires so much physical intimacy.

The extensive sensuality of pro wrestling is, of course, inherent in all forms of wrestling, but in high school (or Olympic) wrestling, the objective is to defeat one's opponent, and hard, firm grasps are mandatory techniques used to pin opponents and win. Pro wrestling shares this physicality but is more tenuous because actions are not motivated by actual competition or domination. To avoid injury and only appear to be in conflict, participants extend soft, caring hands and light touches of one another so they can move in graceful, if brawny, synchronicity.

Wrestlers are encouraged to maintain this light disposition outside the ring as well. I learned how this rule transcends the in-ring interactions and is enforced throughout the indie scene early in my fieldwork:

> At about 9 PM Tony circled the outside of the ring giving parting handshakes. When he got to the corner of the ring where I was standing with some newer students, one of the new guys reached out and shook his hand, apparently too hard. Tony said "Light! . . . light . . . light," to

the new guys. The others came over and, one by one, gave him a light grip. He turned to me and I feigned a huge, vigorous handshake before giving him the softest dead-fish shake I could. "Perfect!" he said.

In pro wrestling light, soft touches are valued—both inside and outside the ring—inverting the hard norm of masculinity. This would presumably be disconcerting if not for the fact that every other member adheres to the convention.

However, despite living in a postcloset era and knowingly investing in an activity that requires endless amounts of touching and intimate maneuvers, men in the indie scene incessantly police one another for conduct that might even suggest "gay tendencies." Everyday examples include "Do you have to be so gay when you do it?" and if, for example, someone is sitting with his legs closely crossed, "You aren't gay . . . don't sit like that!" Even with this policing, sexualized behavior is an everyday occurrence in the training space.[14] While it is impossible to know the actual intentions of those who initiate it, mimicking sexual acts was almost always a symbol of dominance. The most common form is wrestlers dry-humping other members of the group (a man stands behind another group member and mimics the motion of anal penetration). The simulation is performed when the other person is either unaware of it occurring (as a result of being pinned face down to the mat, for example) or in a subordinate position—such as being on his knees and reaching for the bottom rope or, as in the following example, bending down to tie his shoes:

> Just before we all left for TGI Friday's, Tony came up and started dry-humping Donny. He pumped his torso back and forth a few times while Donny was bent over unlacing his boots. Donny then moved away from him and said, "You got two more days and then I'm no longer gay!" (referring to the upcoming change in his public wrestling character). As Tony saw that I had been watching this whole exchange, he explained, "Don't worry, in real life I am actually a total homophobe."

While this incident corroborates research that finds that men's homophobia is heightened when they are concerned with emasculation, it also shows how homoerotic behavior (in this case dry-humping another member of the group) functions as a performative act of dominance.[15] An act like this is unlikely to occur if no one else is there to witness it, and because the act's recipient is of equal or lower rank in the hierarchy, it is

FIGURE 4.5. Solidarity with (and care for) "opponents." CREDIT: Justine Stehle.

a show of dominance. (Never did I witness a subordinate simulate a sex act on a superior.)

The sexualized terrain is difficult to navigate because, for one thing, mixed messages abound about what degree of displayed affection is permissible or offensive. Second, status often determines the homophobic penalties one might receive, and status is usually in flux. It may rise or drop based on wit, audience response, or cool indifference to injury, among other things. Most importantly and obviously, wrestlers *must* touch one another in order to actually wrestle.

The following two examples from training (they took place on the same night) demonstrate the ubiquity of homophobia and how status shapes the responses to it.

> Al and JD are in the ring wrestling, and Al is lying on JD's back, both facing the same direction. Things seem rather ordinary, and most guys are not paying close attention as they stand below the ring or on the apron of the ring. From nowhere, Dan, noticing their positioning, exclaims, "What the hell are you doing, Al? Sticking your cock in his ass? Where did you get the idea for that move from?" Al, looking very

concerned, doesn't have a chance to defend himself, and no one really cares to hear his explanation.

Donny is in the ring demonstrating a new move to Al, Brett, and Alex. He is on his stomach lying on the mat and he has his legs spread apart. He raises his buttocks in the air while his elbows remain on the mat. Hammer is standing outside the ring and he shouts, "That looks so gay!" Donny changes his positioning and replies, "Yeah, well, it's wrestling. Get used to it!"

Despite the necessity of the sensuality, these examples show how participants remain hypervigilant about the ever-possible doubt of their sexual desires.[16] Depending on one's place in the hierarchy, the sanctions may or may not be easily dismissed; subordinate wrestlers can be subjected to homophobic sanctions at nearly any moment. In fact, the homophobia can be so stifling that it impedes the acquisition of wrestling skills. Ironically, the greater fear a wrestler has of being labeled gay, the slower he develops his skills and advances as a solid performer.

The homoeroticism was at times a challenge for me in my role as a researcher as well. Take, for example, the following conversation regarding gay pornography.

I asked Nic where they got the wrestling ring. He said they bought it at an auction for $5,000 and they ordinarily cost much more (like $8,000). He explained that he got a good deal on it because he bought it from a guy who turned down the highest (and first) bidder because apparently, the original high bidder "wanted to use it for gay porno." Nic made his agreement with the seller's decision to me very clear.

In not questioning whether the gay intent or the pornographic intent was what concerned him, I erred as a researcher—and also contributed to a certain taboo around homosexuality. But I felt that asking for clarification might flout the group's tacit rules.[17]

PSEUDOSPORT

Traditionally, men participating in organized sports, especially contact sports, are granted a pass as to their masculinity. Some scholars find this the main impetus behind the proliferation of organized sports in the late nineteenth century (Guttmann 2000, Sage 2000).[18] Athletics offer boys and men an opportunity to prove their manliness, and all boys, to a greater or lesser extent, are judged according to their success or failure in competitive sports (Eitzen 1975, Sabo 1985). As Varda Burstyn states, sports provide "perhaps the one constant in an ever changing world where the requirements of manhood and masculinity are so hard to fulfill" (1999, 25).

Today openly gay athletes are increasingly accepted in sports. However, this hallowed terra firma is especially muddied in pro wrestling because the functionality of the athlete and the testing of character—key features of legitimate sports—are missing.[19] The bodily logic is more akin to ballet than battle as wrestlers *craft* an act of dominance instead of truly winning one. Rather than destroy an opponent, a pro wrestler actually trusts and protects him; success comes to both from helping each other look powerful and skilled. Some sports may share this effect, but pro wrestling maintains the fraudulence (and the emphasis on lightness and safety) within the framework of sports entertainment.

The fakery that is central to sustaining physical storytelling also represents wrestling's bane. Detractors harp on the fact that it is not functional violence. The male sports world trades in hard, bruising contact, and the public's valuation of a sport is highly correlated with the degree of violence in it. That international rugby players tease American football players for their use of pads and helmets while American football players razz soccer players for their noncontact play illustrates this valorization of violence. But even in the "softer" endeavors of soccer and baseball, the objective is still to beat your opponent.[20] In pro wrestling you dominate only as an act, a collective act built on audience recognition and participation. Yet performance constitutes a very small proportion of the time wrestlers spend together when compared to their overall time input. While the pageantry, intimacy, and display are directed toward the ephemeral *onstage* show, the homosocial practice space—where most of wrestlers' time together is spent—lacks a paying audience. Since the audience defuses the homoerotic tension, yet it is not a large part of their time spent together, their work with one another is often a disconcerting, self-conscious experience.

RECASTING THE DRAMA

The learning and performing aspects of pro wrestling are characterized by nuance and complexity. Much of the complexity stems from the need to unlearn "hard" instincts (those helpful in a *real* fight) and adopt the counterintuitive bodily skills of remaining loose, relaxed, and trusting. It is difficult to look angry when in fact you are trusting or to slap your arm widely and loudly without actually inflicting harm.

At the center of this challenge is a conundrum: how do participants maintain a normative masculine habitus, one generally upholding a rigid, unforgiving definition of masculinity, when their training and performing contradict several of its rather stubborn precepts? Put otherwise, how does one train for and participate in a performance that seems a celebration of and forum for manliness but that is in actuality an ambivalent exercise in which intimacy, pageantry, expression, and choreography are the essential ingredients? How does a wrestler navigate this world of contradictions, and what meanings does it impart?

A closer look reveals that wrestlers invert and reinterpret their effeminate, homoerotic acts. Instead of language and meanings that realize the intimacy, theatricality (choreography), and pageantry, the group emphasizes the routine pain, business, and intragroup validation. Two sets of meaning uphold masculine credibility: first, homosocial solidarity, consisting of the bodily duress (pain, injury, discipline) and dominance intrinsic to the experience; and second, the professionalism of show business, consisting of business acumen, technical expertise, and showmanship. The homosociality of the training buttresses these interpretations of behavior; all-male contexts are a common proving ground, since men are most often concerned with getting validation not from women but from other men. Fellow wrestlers, especially veterans, sanctify their achievements, although the homosociality nonetheless presents certain risks.

SOLIDARITY THROUGH BODILY DURESS

Mike M. takes pride in his ability to get back up despite the pain of being thrown around hard by the older guys. He explains the thrill of getting slammed by a veteran during one such session.

> I got to referee a match today with Rage, he was the heel in the match. You know, it was just in front of the other students and Timmy. [He pinned Slaughter.] I raised Rage's hand, he wins. [Then Rage] was like, "Can you bump?" I said "A little bit." He picks me up and shoulder-slams me. That guy's huge, too. But the rush, you know! I wasn't hurting at all, I got up smiling. The next day it hurt. But when everyone's there, it's like, "Oh, you look good."

It is noteworthy how the pain is not only denied, but muted by the fact that "everyone's there" (in actuality only ten other fellow wrestlers were there). Legitimacy derives from the intragroup acknowledgment of the achievement, not from fan appreciation.

For younger, less experienced wrestlers, the intragroup response often bestows the greatest validation, reinforcing the idea that masculinity is a homosocial enactment. Mike M., you may recall, feels that "to have the boys really like you . . . that would be the best." This perspective represents the notion that it is actually other men who are so important to men because American men define their masculinity in relation to each other (Kimmel 1996). As Brian Pronger states, this is the irony of orthodox gender relations: "Men become segregated from women; consequently, they develop a greater affinity for other men than they do for women . . . the paradox of orthodox masculinity is that the hierarchy of gender difference compels men to find satisfaction in one another" (1990, 178–179).[21]

In Donny's case, having never played sports and coming from a "household full of women," it was less the pain than the achievement of competency and perseverance under bodily duress that made him a man. When he first attempted pro wrestling, the school he was in "beat the shit out of" him. He entered the Rage school doubting that he could surmount the physical challenges. Earning the respect of his fellow wrestlers for enduring the physical disciplining became a realization of Donny's manhood.

> Cuss always tells me now, "Man, look at this tool. I don't think this guy's going to last a day." I know that two other guys didn't think I was going to last either. Now, where I am at, with all the somewhat success I have had for myself, they told me outright, we never thought you would last. . . . When I walked into Rage wrestling school, I walked in as a boy and walked out a man through the wrestling and the training I did. Because you feed off a lot of what guys feed you.

Other young wrestlers see achievement in the newfound association with vets and former stars. Al feels a sense of achievement and solidarity because he is now working alongside wrestling legends he has followed since childhood. These are guys he used to watch on television, men he used to dress up as on Halloween. Now he wrestles (albeit infrequently) on the same card and in the same locker room with them. He may never make it to the big-time of televised pro wrestling, but now he occasionally performs with legends who have epitomized heroism since his earliest

FIGURE 4.6. Mick Foley and the author. CREDIT: Author.

years. Communing, albeit briefly, with former WWE stars like Mick Foley and Marty Jannetty, who at times cameo at indie shows, makes indie wrestling part of something much larger. In fact, when I met Mick Foley at one of the shows, I was also thrilled to connect with the larger history and fame. His brief act in that night's show elicited a visceral crowd response that, to my surprise, even made me tear up.

SEXUAL DOMINANCE

The hierarchy of the group generally correlates with experience; other determinants—physical ability, age, wit/humor, "look"—also shape a wrestler's status, however. In side conversations members reinforce the hierarchy by putting down those of lower status than themselves or praising those above them. Sexual banter affirms status within the group, and homophobia, put-downs, and misogyny are common means of enacting dominance.

Coarse sexual acts and boasts, almost always at another member's expense, are an everyday occurrence. In addition to the acts that mimic anal penetration, there are acts simulating fellatio. When a wrestler is on his knees, for example, with his face at the level of a standing opponent's waist, he might feign receiving oral sex from this man. Such acts of dominance took place about every other time I was in the training space. Another routine act is the degradation of a woman closely related to another wrestler. Early in my fieldwork, for example, the mother of a young wrestler, reportedly very attractive, was pointed out to me: "Have you ever seen Dominic's mom? Phew . . . She's hot!" A dozen times or so, I heard guys crassly state how much they'd like "to do her." Dominic was often within earshot as guys exchanged cuts like the following. Louie says, "She should be a valet."[22] Cuss replies, "No, she should be a hooker." Tony chimes in, "Yeah, I'd pay $20 for that!"

Another representation of this dynamic was the exchange I witnessed involving Tony, Pete, and Fishman, three members of comparable mid-level status. Tony, standing on the apron, boasts during a pause in the group's conversation: "I screwed my girlfriend four times today." Pete, standing below, retorts: "Really, so did I!" Fishman then chimes in by walking around bowlegged and stating that since *he* has had sex with Tony's girlfriend, she now "walks funny." In this aggressive representation, Tony initially attempts to flex his virility, yet lacking a better rejoinder, he succumbs to a prowess of another kind: his fellow wrestler's quick wit.

HOMOSOCIAL SOLIDARITY: TRADITION AND PATERNALISM

The subculture of pro wrestling is steeped in etiquette and respect for tradition. There is always a right and wrong way to do things, and many rituals serve to establish or maintain tradition. Newcomers learn crucial customs, such as wiping their boots off on the apron before stepping in the ring, saying "thank you" to the person they have just "defeated" in a show, and shaking hands with wrestlers softly, not firmly.

Matt, a veteran and longtime mentor, places great emphasis on the lore, tradition, and rituals of pro wrestling. He subscribes to an adversative model of hard knocks and ritualized ardor; he considers pro wrestling a profession, a high-skilled art that is only for the select few who are respectful, tough, and disciplined. He had been roughed up early in his career by a more senior wrestler who asserted physical dominance while they were in the ring. According to Matt, after the bruising, he boldly asked the veteran if there was something he was trying to show him.

He had heard that I thought I was the big king of the ring, so I said to him, "With all due respect, um, I think you can tell by my character right now that what you heard was probably untrue, probably from someone who just wanted to see me get mine." And he says, "Well, if that's the case, that's fine. Because you took whatever I gave you like a champ, and you came over and asked me. And now I know the truth about you."

Matt understood this moment—when he stood up to an established vet and got his approval—as his benediction. After the confrontation, the senior member recognized that Matt "knew what he was doing." Matt drew an analogy to baseball to make a point about competency and attaining recognition from more senior members of the indie scene: "Roger Clemens isn't going to pitch in a little league game. It's just not the way. And if you can't handle yourself, it's obvious from the first forty or fifty seconds [in the ring] that you don't know what you're doing."

Going further, Matt relishes this older brother role. "I think I have the act down to a science. I look around when I walk in a room and I can't avoid the fact that I am someone they look [up] to. Guys come up and say, 'Hey, can you come watch my match?' And I like that. I like being there to help people." Cuss, too, enjoys expressing supportive paternalism. Wrestlers are grateful for his generosity with time, expertise, and money, as well as for his tough love. In one way or another, Cuss frequently invokes family and how everyone's there to help each other. Having received extensive fatherly support from Cuss, Tony spoke of the value of his enduring love: "I would definitely like to give young guys the same opportunity that guys like Cuss [have given me]—helping kids fulfill their dreams, 'cause I'm forever in debt in my eyes. No matter how big I ever make it, I would also work for Cuss. Always. Because without him, there would be no 'me.' I owe him so much."

PROFESSIONALISM: SHOW BUSINESS AND TECHNICAL ACUMEN

Muscles, athleticism, and physical size showcase masculinity, but what happens with men who are physically unremarkable, on the small side, or maybe even heavyset? Take Patrick, who is pale and unchiseled and stands about 5′8″. He teaches sixth graders with special needs when he is not ensconced in pro wrestling, but that is very infrequent: he is fanatical about being part owner, booker, and occasional wrestler within the promotion.

Having a relatively flabby body type and more autonomy in the story lines, Patrick's character is more reliant on irony and self-deprecation than high-flying stunts and glitzy muscularity.[23] He gets huge pops when he interrupts the grappling, leans forward, and slowly brings his arms together to flex his jelly-like physique. His pride comes from his artistry and ability to "fill seats." Instead of physicality and brawn, he revels in an ability to "have the fans in the palm of my hands, right where I want them." As with the pride Timmy takes in his "knack for controlling people's emotions," Patrick understands his wrestling achievements through the prism of his intellect and more skilled acting. Credibility derives less from his body's semiotics and more from crafty performances, creative thinking, and authority.

This standpoint, while less common, correlates with his body type and years in the business. Those who are less physically daring (or rather, less inclined to risk harm) tend to be older and more experienced, for any of a variety of reasons. For one thing, injuries and bodily destruction slow down guys who have been in the business a long time. Second, new guys want to get noticed and prove themselves, and they are more likely to believe that high-risk maneuvers are the means to achieve this. Third, experienced wrestlers find ways to use charisma and psychology to get the crowd going. You may not need to generate heat with high-risk table and ladder stunts when you are adept at mic skills, irony, and passion work.[24]

Pro wrestlers routinely speak of their collective ruse as a type of labor. Much pro wrestling jargon is language based on economics and production (e.g., a "work" is a scripted, deceitful act; "working the crowd" means keeping the crowd in suspense and captivation; "jobbers" are lower-level wrestlers who help bigger-name performers look good). Over time, wrestlers become more likely to measure their success (and skills) by both their authority and the number of seats they fill. Good performers become central features of the show that fans come to see. The better a performer you are, the better your chances of getting booked and being able to wrestle in the show's main event. Your worth is measured by your understanding of show business. Like Patrick stated, "If you make people's shit look good, you're gonna get booked."

Show business success as a form of status is evident in the practice of delegating ticket sellers. In almost all indie promotions, younger, lower-status wrestlers are asked to sell tickets for the upcoming show. Ticket sellers are required to sell 100 percent of the tickets the promoter or booker has allotted each wrestler. This onerous, time-consuming task can even be tied to being awarded a performance slot in the show. In such cases, if you do not yet have a name or have not yet earned the respect of the veterans of a particular federation, you must succeed at ticket sales to be given a match in the show. Correspondingly, those who have been crowned as "established" are not typically asked to sell tickets. Wrestlers at the highest level of the indies consider it a slight to even be asked. When Tony was asked to be part of another federation's show, the stipulation was that he would sell a certain number of tickets prior to the event. He was offended since, in his estimation, people come to see *him*; he should not have to hustle on behalf of *that* promotion. "I really can't sell tickets to be on the show. I'm better than that. Not to, like, pat myself on the back, but you know what, I don't want to be known as that. 'Oh, Tony had to sell tickets to get on [the card at] Federation USA.'"

SUMMARY

The backstaging of pro wrestling shows how the violent, hypermasculine performance onstage contrasts with the intimate, homoerotic, and choreographed behavior—arguably gay and undoubtedly effeminate—of the backstage. Paradoxically, performing violent masculinity is a nuanced, self-conscious, and collaborative activity.

When the intent to defeat or harm is removed, rolling around on a mat with other half-dressed men is a very tenuous exercise for men who pride themselves on their adherence to heterosexual ideals. In fact, even in high school (or Olympic) wrestling, where dominating an opponent is the stated objective, young men now face similar challenges regarding the fine line between what is considered acceptable physicality and sexual behavior.[25]

Participants come to recast the touching, toning, tanning, and disparaging. These behaviors are given new interpretations: homoeroticism, intimacy, and coordination recede in significance as alternative meanings—pain and bodily duress, business acumen, solidarity, intragroup dominance—are stressed. It is not a direct substitution in which the thorny, awkward homoerotic elements disappear from consciousness. Rather, it is a redirecting in which the homoerotic, uncomfortable edges of homosociality are smoothed over, albeit not smothered.

Ironically, doing pro wrestling puts wrestlers' gender identity in a precarious place. Being a pro wrestler risks revealing the social construction of masculinity; when an act is poorly done, it is seen as a big act that anyone can do—the lie and fragility of masculinity itself are exposed. The tension participants experience derives from the potential revelation of masculinity's very act.

In the chapter that follows, I bring wrestling's dual nature to the analysis of pain and injury. Like the dialectic dimension of their intimacy, pain is both a punishment and a reward that performers must endlessly negotiate.

CHAPTER 5 ★ PAIN IN THE ACT

SATURDAY NIGHT SHOW

Around four o'clock, just after arriving at the community center, I see Donny in the hallway walking toward me. "I'm scared," he blurts out as he approaches. I'm caught off guard by his admission, as fear is not usually publically verbalized, but then I remember the plans for "Dickie," Donny's character, to be thrown from a ten-foot-high ladder through a trapdoor in tonight's "main event."

At their prior Thursday training, I had seen the planning for the trapdoor gimmick. A tried-and-true crowd pleaser, it requires replacing the usual lattice of plywood and light metal pipes underneath the canvas mat with a massive 20′ x 20′ wood platform (the size of the ring) and a 5′-square quadrant, which functions as a trapdoor that can be latched closed (as it is for most of the show) or unlatched to drop open to the ground below. Once someone crawls beneath the ring and unlatches the trapdoor, a performer can fall through the ring via the trapdoor, presenting the effect of breaking through the entire mat by sheer force.

It is now two hours later, almost ten minutes into the "main event." There is a house full of raucous fans—250 seated and about 40 more standing. Dickie is in the ring, outnumbered by three opponents, Brickman, the Greek, and Slaughter. Although Dickie started out in charge, he has ceded command and is now receiving a bruising punishment from Brickman, a muscular 6′3″ opponent who resembles a light-skinned version of the Rock. Brickman, wearing nothing but boots and spandex shorts that have BRICK stitched down one side in red, is performing masterfully—taking his time teasing and taunting Dickie as the crowd roars in appreciation.

I am standing with the rest of the audience soaking up the drama as Brickman continues his mayhem. Meanwhile Slaughter, his tag-team partner, has begun sliding a ten-foot-long aluminum stepladder into the ring. Simultaneously, Patrick sneaks underneath the ring. Seeing Patrick disappear, I remember the fear Donny mentioned when I arrived earlier that evening. How could I forget?

Brickman continues a rather extended finishing move by striking Dickie/Donny with a forearm. He stumbles around the ring appearing to be in a semiconscious state. Slaughter and another performer have by now stood the ladder upright and are unfolding it. As Dickie staggers about, Brickman wraps his arms around Dickie's chest and heaves him up and over his head, draping him over his shoulders in a fireman's carry. He takes four or five steps up the stepladder and makes several awkward maneuvers on the rung necessary to turn 180 degrees with a grown man sprawled across one's shoulders. With a triumphant sneer on his face, Brickman looks toward the crowd and bellows, "Now you're gonna pay!"

Brickman then heaves Dickie's listless body ten feet downward to the mat. Dickie's body crashes *onto* the mat (instead of *through* it), producing a loud thud. He lands on his right side, his mouth open. The right temple of his head does a second, ricochet slap on the mat. With no expression on his face, he lies in a fetal position, hardly moving. The ensuing stillness—fifteen seconds or so—is far too long to be an effective pause of suspense. Moreover, every other performer stands motionless, all looking confused. The scene has become palpably stilted—eerily awkward for what's usually an action-packed depiction of mayhem, combat, and destruction. Now that things have gone awry, the performers seem unsure of how to proceed. Or are they? I of course know that the trapdoor failed to break through, and I am sure the planned crash through the ring was intended to be the culmination of the entire show. But nothing is certain. And is Dickie hurt?

From the corner of my eye I catch Patrick crawling underneath the ring. Brickman, after his uncertainty, reestablishes his ferocious character and begins his routine again. He climbs down from the ladder and repeats the sequence, picking up Dickie where he lies limp on the mat, climbing the ladder with him over his shoulder, slowly turning around from halfway up the ladder, yelling a taunt to the crowd, then tossing Dickie to the mat. This time, his body hits the mat and crashes through the canvas to the floor. His body, enveloped by the sagging, light-blue canvas of the mat, has disappeared. A few hoots, hollers, and whistles are heard, but nothing like the eruption that usually accompanies the finishing move at the culmination of a main event. The entire auditorium has grown quiet again. And the scene turns very strange.

The wrestlers mill about above the collapsed quadrant of the ring, looking downward into the gap. They don't have the customary swagger and effervescence that follows such a closing triumph. As we all await Donny's emergence from the canvas crevasse, I look around the auditorium and notice that Clara, Donny's girlfriend, is standing in the doorway behind me, sobbing. Tears are running down both cheeks. Since it is common for performers to go to great lengths to dupe fans, I think she is part of the act, too. Not to be hoodwinked, I ask—with a knowing smirk on my face—why she's upset. "He was supposed to go through the first time!" she snaps.

Her emotion is more palpable than anything I've experienced during all of my fieldwork. I let out a nervous laugh, embarrassed about my earlier smirk, and become truly worried myself. If she is acting, this is the most convincing collective gimmick I have ever witnessed. I feel sick with concern, but I still hold out hope that I have been duped. As far as I am concerned, neither scenario is good: either Donny is truly destroyed, or they have just taken their act to a new level of manipulation that makes me feel very uncomfortable.

Everything continues to appear wrong in the ring and throughout the entire auditorium. The spectators are nearly silent—the somber atmosphere and unusual stillness reminding me more of a memorial service than entertainment. Parents are at a loss for what to tell their children, whose faces cannot hide their confusion. The wrestlers' slow motion goes on for what feels like an eternity. It is obvious that Clara and I are not alone in wanting to see whether Donny is okay. I hear a nearby seven-year-old fan ask his father, "Is Dickie okay, Dad?" A wrestler in the ring finally yells for someone to get the doctor.

Very quickly I go from feeling nervous to outright fright as evidence starts to cascade: Donny had expressed how scared he was before the show; he fell from a height of more than ten feet and landed on his side not once but twice; his girlfriend is sobbing uncontrollably; several people are now yelling for the doctor; and performers are at a loss for what to do. The flow of the show is completely disrupted. If they are screwing with us, they need to get Donny out of the ditch right away. But for some reason, they don't. It is taking *forever* to retrieve him.

About six minutes pass as the crowd watches the following: one wrestler comes in with a stretcher board; two performers step into the crevasse and work to pull the body out; the state-mandated doctor comes running from the locker room with a stethoscope around his neck; Donny's listless body is fished out of the hole and carried out on a stretcher by a paramedic and two wrestlers. But contrary to what injured athletes customarily do, he never raises his arm to indicate he's okay and conscious. I hesitantly approach the stretcher to see how he looks. He is still, his eyes are closed; there is blood next to his mouth, but it is smeared.

Twice I called Andre, the only person whose number I had at that point, to see how Donny was doing, but he never picked up. In the pit of my stomach I sense that this is the horrific moment I had been anticipating since my research began. In a stunt that I am complicit in by virtue of being in attendance, something goes terribly wrong, or at least too far, and a group member becomes permanently maimed. I had no way of finding anything out other than visiting the group about twenty hours later at their practice space.[1] Driving into the parking lot, I anxiously scan the lot for Donny's or any other recognizable car, fearing that the whole operation has possibly collapsed following such a serious accident.

I get out of my car and walk toward the training space, the former auto body shop tucked into the corner of the worn-out strip mall. Ordinarily, upon approaching I would hear the thuds of wrestlers' bodies crashing upon the mat, but not this time. Walking in through the rusted metal door, I'm shocked to see Donny, awash in exuberance as he sits in a dented fold-up metal chair, holding court as five younger wrestlers listen to him with admiration. I admit to them that I was so worried that I combed the Web message board and called another performer's cell phone to check on his status. Hearing this inflates Donny's pride even further; he exclaims, "It was a *work*!"

He confirms that the trapdoor was supposed to open the first time. As he slowly gets up from his chair, grimacing, he concedes a gnarly bruise to his coccyx. I ask about the blood that had been on the side his mouth. "I bit a fake blood pellet" he explains, "but it tasted like shit, so I spat it out and wiped it off." Needless to say, Donny saw the whole episode as nothing but a huge success, one that *made* the show.

The culmination of this main event captures the peculiar experience of trying to avoid pain and injury while performing in a show that glorifies violence and pain. Indie wrestling is undeniably dangerous, and injury and pain are frequent outcomes of the crafted combat. For performers, the pain can be everything from thrilling and flaunted to suppressed, debilitating, and agonizing. In Donny's experience recounted above, it was all of these things.

The field note begs several questions that I address in this chapter: What is the individual's attraction to pain? What, if any, is pain's benefit to the entire group? Within a context that rewards good acting yet also espouses stoicism, how do participants think about, feel, and manage everyday pain and injury? Are participants being hurt—or hurting themselves? Lastly, as analysts, how are we to interpret a phenomenon such as physical damage when it may be experienced as beneficial?

Historically, understandings of pain have been governed by two institutions of knowledge; the realm of the body was studied by the field of medicine, and the realm of the mind and soul was studied by philosophers and theologians (Zborowski 1969). In Western discourse the phenomenon of pain has been primarily analyzed with regard to physiology, and understandings of pain and suffering continue to be almost exclusively explained by the field of medicine (Morris 1991). Consequently, pain is conventionally understood as a bodily reaction involving the transmission of nerve impulses. As the International Association for the Study of Pain defines it, pain is "an unpleasant sensory or emotional experience associated with actual or potential tissue damage, or described in terms of such damage" (International Association for the Study of Pain 1979, 249–252). There are sometimes external markers for this "sensory or emotional experience," but pain itself is an unseen, subjective experience.

Pain, like other corporeal phenomena, has little meaning for anyone beyond the individual sufferer until it is manifested socially. Through material signs (casts, crutches, bandages, scars) and a range of behaviors (wincing, moaning, clenching teeth) an individual's subjective experience is made social—an "objectivation," according to Berger and Luckmann.[2]

There may be information or signification from the incident (or disease) that caused the pain (if witnessed, for example), but without this information, it is unseen. This invisibility, combined with a dearth of language that might help convey the experience of pain, makes the sensation even more troubling and isolating (Scarry 1985). What's more, sufferers of physical pain feel obliged to keep expressions of anguish within the bounds of local decorum—a dynamic that applies crucially to professional wrestlers.

Even with visible markers of injury—a cast, a crooked nose, bleeding—we do not necessarily have a valid indicator of the degree or extent of the pain or damage. There are no objective tests for detecting pain or measuring its intensity (Osterweis et al. 1987). Given physiology and medicine's quest for measurement—the scientific credo suggesting that "if it can't be measured, it doesn't exist"—scholarly understandings of pain remain troubled. Importantly, most medical research fails to explain how pain is socially experienced; moreover, it is ill equipped to account for the potentially seductive aspects of the phenomenon.

The shortcomings of this strict physiological perspective have been highlighted in an emergent body of social science research that examines pain and illness as a social phenomenon. Interactions are crucial to the analysis of pain, and research like that of Arthur Kleinman (1988) has examined how the meanings of illness are shared, negotiated, and deeply embedded in the social world.[3] David Morris, in turn, finds that pain is a powerful force that is far from a strictly corporeal phenomenon; it is a varied experience that we endow with assorted meanings and interpretations depending on time, place, and person(s). As he contends:

> We experience pain only and entirely as we interpret it. It seizes us as if with an unseen hand, sometimes stopping us in mid-sentence or mid-motion, but we too capture and reshape it. . . . It is never simply an impersonal code of neural impulses, like changeless, computer-generated messages sent over an internal telephone line. Human pain is never timeless, just as it is never merely an affair of bodies. (Morris 1991, 29)

Hence the relationship between physical pain and the social processes that rule its perception, experience, and meaning is best understood when researchers contextualize the suffering and the sufferers. Pain is not perceived in any universal manner, and pain stimuli are understood within a larger signification system; depending on the time, place, and person (or group) involved, pain can be given different meanings. Interactions of all kinds influence how the mind and emotions may exaggerate or diminish the perception of pain.

A small collection of empirical studies reveals how identity can be shaped by the experience of pain and injury—for pain presents the possibility of developing new interpretations of the relationship between body and self.[4] In general, social science research has focused on pain and injury as it relates to sports and athletes.[5] Nixon found that sports promote a "culture of risk" where injury is normalized (1992). Frey contends that such risk is directly tied to the athletic performance's overall meaning (1991). Howe's research on pain among elite athletes shows how health and well-being are ultimately a personal responsibility (2004). Gender scholars commonly find that how pain is suffered is highly correlated with traditional notions of masculinity such as stoicism and the "sport ethic" (Messner 1990, Malcom 2006).

In this chapter I explore what the wrestlers' interactions, interpretations, and experiences tell us about pain. Pro wrestlers conduct a dangerous, high-risk performance where violence and pain are often revered, even sought after, even though their unfortunate but common outcome—injury—is to be avoided. In this setting, their interactions affect the very likelihood of pain and injury, the control and understanding of the bodily experience, and importantly, the rewards of hurting. These attractions revolve around themes of authenticity, status, and the solidarity generated through the sacrifice of self.

IN SEARCH OF NEGLECT

Although wrestling matches' outcomes are fixed and opponents usually choreograph movements with one another before the match, participants experience pain and injury all the time. The injuries come in all shapes, sizes, degrees, and even pigments; they range from subtle to catastrophic, internal to external, silently suffered or audibly alarming.[6] Some injuries have only short-term effects, like a charley horse to the thigh that sidelines a wrestler for thirty minutes; others are career-ending, such as a shattered forearm or irreparable nerve damage to a wrestler's spine.

Every single member of the group was injured at least once during my fieldwork, in most cases repeatedly. Nine out of ten times when attending a practice, I witnessed an injury. On at least four different occasions, wrestlers were sent to the emergency room—twice by a racing ambulance. Fatal consequences are very rare but certainly possible. Serious long-term injuries are common. Spinal and neck trauma, concussions, bruises, broken noses, and damage to the knees and other joints happen all the time. Very many injuries are never visible yet felt intensely by the performer, such as nerve stingers that immediately end a match and send the wrestler skipping around the ring, forcefully exhaling through tightly clenched teeth. Others, like concussions or neck twists, leave the person dazed but coherent enough to leave the ring unassisted. Every few weeks an injury is painfully obvious—for example, a forearm broken so badly that any onlooker would bristle because bones just should not go in that direction.

Fishman, the beefy twenty-eight-year-old performer with four years of experience, gives an account of his pain and injuries during the last four years:

> Pinched nerve in my neck, several broken fingers, broken wrist. I have never seen the doctor about injuries in my knees but they're wearing down. I use to wear just pads, then went to knee pads, knee braces, and now it's knee pads and knee braces with the springs in the sides. Eventually I'll be moving up to hinges, I can foresee it already. I limp to work a lot of days. When it rains, it's hard to get up. And for a young guy, that's not something you hear. I have arthritis, torn rotator cuffs.

Timmy, the more veteran wrestler who is thirty-three years old, gives an account of his body:

> I broke my ankle. I broke both my knees. I have no ACL in this knee.[7] This knee has an ACL, but it's just kind of on the verge of being gone. They can't even find this one; they don't know where it is. I have bone chips in my knees. I have a tendon that's displaced; it actually goes over my kneecaps, so if I go on my knees at all, it kills. I have two herniated discs in my back. There's now something wrong with my neck. Don't know what the hell is wrong with it. I had a hairline fracture in my wrist for about three years that wouldn't go away. I've dislocated this elbow. I've broken this shoulder. Fourteen concussions.

As these accounts reveal, and as any spectator would infer, the health consequences of pro wrestling are severe. Even professional football players, participants in what is often considered the most brutal of sports, have suggested that pro wrestling is more punishing than football.[8]

Yet pro wrestling's distinction as pseudosport entertainment, its bane and its beauty, shields the performance from the wider scrutiny of state

FIGURE 5.1. The state-mandated doctor sitting backstage during a show. CREDIT: Author.

health agencies.[9] In general, indie promoters skirt the regulations of similarly situated promotions (like boxing) and can therefore exhibit little to no regard for most wrestlers' long-term health. There is no provision for health insurance, sports medicine, or medical trainers despite the fact that access to such care is essential to how an athlete copes with pain (Howe 2004).[10] When an injury occurs, performers must seek out and obtain treatment and rehabilitation on their own (if they do so at all). There is neither a preventive health treatment nor any precautionary intervention, so a nagging strain usually worsens as it goes unattended. While there is a doctor backstage at Saturday night shows—by mandate of the state regulatory agency—he only takes vital signs (pulse, blood pressure, and the like, of course also noting obvious signs of distress), and he does not attend training sessions, where in fact more injuries occur.[11]

The long-term consequences of the harm, often more severe than fans suspect, are mostly hidden from the audience. The cumulative effect of this battering, coupled with the denial of its occurrence, makes it particularly grave. The average career of a performer in the indies, like the brief but more enchanting (and better-paid) careers of some pro athletes, ends long before the age of thirty-five, despite skills that could continue for a decade or so longer. In addition to early retirement, pro wrestlers can expect a reduced life expectancy, a fact brought to the floor of the US Congress in 2007 by Congressman Cliff Stearns.[12] In fact, 25 percent (14 out of 51) of the wrestlers from the 1991 marquee Wrestlemania have already died from accidents, violence, or drug overdoses.[13] These long-term like-lihoods demonstrate the inherent danger of this physicality, the general neglect for health within the wrestling community, and the many ways the performer's body is central to the sense of identity.

Despite the group's general neglect of the consequences of harm, the social costs of an injury to a wrestler cannot be overestimated. First of all, for a young man whose socioeconomic status is more dependent on bodily capital than that of his middle-class counterparts, an injury means far more than taking a few weeks off from wrestling. An indie wrestler's day job, despite its low priority as a mere means to keep wrestling, pays the bills and usually requires him to be physically capable.[14] Second, once you are too injured to wrestle, you lose your spot in the upcoming shows that your life has been organized around. Third, health insurance coverage is rare, and expert medical attention is hard to come by. Most importantly, once sidelined, wrestlers who cannot physically participate become im-mediately alienated; they risk invisibility because physicality is the group's medium of connection and solidarity.

RELATIONAL HURT AND SUFFERING

As Roland Barthes pointed out, "what [pro] wrestling is above all meant to portray is a purely moral concept: that of justice. The idea of 'paying' is essential to wrestling, and the crowd's 'Give it to him' means above all else 'Make him pay'" (1972, 21). To tell this moral story, wrestlers follow a set of rules similar to those governing magicians: make your move ap-pear as real as possible without actually *being* real. Wrestlers groan, grunt, and verbally taunt, but it is primarily the body movements that tell a story and give meaning to the duels. Unlike other moments of athletic triumph (whether baseball's home run or basketball's three-point buzzer-beater), excellence in professional wrestling can come only from physical interac-tion with your opponent. The dialogue of this story requires a high degree of close physical interaction during which reliance on one another is es-sential.

Paradoxically, it's these fellow collaborators who are implicated in the participants' pain and injuries. In other sports, pain and injuries com-monly stem from efforts to improve athletic performance (e.g., overtrain-ing); in wrestling, injuries usually stem from misunderstandings between the two performers (or between bookers and performers), misunderstandings that could have been avoided had there been better communication, understanding, or synchronicity.[15]

For example, jumping off the top rope when the opponent is not in the proper place to break the fall can result in an injury. I witnessed Johnny crack a rib when he did a flip from the corner and landed flat on his own chest, missing the opponent meant to help break his fall. Conversely, jumping and landing on an opponent can also cause injury. Such misunderstandings can easily result in a painful knee to the face or crushing bruise to the sternum if the jump is off by a split second. Johnny articulates this when recounting a match at another federation:

> I shattered my nose in a Battle Royal.[16] I mean, miscommunication with one of the guys. Turned around and he clocked me right in the nose, completely shattered my nose. I had to get reconstructive nose surgery . . . yeah, the bone's sticking into my eyeball. . . . He was supposed to wait till I turned around. I had turned around and he wasn't in the ring yet, so I figure I turn [back] around for a little bit longer. And I turn around again later, for the second time, [and] he didn't think I was turning around again. So [he intended to] hit me on the back of the head [but] I turned around—and it hit me right in the face.

Here, surgery was required because the timing was just slightly off. Such accidents become normalized, however, because of their frequency and their centrality to the group's cohesion, as I will explain.

Blame as such is rarely allocated, even when a painful injury results. After witnessing Donny injure his hip during practice, at the next practice I asked how he was doing. He claimed to be "doing better," lowering his pants enough to reveal the evidence—a purple baseball-size bruise eight inches below his grey briefs. Having witnessed the collision, it seemed to me that it was Drew's fault because he had not tucked his hand inside closer to his own body; however, Donny was reluctant to cast blame. "I don't really like to call it anyone's fault. Those kinds of things just happen. It is just part of it. Mistakes happen. It wasn't his fault or mine."[17]

In tag-team matches, where a team of two wrestlers is pitted against another team of two, performers must coordinate with three other people. Not infrequently, the story line calls for a performer to exact punishment on one of his two opponents—and immediately afterward receive retributive punishment from the second opponent. Take Tony's account of his pain in a tag-team match where he jumped off the ropes toward his opponent, Vinny, and then had to immediately turn around to receive Terror (another opponent jumping toward him). "I did a flying clothesline to the outside, and Vinny didn't catch me. So I landed on my knee. If you watch the [video]tape, you'll see me limp. I get up and I limp [over] because I'm like, 'I have to catch Terror.' And once Terror did [his move], I just lay down. Oh, that was the worst pain! My girlfriend and I went home that night. She said that in my sleep I was moaning and groaning. She said it was so bad she had to sleep on the floor."

As the expression goes, Tony "takes one for the team"—not just his tag team but the collective team of wrestlers who all look out for one another. Hurt by a wrestler who made a mistake, Tony then sacrifices his body on behalf of another wrestler. Of course, a price is paid in this exchange, but pain, the currency that circulates in this market, pays dividends.

Pain and injuries can also stem from an anticipated synchronicity with your opponent that fails to develop because of faulty assumptions. After witnessing Fishman, a midlevel wrestler, injure Vinny, another veteran, during a roll-up maneuver, I asked Fishman what had happened.

> "He didn't know what move I was doing," Fishman explained, "or he thought I was doing something else. And he didn't know how to take the bump I wanted him to take. And so there was a miscommunication between the two of us that resulted in him getting hurt. As far as I'm concerned, that was a mutual miscommunication. Because when he said, 'Use your finish on me,' I don't think he'd ever seen me do it . . . and that resulted in an injury."

This mutual miscommunication sent Vinny to the hospital. His painful injury could have been avoided had the performers improved their communication and synchronicity.

All injuries, nonetheless, have a latent function because real injuries blur the line between real and fake for both audience *and* participants. Each one benefits the business of pro wrestling, since spectators always experience a potential for real violence. In fact, the WWE routinely plays with this reality. A popular WWE T-shirt is a case in point: below the bloodied face of the megastar Mick Foley (aka Mankind or Cactus Jack) on the front of the T-shirt is the phrase "Fake wrestler." The back of the shirt says "Injuries" and lists nearly twenty different matches with the exact injury sustained, the date, and the arena. However, like the fiery high-speed crashes in a

NASCAR race, these accidents are ideally avoided, and if they cause known harm on a repeated basis, they are likely to lose their appeal.[18]

PRIDE AND PUNISHMENT

Despite the performers' need for exuberant, emotive displays in the on-stage show, pro wrestlers make extraordinary efforts among themselves to conceal, endure, or overcome the feeling of pain. In most respects their efforts to endure pain mirror the larger zeitgeist. which has it that over-coming pain is a necessary passage on the path to achieving strength and success. Their beliefs reflect what Don Sabo identifies as sports' "pain prin-ciple": the "cultural belief that pain is inevitable and that the endurance of pain enhances one's character and moral worth" (Sabo 1994, 3).[19]

The culture at large abounds in clichés and adages proclaiming that, for example, "pain is weakness leaving the body." While pain may not neces-sarily be desirable, it is seen as a crucial stage of physical, even moral, de-velopment—"no pain, no gain." The message that saturates us and meshes with the zeal for victory in our competitive capitalist society is that "pain is only temporary, but victory is forever."

Since stoicism and invulnerability are cornerstones of our heralded masculine ideals, wrestlers are already groomed to "suck it up." Custom dictates an act of "no fear," just as a popular T-shirt or rear-window car de-cal might implore. Combine these obdurate ideals with wrestling's imper-ative to be combative and strong. Few identities, even soldier and boxer, automatically connote the hardened manliness of "wrestler."

Despite the socialization toward being hard and the group's emphasis on toughing it out, it often is not easy for a young man to "grin and bear it." Experiencing pain is not a natural fit for many. Those who seldom played sports, who escaped street violence, who were raised, for example, by a protective parent who just couldn't bear to watch the violence of pro wrestling—those from such backgrounds find that pain takes some get-ting used to.[20] Of course, some people are just better at performing the emotional labor necessary to conceal fear or agony. Thus, some students never get past the initial fear of hurting themselves. As Cuss, the head of the school and now a veteran, explains: "A lot of the time, it's just fear. It's not natural to fall backward and expect to be okay. Some people can get over that, some can't. If you can't, you're in the wrong business. We've had students that I've actually told, 'You're not cut out for this.'"

For those who make the initial cut, this stoic imperative is only magnified because the group actively polices the weak—rather, those who dare admit to vulnerability and weakness. When wrestlers with less status express concern, hurt, or agony, it usually meets with a veteran's harsh dismissal. When, for example, JR sat down and rubbed the back of his right knee as he stated, "My knee is fucked up," Timmy said, "You are only twenty! It couldn't be that fucked up! Just you wait. . . ." Other common retorts include "You still bitchin' about your neck?" and "You don't need your ACL anyway! I don't have one in either knee." As participants' responses to hurt are policed, potential confessions of suffering are silenced, and higher-status guys maintain a greater say about the intensity of distress and possible need for resources. If and when benefits to health consciousness (or maintenance) are acknowledged, they are usually noted as a private aside. The ethos echoes Scarry's contention that "to have pain is to have certainty, but to hear about pain is to have doubt" (1985, 13).[21]

Cuss recalled his ambivalence about speaking up after his very first injury eight years prior:

> The first injury in training, I fractured two ribs. So I was out for like four or five weeks. I had two fractured ribs, [but] you know, you don't know what happened, what it is at the time, and you don't want to look like a sissy, so you know, you do more. Then it happened, and I'm like, "Yeah I'm okay, I'm okay." Then you get thrown around again, and I'm like "Ah, maybe I'm not okay."

Despite fracturing his ribs, Cuss tries to conceal the hurt out of concern for looking like a sissy. Ultimately, it is so bad that he must speak up and state his limitations. This illustration of unwelcome pain, pain understood to be poorly received by teammates, trainers, and others (Young 2000), shows how far members go to avoid others' judgment of their pain management. Much like the professional piano players in Alford and Szanto's study, wrestling participants face a bind: they are continually exposed to pain and risk, but they do not want to abandon a lifelong dream, and they cannot openly acknowledge hurt or seek help for it without negative consequences (1996).

Importantly, at the same time that wrestlers are penalized for admitting distress, they can be rewarded for overcoming it. When pain is nondebilitating and can be controlled, enduring it extends energy, valor, and status to the sufferer. Once repeatedly well managed, it becomes heroic. As with Morris's description of patients in Zborowski's study of pain (1969), "taking pain is an action, not passive suffering, and the ability to absorb punishment becomes a semiheroic sign of courage and endurance" (Morris 1991, 54). Nevertheless, complications abound when physical distress is invisible and lacks verifiability. Cuss's ribs are cracked, but who is really to know?

This denial may be quite detrimental; we know that pain is oftentimes the canary in the coal mine signaling a harmful root problem—a fracture, a traumatic brain injury, a torn ligament—that requires immediate medical intervention or, at the very least, rest. In fact, recent research on former professional football players has brought to light the severe long-term consequences of ignoring or denying head trauma.[22] Yet denial is not automatically harmful. Denying pain (or rewarding the denial of pain) can be a double-edged sword, depending on the person, ailment, and medical and social support, because there can be some benefit to denial: it allows you to carry on, reduce atrophy, and maintain the active lifestyle and functions that can foster a quicker recovery.

INJURY VERSUS PAIN

The leaders' official stand on pain and injury is fairly simple: pain is OK, perhaps even good, but injuries are bad.[23] As Fishman, the four-year veteran, made clear: "Nobody gets hurt. That's the end-all, be-all, of a wrestling match. First, at least as far as I'm concerned, before psychology, before getting the crowd behind you, it's making sure you and the guy you're with can both drive home." Tyler, the lead booker, corroborated the collective goal after I asked what constituted a bad match. "I consider a failed match [to be] when somebody gets hurt. That's when I think somebody fails. Whether it's a good match or not is a matter of opinion."

From the standpoint of the organization, debilitating injuries are problematic because they remove potential talent from the shows. Accordingly, avoiding injury is a central tenet of their training. While ringside one Tuesday night, four days before a Saturday show, Tyler and Cuss are leaning on the apron, quietly discussing plans for the upcoming show. Suddenly Brickman, who has been in the ring wrestling Tony, is clutching his right shoulder with his left hand, squinting his eyes, and muttering an obscenity as he circles the ring. Tyler looks up from his conversation and angrily exclaims, "Hey! If you are wrestling on Saturday, get out of the ring. No one should do any more wrestling if they're wrestling Saturday! We don't need any more people getting hurt!" Brickman hobbles out of the ring to walk it off, as Fishman, turning to me and Mike, confides, "Yeah, that's why I am not coming in on Thursday." Tony, responding to Tyler's demand about Saturday performers needing to leave the ring, states with smug disappointment, "Well, that's *everyone* here."

Tyler's outburst demonstrates how the injured individual is secondary to the show business. In addition, it highlights the normalization of harm. Perhaps respecting the creed that is tattooed on his shoulder in Japanese characters, "path of the scholar warrior," Fishman will skip the upcoming training out of a concern for possible injury. He is mindful of its frequency—and the rewards of Saturday's show are not worth the risk.

Which of the myriad reactions to a painful experience one receives— fear, anger, laughter, sympathy, or nonchalant indifference—depends on several factors, including the degree (and indicators) of pain (e.g., blood or being unconscious), the symptoms expressed, the adrenaline, and the status of the wrestler. On the night that a low-status, relatively new wrestler named Josh lost consciousness after a painful knee twist, we were forced to call an ambulance because he did not come to. It was a harrowing several minutes in which Josh lost all color, breathed irregularly, slumped to his side and then crumpled over. I recall the alarming demand made by Chris, himself an EMT, as he slapped Josh's face with the palm of his hand, "C'mon. Josh. Hang in there, Josh! Stay with us, Josh!"

Fortunately, just after the paramedics arrived, Josh regained consciousness and was able to hobble to the ambulance with only light assistance. Before his final step out of the gym, Josh turned to us and began to say, with embarrassment, "I'd just like to thank everyone," but Cuss cut him off with, "C'mon, cut it out." Despite his gruff response, Cuss had certainly been unnerved by it all. Three minutes prior, just after Josh regained consciousness, Cuss relayed to me with palpable relief, "*That* was scary!" It is hard to say if his relief came from seeing Josh escape a worse fate or from knowing that he and his school had just escaped a worse fate. (It could have been both.) Cutting off Josh as he said thanks did more than reveal Cuss's discomfort with any heartfelt sentiments. It indicated the rules: injuries are just part of the business, you will get over it, and there's no need to be grateful for people's support. It's no wonder that Josh rode off to the hospital in the ambulance unaccompanied by any of us.

When a senior member gets injured, as on the night Tyler twisted his neck, there's likely to be collective concern and a complete halt in the training. Once the extent of Tyler's injury was realized, the mood shifted from happy-go-lucky to one of harsh silence. Donny, irritated by the students' blasé reaction to the injury (and also wanting to assert his authority), quickly climbed into the ring and reprimanded folks about their failing to communicate needs and limitations given wrestling's risk. He stated, "God created this one little word . . . and it is 'No'! If you don't feel comfortable doing something, you can always say no!"[24]

In terms of pain that is not debilitating at the onset, leaders have a different stance. Conditioning is akin to the adaptation in boxing where one must "harden oneself to pain, to get one's organism used to taking blows: to get hit regularly and progressively adjust to it" (Wacquant 1992, 246). In Fishman's experience, wrestlers must adjust the body to routine pain: "If any wrestler tells you they feel fine, they're lying. . . . There's a certain instinct you fight when you learn to wrestle because you're throwing yourself at the ground on purpose. . . . It's probably something you shouldn't be doing." Jimmy echoed this idea of pro wrestling as being defined by its suffering. "In professional wrestling you learn how to fall, [but] I'll tell you right now, there's no way to learn how to fake a fall on concrete. You hit concrete, you know, how are you gonna fake that? You know, you take a steel chair and smash it in your face, you know, it hurts." Likewise, Cuss stated: "Guys get hurt all the time. Hitting the ring hurts. Hits on the mat hurt. Getting punched in the face hurts, even though you try not to do this."

Few physical sensations require so little conscientious effort in presentation of self (i.e., a grimace comes fairly naturally with true suffering) yet so much internal effort in the impression management (of endurance). Expressing feelings about being in pain is at times permissible, but navigating the codes of appropriate expression is a shifting puzzle. Pain (offstage) must be exhibited so it is not construed as weakness or vulnerability. Blood, bruising, and expressions of pain are exhibited triumphantly when the sufferer has control of the emotions that have been prompted by the bodily experience. In this sense, an indie wrestler's "pain management" requires two things of the sufferer: parading the experience (or effect) of pain and assuming the demeanor of one in control of (indeed, overcoming) the pain.[25]

Here is an example illustrating a "good" act. Following a head-to-head collision that brought both Cobra and Tony to their knees, Tony yells, "I am juicing, I am juicing!" as he holds his right palm to his forehead and

FIGURE 5.2. A match moves into the crowd as wrestlers incorporate chairs. CREDIT: ©2006 Mark Stehle Photography.

blood spills between his fingers. This is an ideal injury (if there is such a thing) because two heads collide and audibly crack, with blood spurting out of one, but the collision is just light enough to be nonconcussive, and Tony remains wrestling. Only if Tony had *not* called everyone's attention to the blood (while still having everyone notice it) would this have been a better exclamation of stoicism, grit, and the ability to deny.

Therefore, in one instance a wrestler's experience of pain is hidden and obscured; then in the next, it's amplified and hyperbolized. Backstage a wrestler might downplay true feelings of hurt and then amplify the same feeling (from the same injury or sensation) onstage. This code switching, coupled with the pain's invisibility, is the bugaboo of pain research. Furthermore, because pain is experienced in myriad ways and individual responses vary considerably, I often lost track. For instance, a guy I had confirmed as suffering a concussion during a match returned to the ring a few days later and carried on as though there had been no damage. Conversely, a guy who quietly climbed out of the ring after taking a hard hit but giving no sign of distress disappeared for six weeks; he explained upon his return that he had ruptured his spleen while wrestling with a case of mono. Arguably, the worst part of such variation of symptomology, especially for a lower-status wrestler, is that there is little to no glory in it; there is no evidence of the pain nor any indication of the individual's ability to overcome it.

Consider this example from the locker room of a Saturday night show. Pete is fiddling with the ACE bandages covering the splint on his broken right forearm. I ask what he is doing. He says, "It's part gimmick"—the extra bandage will help sell the story of his bruised and battered character during the show. I had seen the splint earlier that evening when he first arrived, so I knew the splint would help protect and heal his actually broken arm. Functional devices that assist in healing are therefore also potential props to help tell stories about pain and agony—pain and agony simultaneously real and fake. Ironically, such faked trauma can mask real feelings of pain in the stoical backstage.

TREATING AND COPING WITH "UNWELCOME PAIN"

Indie wrestlers' treatment of their pain and injuries is shaped by several factors. Most notable is the ethos of stoicism and invulnerability, with its rewards for those who tough it out. Another factor is that many guys are distrustful of the medical establishment, with the result that the leaders of the promotion—and by extension the wrestlers themselves—do not want to raise any suspicion among health authorities. Utilizing formal health care might draw state attention to the promotion's all-too-frequent injuries. One night, for example, just before Dan was taken to the emergency room by his girlfriend, Cuss sternly admonished folks about giving information to health practitioners. No one was to mention the wrestling school in any treatment—in effect, an unofficial denial of the association between the Rage school and harmful risk.

Significantly, even when formal treatment is required rather than simply encouraged, most wrestlers lack health insurance or the resources to pay for care. As Tony stated bluntly: "Right now I'm in a lot of pain all the time. I don't know, it takes it out of you, you know. It's definitely my back, my neck, my knee, just everything. I'm always on Vicodins. . . . Yeah, Vicodins and Percocets, you know. I don't believe in doctors. I try to stay away from them as much as possible because if I went to them every time I had a little pain or something, I'd be broke."

A further impediment to care-seeking behavior is one plaguing all of us—no one likes hearing bad news, especially if the news is your doctor telling you to "hang up the boots." Any ethical health practitioner would have to inform a pro wrestler that participation is harmful to his health and ought not to be continued. Who wants to hear this when you eat, sleep, and slog through a boring day job just so you can be a pro wrestler?

Given that there is only so much battering and denial a body can take, how do wrestlers endure it? For those without easy access to quality health care, including most wrestlers, over-the-counter and subscription-strength painkillers are common palliatives. I could not verify how many pills wrestlers take on average, but they are readily available and circulate copiously within the scene. Several journalists have noted the routine abuse of painkillers by pro wrestlers and the easy slide into addictions—and at times death—as wrestlers up the ante and mix drugs.[26]

One approach, which I heard the backstage doctor share, was to visit the local hospital's emergency room in the middle of the night. Mayhem strained his shoulder, and after unsuccessful attempts to ignore the pain, distress prevented him from wrestling. I heard the doctor state that from what he could determine, it was not likely to heal on its own. Mayhem clarified that he had no health insurance. The doctor shrugged and said, "Just go into the ER and have a guy look at it, then get a referral to an ortho clinic. The hospital's open twenty-four hours, so go in there at 3 AM when no one is there. It's right on Route 212, just drop by some night." He suggested that if he used the right channels, he could "go a long way" without insurance.[27]

Even the few who are fortunate enough to have health insurance can be reluctant to voluntarily seek treatment from medical professionals. This stems from concern about their status at their day job or simply from mistrust of the medical profession. One hot summer night, for example, I asked Peter, 24, about the shoulder he had aggravated two nights before. He explained that he initially hurt it the prior summer when sliding headfirst during a softball game and that it's "been fucked up ever since." Very casually I mentioned that maybe he should get it checked out because often people do not realize that they have a torn rotator cuff despite its being a very common injury. "Well maybe," he replied, "but I haven't been to a doctor since eleventh grade."

Other times, people follow folk wisdom on the treatment of sprains, twists, or hematomas. Reminiscent of Jack's treatment for his fall in the Jack and Jill nursery rhyme, Matt swore by his vinegar. "I was taught a wonderful remedy. Warm vinegar. Hot vinegar on a towel, wrap it around your injury, ACE bandage. I have avoided casts and surgeries. Doctors have been adamant. Oh, six weeks, six months. Vinegar for three weeks—and I'm right back out there."

Dan, known for his high-flying stunts off ladders and tables, has a self-administered mechanism to pop his shoulder or hips back in place whenever they get dislocated. "I popped my hip out of place on a fall. . . . That hurt so much! Indescribable pain. It popped out, and I popped it back in real fast 'cause if you let it sit, then I'd be hurting so much bigger, so I just jammed it back in and laid there. . . . As long as you apply pressure, it'll pop in real fast. If it doesn't pop in, then I'd be in the hospital. . . . If you just let it linger and *then* pop it back in, the pain hurts so much worse."

While it is hard for me to verify this remedy's success—much less stomach it—it nevertheless conveys the contours of the wrestlers' lay understandings of effective treatment. As Matt has his vinegar, so Dan has a unique alternative medicine that he understands as a palliative. But if placebos have such profound effects for subjects within a countless number of health studies, why not vinegar and self-administered joint relocations?

Cuss undoubtedly received the best care thanks to his more privileged, white-collar occupation. When he is injured, he simply goes to the doctor right upstairs from his office at the financial firm where he works in Manhattan. The firm has its own "doctor's office with X-ray machines and physical therapy in the building," Cuss explained. "[I'd say] I'm going to go upstairs to the doctor, I'll be back in twenty minutes, or whatever. After I started wrestling I was a regular up there. . . . Sometimes I'd lie to people about the injuries up at the medical office. And I guess this one nurse just got so used to seeing me up there she said, 'Well, what happened to your . . . ?'—I don't remember if it was the ribs or shoulder—and I just told her I got double-teamed by two guys. She just looked at me like I was nuts."

MEASURING UP

It is disconcerting to be part of any group where you constantly worry about the other members' health and welfare, oftentimes when the members themselves do not. I tended not to cast myself outside the calm, invulnerable, intrepid vibe that pervades the scene.[28] Being older and less invested also meant that I was saddled with the burdensome perspective of foreseeing moves and situations that had great risk (and the risk's long-term consequences). Despite the prevailing nonchalance and denial, it was so hard to ignore the physical, mental, and social costs of injuries that, perhaps to a fault, I trained my eyes (and notes) on their ever-present possibility. I often dwelled on how a mere centimeter of error could mean the difference between an active, able-bodied life and a life confined to a wheelchair.[29]

Research was most distressing, not because it had to do with high risk per se, but because of how this risk was managed and how leaders responded after harmful outcomes. No one is surprised that when people jump off ladders and get thrown through tables, they get injured. But high-risk theatrical productions are not de facto harmful. Big-budget Hollywood and Broadway productions prove that if dangerous acts are carefully planned and actors are well trained, injuries will only rarely occur.[30] However, indie wrestlers routinely do stunts that are *not* very well rehearsed or planned; moreover, the majority are not autonomous enough to opt out of a clever but dangerous new gimmick that an excited promoter has recently contrived. Being in a position to determine the conditions of the stunt is improbable, especially for a low-status wrestler striving to impress.

At the same time, wrestlers are walking a fine line, because the experience of pain is generally flaunted, indeed cherished. As Kyle Green discovered in his study of mixed martial arts fighters, wrestlers also seek the "temporary fleeting pain . . . that shocks the system before fading away, leaving only a dull ache that serves as a reminder" (Green 2011).

ROYAL PAIN: STATUS AND DOMINANCE

The bulk of painful physical suffering occurs during training because this is the space where veterans enact dominance and younger wrestlers jockey to impress superiors and one another. Every couple of weeks or so, trainers initiate a set of highly physical rituals and exercises that, while tangentially related to building pro wrestling skills, primarily function to maintain cohesion and stitch up fissures in the group's hierarchy. "Amateur," "shark bait," and beatings are examples of what purport to be cardio drills but in fact add little to the development of being a good pro wrestler.

Shark bait is a drill featuring competitive, Olympic-style wrestling, except that one wrestler remains in the ring trying to elude a pin while everyone else takes turns cycling in and out. The stiff, aggressive physicality enhances cardiovascular conditioning, especially for the subject who must stay in the ring. The drill demonstrates who is the strongest and most capable Olympic-style wrestler under the very arduous conditions of having no break (and having a fresh, new opponent thrown at you every two minutes).

Ironically, shark bait does little to help one become a great performer; its main benefit is to the social order. These exercises in dominance, which vets can opt into or out of at their leisure (younger, lower-status wrestlers have no choice but to participate), reinforce a code of hard, tough self-reliance, even though this is not an essential ingredient for becoming a great wrestler. The best professional wrestlers need only *appear* tough and violent, not actually *be* so.

I asked Slaughter, a lead trainer, about the function of shark bait. "It's very good cardio," he begins, "and it gets the guys used to being roughed around a little bit, should they ever be in the ring with someone like Perry Saturn.[31] [It's] so they can really take it to him and be a little tougher in the ring. It just . . . toughens them up a little." I ask how often they need to do it, and he states, "I don't like to do it too often. It doesn't really help at all. It's good cardio. But you don't really learn anything."

Another form of exchanged pain is the "shoot," a true fight where wrestlers exchange painful "stiffs" and implicit trust disintegrates. In any given match, either during training or in public performances, there is the ever-present possibility of a shoot. There are two different kinds of shoots: one is premeditated (set up before the match begins), the other occurs when someone accidentally stiffs an opponent during the match, triggering an escalation of exchanged stiffs. The premeditated type is very rare, whereas the unintentional kind of shoot "happens all the time" because it is so easy to stiff someone accidentally.

Premeditated shoots are highly threatening because the typical need for a "loose" and "light" disposition makes the wrestler virtually defense-less. A person anticipating a soft, loose grip or contact who instead receives a firm arm thrust at him becomes extremely vulnerable. There is more vulnerability here than in almost any other violent encounter (such as a car crash or fistfight) because one cannot tense up or flinch in preparation for the strike.[32] Tony, a participant who was fortunate enough to have a split second of anticipation, explains such a threat:

I knew it was coming. You can kind of tell by somebody's demeanor. Like, the way they grab you . . . when somebody grabs you in a different way. I guess when he flipped me over, I was like, here it comes. So just brace yourself and take it. But I wasn't expecting it at the level in which he nailed me.

Premeditated, intentional stiffs and shoots maintain the group's hierarchy and are considered justified when a participant is disliked for getting "too bigheaded" or for appearing to disrespect pro wrestling's traditions. Losing the group's respect (more likely the respect of one of the veterans) is therefore extremely dangerous. The target often has no warning, so added to the formidable challenge of defending oneself is having no time—not even a split second—to find out what you are in for. Tony describes delivering a premeditated stiff:

When I do the kick in the corner, if I don't like you or you've done something to piss me off, I will just rip you in the corner—and I'll do it. And you'll usually catch it pretty bad. But if I like you, I'll grab you by the wrist before I whip you and kind of talk to you, like, you know, "turn your face to the right." So that way when I hit the corner, as I'm about to come up with my foot, they can turn their face and I plant my heel on your chest. My toes will glance off your chin, and I'll just slide off. So it really doesn't hurt. But if I don't like you, you're catching that shit [laugh].

The second type of shoot—an accidental stiff that triggers an escalated exchange of stiffs—is far more common. An opponent may intend no harm, but since a real fight is being simulated, each performer repeatedly flirts with, say, drilling his opponent's cheek or clocking his opponent's testicles. As Slaughter states, "Sometimes you accidentally stiff someone. Sometimes you just can't help it. . . . But if somebody's going to blatantly stiff me, then they're getting it back. You know what I mean?"

Every seasoned wrestler knows that the standard response in such instances is a firm shot back, known as a receipt. As described earlier, the rules of the interaction are not verbalized but, rather, physically negotiated. Fueling the precariousness of this negotiation is the fact that at public shows the crowd is cheering, adrenaline is flowing, and wrestlers (are trying to) embody their brawny characters.

When describing his wrestling style, Tony shared an example of how an accidental shoot ever looms because of the fine line between harm and routine maneuvers.

I do a lot of things that you feel, but I'm not blatantly stiff[ing you]. I do moves that are portrayed as stiff, like the "hot hand." I feel terrible. I wrestled Tyler, who I've been good friends with, and he had a handprint on his back for two weeks. . . . Yeah, it was bad. . . . He said it really hurt. So the second time I wrestled him I tried getting more on the meaty part. He kind of hunched over a little bit more. There was a little more muscle exposed. He said it didn't hurt as much.

In this scenario, it's likely that their great respect for each other de-escalated an accidental shoot (because Tyler let Tony know he had hurt him), and ultimately Tyler just shrugged it off.

Matt described his experience with an intentional shoot, the result of his being considered too bigheaded. Sometimes younger, less experienced wrestlers need to be "broken in," and the exchange of pain enables veterans and other superiors to maintain status by vanquishing any perceived threats to the group's hierarchy. An exception proving the rule is found in how Slaughter distances himself from this practice.

I've had instances where guys have shown me very roughly that you do this this way and that way. I don't have that streak in me. It takes a lot for me to purposefully inflict a great deal of pain on somebody. I mean, I'll put a move on tight and let it go. But I'm more of a talker. You know, "Hey listen, do you know why I did that?" Or "Hey, listen, I just wanted to let you know, you're doing this wrong." . . . But I was shown one way, and that's the whole thing. You give me something, it's my job to give it to him, and three years from now he gives it to him. So you keep the wheel going.

Nevertheless, this account still shows that pain is a valuable instrument in maintaining the tradition of adversarial training.

Donny shared with me his initial experience at a wrestling training school he once belonged to.

They would beat the shit out of you, [do] cardio, then they'd put you in the ring, [and] something just didn't seem right. I had learned too much in one day. I was just getting my ass kicked. If I did the slightest thing, if I just took a step the wrong way . . . one of the trainers would choke the shit out of me. I was getting thrown around and choked out. I mean, they really just slapped on a nice choke hold on you and said, "You think wrestling's fake?" So something didn't seem right. So [I] said, "Screw this, maybe wrestling isn't for [me]." . . . I found out later that it was an old-school way where guys would just have the shit kicked out of them to show you how tough you have to be, and [to see] if you came back the next day to wrestle.

Not surprisingly, this school did not last. Regardless, conventional wisdom still holds this as the norm for wrestling schools—that you will learn that pro wrestling's "not fake" by experiencing, enduring, and overcoming pain.

While few would dispute that pro wrestling can be painful and dangerous, this book reveals how trust between performers is a crucial element of a successful (noninjurious) act. Despite this crucial ingredient, trainers I interviewed never framed trust as the key locus of success. In many respects, it was just the opposite: leaders perpetuated a belief in adversity as the central tie between performers. Matt, who went on to work in the wwe's "incubator league" in Kentucky, consequently earning great respect from the group, stopped by several trainings and served as an interim trainer. Sharing with the group what he had learned as a new student at the wwe-affiliated trainings, he said, "The way I learned was that everyone in the ring is a potential threat. You don't want to leave yourself exposed. You should be aware of limbs and extremities being exposed or away from your body. Remember, you are the master of your own destiny!" This highlights the mixed message received from experts: beware of "potential threats" *and* remain self-reliant even while exercising the true need to rely on one another.

The self-reliance, constant bruising, and stoicism that saturate the ethos of indie wrestling might be taken for granted, given that the objective is showcasing fighters who exact pain and frequently get injured. However, the hard ethos is largely contrived, not necessarily beneficial to wrestling development, and, I found, a sublimation of the anxiety about pro wrestling's intimate, homoerotic, and fraudulent underbelly. This underbelly, which remains largely tacit, animates a hyperhierarchical arrangement of wrestling superiors who leverage their status with not only expertise and braggadocio but a heavy dose of inflicted pain.

SOLIDARITY

A by-product of the fine line between real and fake violence is the solidarity generated by safeguarding one another from harm. Injury and, potentially, agony are the likely outcome when one person is careless or incompetent and things go astray. Yet if movements are synchronized and you have *achieved* an act of unbridled hatred while actually avoiding harm, you have successfully led one another through a threatening gauntlet and come out alive. Like soldiers in combat, helping one another survive a dangerous context engenders an invigorating solidarity.

To outsiders, nearly every single wrestling maneuver presents a "compromising position." Recall the words used by Hammer to characterize the extremely fine line separating a match having trust from a match with animosity—or rather the line between painful injury and intimate protection: "You're allowing me to put my hand behind your head. You're allowing me to hold your arm—which can easily be turned into a very compromising position."

Often what's more frightening than being pained or injured is the omnipresent threat of hurting someone else. The following excerpt from my field notes is a case in point.

> Rich and Al are in the ring. They have attempted a hip toss where Rich was the giver and Al the taker. Al was flipped and landed, but Rich immediately stood up and looked spooked. He could not see Al behind him. His eyes were wide open and he had raised eyebrows and was looking straight ahead with a ghost-white face. Fishman, standing next to me, knew exactly why Rich looked frightened. Al had not properly executed the move and it was *not* clear to Rich that Al was going to be okay when he turned back around. Al was fine. In fact, he was smiling like a proud young child who's just retrieved the ball from a busy street, unaware of the speeding cars. Rich was immensely relieved. Al was then sharply criticized by three vets for his mistake. I ask Fishman, "What was it that he did wrong?" With utter disgust, Fishman states "It?! . . . He did *everything* wrong! . . . he didn't jump, he didn't tuck his head under, he didn't put his hand on Rich's back. . . ."

Since performers take their craftsmanship seriously and because it is high risk, incompetence in any form is frowned upon. A big mistake such as Al's is usually met with disgust even if no one ends up injured. The angry reaction reveals the emotional burden carried by performers who are responsible for one another at all times while in the ring. When minor mistakes happen, such as a foot being slightly out of position, performers tacitly acknowledge it and move on. But individuals who are repeatedly reckless do not last long in the group because participants ostracize those who do not respect the inherent risk and harm.

As Damon conveys below, being a good pro wrestler goes far beyond being a good entertainer; it means bearing the responsibility of protecting opponents from pain and injury.

> So I mean, let's say I go in there and I have a bad spot in the match or I fuck up royally, or I do something to hurt someone else. . . . You know, it turns your great day into a shit day.[33] So that's why a lot of people don't realize [that] when we say "work," there's actually work involved. You're not actually having as much fun as people think out there. So you can actually see someone's attitude change and one guy can be "Oh wrestling is great, I can't see my life without it." By the end of the night, he could be looking at it as "I don't know why the fuck I'm doing this shit, 'cause all I'm doing is fucking up."

This illustrates the central, albeit unmentioned, tenet of performing: participants are responsible for their opponents, and being open to such responsibility (and vulnerability) with the other person can foster an intimate, though tacit, connection. In fact, a mistake that results in injury can actually bring two performers closer together. Many times I witnessed a painful injury—such as a knocked-out tooth causing blood to spurt all over a person's mouth and neck—cause initial indignity, which was then followed by tender empathy and affection. Performers identify with how easily they could have been on the flip side, having given the injury and been the one who made the mistake. And common weapons and props such as fire, trashcans, tables, ladders, and sticks increase the stakes of the implicit bargain. If the padding on the turnbuckle in a corner of the ring slips off, for example, a performer's head is exposed to the hard metal underneath.

AUTHENTICITY

Since pro wrestling is always subject to charges of fakery, pain authenticates the realness for fans and participants alike. On the individual level, these experiences provoke what Drew Leder calls "sensory intensification," where "a region of the body that may have previously given forth little in the way of sensory stimuli suddenly speaks up" (1990, 71). On a group level, pain and injuries demonstrate that wrestling is in fact real. It is an indisputable rebuttal to the relentless charge that pro wrestling is

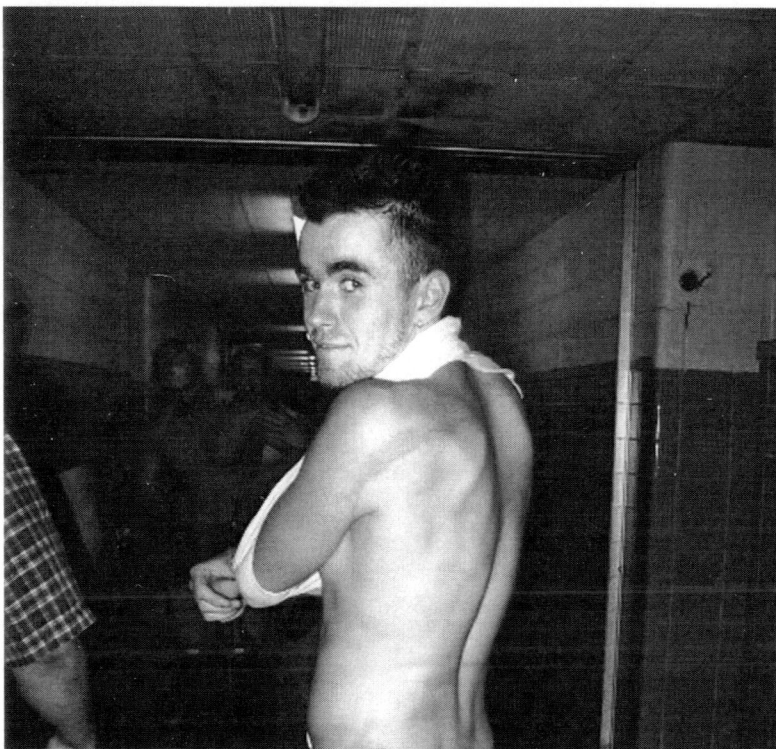

FIGURE 5.3. Flaunting scars. CREDIT: Author.

nothing more than a soap opera. Crutches, limps, and casts confirm its violent reality.

Participants in the group frequently flaunt their scars and bruises in sadomasochistic rituals that verify their suffering. Visible indications of pain, such as limping, bruises, bleeding, scars, and red marks, are commonly flaunted, especially when they are nondebilitating, because they legitimate the hurt, sacrifice, and dubious combat itself. For example, a bright red handprint from a direct, hard slap on the back (a "hot hand") is understood as a tangible badge of punishment and pain. In certain cases of damage, denial is not possible; it simply hurts.

Certain training exercises are organized around the giving and receiving of pain. Every few weeks, when they had the right combination of low- and middle-status wrestlers, spare time, and giddy energy, senior wrestlers would dispense kicks or hot hands to lower-status wrestlers. These performative exchanges—analogous to s&m play, where dominance, legitimation, and affect are desired ends (Newmahr 2011)—are rule-bound play in which a wrestler will slap or kick another wrestler on the chest or back as everyone looks on. As the open hand or foot of the inflicter hits the meaty flesh of a subordinate's lower back or upper chest, creating an audible smack, you hear a collective "Ooh!" from group members. This ritual, usually occurring when the most senior members are absent because the ritual has little direct utility, is followed by a collective display of wounds. The lower-status wrestler who received the blow lifts up his shirt to reveal the marks. The most rosy-red flesh, the result of the many broken blood vessels, elicits a praiseworthy "God damn!" from either a veteran or the whole group, thereby affirming not only the extent of the damage, but also the glory of having endured it. In this sense, the red mark represents a bold and simple proclamation: I have been hit, I suffer, and I am alive. As Fishman said to me, "It's just pain. Pain is God's way of letting you know you're not dead."

SUMMARY

Wrestling causes real, harmful health outcomes, including damaged tissue and broken bones. Research on such pain tends to focus on the phenomenon as an isolating experience that is invisible, individually experienced, and debilitating. In light of this, indie wrestling might be understood as an unnecessary, dangerous exercise of personal neglect.

However, the consequences of these physiological experiences are shaped by the interpretation of those who are bruised, battered, and broken. For wrestlers, experiences with pain gain meaning not just through exchanges of slaps and strikes but through their grimaces, clenched teeth, and offerings of ice. As Kleinman illustrates, "Experience is . . . constituted out of smiles, stares, gestures, stories. Experience is the pain I communicate to you with my grimace, and it is taken up and made up out of my efforts to explain (or deny) what I feel, and out of your efforts to hear me, help me, or avoid me" (2007).

The closer look at wrestlers shows how pain can be a seductive means toward solidarity, self-realization, status, and authenticity. Their pain is a type of currency that is traded and exchanged with one another. It is a clear, tangible index of sacrifice—they save and protect each other from routine hurt as well as from catastrophic possibilities like paralysis and death. The currency is also used, though less commonly, to dominate others. Pain is doled out on occasion to establish who is in charge and who is subordinate.

At times, feeling pain is an experience of suffering or agony; at other times, it is a tantalizing experience because being in pain is attainable, certain, and more appealing than feeling *nothing*. Living in a world saturated with narratives championing toughness, invulnerability, and stoicism, suffering pain offers an affirmation for those who want to make good on an elusive goal. Most ideals of modern Western manhood are difficult, if not impossible, to accomplish, especially for young working-class men. As a pained wrestler, however, a young man is one step closer to making good on these elusive ideals.[34]

★ CONCLUSION ★

In the previous chapters I have shown how certain young men experience and make sense of pro wrestling. In this final chapter, I make the case for why this matters: What does this high-risk, collaborative performance say about larger social issues?

Masculinity is frequently analyzed through the lens of a "crisis."[1] Scholarship has been primarily concerned with the political implications of Western masculinity: how male dominance or adherence to "hegemonic masculinity" (Connell's term for the most esteemed version of masculinity) contributes to racism, homophobia, misogyny, everyday violence, war, and other social issues. This common "crisis" designation, of course, presupposes a certain period of stability prior to the present turmoil and angst. This presumed order—or assurance—regarding men, gender, and masculine institutions is largely mythical, however. Western masculinity has never been *un*troubled. Masculinity "is not in crisis," as Tim Edwards states, "it *is* crisis" (2006, 17).

When masculinity is understood as a set of ideas that are contested and in flux, complexities and contradictions come into better view. Scholars recognize the range of men's experiences—young middle class white gay men and urban black working-class straight men, for example, encounter different opportunities, incentives, and punishments—and the respective categories are hardly static; moreover, contrasting principles provoke paradoxes and complications in the everyday practice of masculinity.

Indie pro wrestlers, like other young men, make their way through a tumultuous, evolving gender discourse that is ever modified and contested. Within this pursuit, wrestlers adhere to and reject ideals, variations, and contradictions of masculinity itself. Many ideals have opposing poles—compelling and rewarded in one situation, devalued and deplored in another. The experience represents an ongoing navigation of masculinity's turmoil and ambivalence; wrestlers navigate the tension between ridicule and recognition, glory and pain, homoeroticism and homophobia, and sympathy and dominance.

Wrestlers engage in violence, yet they care for one another and try to remain unharmed. They interact closely with other men while the specter of homophobia polices and penalizes intimacy and any show of actual affection. They batter and destruct their bodies during a period when male bodies take on even greater prominence as the locus of self-worth. They are personally responsible for maintaining their emotional and physical well-being in the midst of exhortations to deny, repress, or ignore it. Risk taking is bold and venerable and then harmful, reckless, and grounds for ostracism. Their paid work is generally not fulfilling, either financially or otherwise, yet a strong, enduring cultural tie remains between occupational status and their gender identity. Dignity and respect are cornerstones of identity, especially male identities, yet they seek recognition in a pursuit that operates on the fringes of respectability.

In *The Male Body*, Susan Bordo identifies this dynamic as the "double-bind of masculinity," where a person is directed to fulfill two mutually incompatible instructions at the same time. "We fabulously reward those boys who succeed in our ritual arenas of primitive potency," she explains, and "at the same time, we want male aggression to bow to civilization when a girl says 'no' and to be transformed into tender passion when she says 'yes'" (1999, 242). Consider, for example, the messages regarding violence. Violence holds a prominent mantle within US culture and, more specifically, our masculine value system (Collins 2008, Gilligan 1996, Kaufman 1996). Although violence saturates American media and is endorsed by many families, peers, and organized sports, boys are also taught that being violent is improper, uncivilized, and punishable. American men and boys are often steered toward a lesson such as "never start a fight, but always finish one." This message, one of several with mixed exhortations, both legitimates the use of violence *and* characterizes aggression as problematic. This is arguably contradictory and undoubtedly confusing, as the moment a person begins to "finish" a fight, he or she is intensifying it, if not "starting" a new one.

Ideals regarding men's effort can be similarly contradictory. While hard work is a cornerstone of the capitalist, competitive Western world and young men, accordingly, are taught to "give it your all" or "give 110 percent," life is to be conducted with a nonchalant, effortless ease ("never let them see you sweat"; "be cool, calm, and collected"). Being "cool"—what almost every young man strives for at some point—is precisely this: a demonstration of capability and skill executed with little or no sign of actual effort. Since men's behavior is supposedly dictated mainly by natural ability, utility, and innate character, they should not show signs of a learned, practiced response or, even worse, any mistakes. This ideal, of course, like most ideals, is almost impossible to achieve as so few things truly "come naturally."

Wrestling's backstage shows how much work can go into masculine enactments. While femininity has been characterized as an endlessly scrutinizable performance that requires strenuous preparation, internalized discipline, and expressive control, masculinity, in contrast, is considered the standard against which women's behaviors are measured—the invisible, default state of being.[2] Pro wrestling shows an extreme, though generalizable, case of how a "hard" masculinity requires engagement with a set of backstage relations that depend on behaviors not ordinarily associated with the masculine ideal. The hyperbolized world—of imperviousness, autonomy, power, and strength—cannot exist without a backstage of intimacy, interdependence, and collaboration. Behind the onstage display of strength, muscles, and dominance resides a backstage of collusion, intimate dependency, and vigilance of image.[3]

The above dynamic extends beyond the squared circle to various contexts or groups that need (or desire) to be tough—be they athletes, soldiers, or simply young men on the corner or out on the town. I suggest that the greater the show of impenetrable hard masculinity, the greater the web of trust and vulnerability to be shared with one's intimates. That is, such presentations are predicated upon a deep, indeed essential, trust and collaboration. Within locker rooms, fraternity houses, and barracks, to name just a few sites, men adjust and brace themselves to act as rugged individuals but their shared understandings, whispers, and ornamentation reveal a facade of innate utility. It is hardly straightforward, let alone natural, to act like a "real" rugged man; the performance is learned, rehearsed, and disciplined. The look of "natural" strength and cool, dominating indifference takes great effort to sustain.

At the same time, greater awareness of this as an "act" amplifies a tension within many contexts, especially those that are all, or almost all, male. A puzzling reality of Western masculinity is how men fear other men due to the shaming effects of homophobia at the same time that they constantly seek one another's approval. Men's homosocial cultural practices, particularly those organized around close physical interaction and display, are particularly complicated in today's postfeminist, post-gay-liberation era—where many gays live outside the closet and women occupy ever more prominent public roles.[4] These gatherings provoke doubt in a culture that increasingly accepts homosexuality while continuing to venerate heterosexuality: "Why are there no women here?" and "Are these men gay?" are questions posed (or silently considered) in more and more such contexts. A pro wrestler, like many other men who take pains to display masculinity, therefore walks into the very heart of a masculine puzzle: how to completely invest oneself in a "guy thing" that is at the same time considered "so gay."

Indie wrestling fosters close, often tacit, relationships with other men. Indisputably, the violence of the performance veils the expression of empathy between two men who would, in all likelihood, not otherwise share it. Within the ring's ropes and while communing in training, wrestlers find solidarity, protection, and community. This connection, difficult to cultivate in an atomized suburban culture of strip malls and consumer culture, is in fact institutionally encouraged within wrestling. Strangely enough, its broader framework of bravado and violence allows them to find intimacy, revealing a relational yearning in men that is often discounted or outright dismissed. Indie wrestling is an example of young heterosexual men going to great, sometimes physically painful lengths to find relational outlets with meaningful connection to other men. If the situations are not understood as "sensitive" spaces, and exhibit danger with occasional dominance, the more likely the appeal.

Indie wrestlers must consciously (and not so consciously) muddle their way through the power and entitlements of masculinity as well as its toxicity and tolls. Western masculinity has always embodied a set of ideals that are very difficult to achieve, and the effects of the last thirty years of a neoliberal economy have made achieving them only more elusive and, at times, more costly. Paid work, where many men traditionally secure a sense of purpose and identity, has become a less secure outlet for men to affirm their identities *as men*. Maleness (or the male body, if you will) has considerably less inherent value, and the project of proving masculinity—a tentative undertaking under any circumstances—is all the more uncertain as a result.[5] Meanwhile, masculinity (with its various signifiers) remains highly venerated within the culture. Men's continued dominance of women (and more subordinate men) undoubtedly generates a countless number of inequalities. But despite these privileges, young men can be quite constrained by masculinity's limited script, particularly those men with fewer resources. The disintegration of uncontested masculine social spheres, along with the related decreased need for physicality, has been met with a manifest cultural lust for muscles and the virtues they signify. In fact, the muscular male body, now celebrated as never before, has taken on enormous cultural intrigue and symbolic value. Heterosexual men's concern with appearance and body image has never been greater. Indie wrestlers reflect this trend inasmuch as they are heterosexual, work mostly in the low-skilled service sector, and are highly committed to displaying muscularity and bravado. For several of them the drive to display is even so irresistible that it hinders the development of other forms of human capital. In this respect, they are an example of our "ornamental culture," as Susan Faludi calls it.[6]

Yet pro wresters are hardly grappling for glamorous "ornamental" image and applause. While indie wrestling is not utility in the traditional sense, it involves dangerous and difficult work that produces something. This is not as simple a matter as moving the locus of identity from the realm of production to the realm of leisure and consumption. Wrestlers may not secure a sense of self in their paid work, their day jobs, but they nevertheless sweat, toil, and produce—often while in pain. One may read this as ironic: they affirm identity working in a world of artifice and fraud. But is this so different from many other forms of modern work? Wrestlers entertain and excite; their craft transports and thrills. While their labor is designed to deceive and disguise, is it all that different from say advertising or politics?

To an outsider it might look like "masculine compensation" is motivating their participation, but a closer look muddles this commonly applied descriptor. Instead of marginalized men trying to reclaim a lost masculinity by means of "protest masculinity," as R. W. Connell calls it, we see intimacy, cooperation, trust, and interdependence negating hard masculinity and compensating for risk, dominance, and individualism. The pursuit is not the securing of a long-sought-after authentic masculine identity as much as it is a way of expressing, of working through, puzzles and paradoxes of contemporary manhood.

Indeed, the recognition wrestlers garner is premised on the command and display of violence and domination. However, in contrast to groups of young men who campaign for respect through the threat or use of violence, wrestling is relatively safe due to a set of shared guidelines. While still dangerous and very often painful, pro wrestling is dissimilar to combat brutality or street violence and more akin to a very physicalized form of ballet or theater. Indie wrestlers use their bodies, their gestures, and each other to tell stories. Their collaborative efforts allow them to be recognized by fans and find solidarity with one another.

Unlike other, more fungible forms of recognition—such as a high salary or prestigious occupational title—the recognition indie wrestlers win largely remains within the veterans' halls and community centers where they perform. It is generally not transferable capital; it has little or no currency beyond this subculture. When wrestlers arrive for the weekend show, the recognition begins; when the last fan has left, the recognition is over until the next show.

Nevertheless, from this recognition bestowed by both fans and fellow wrestlers, the deleterious effects of meaningless work and suburban ennui—alienation, exploitation, and insignificance—are mitigated, at least temporarily. In the indie world these men find the identity, solidarity, and excitement that the larger world fails to deliver. Tony, a four-year wrestler, sums up this sentiment:

> I had the opportunity to work for the Long Island Railroad [but] because it would be a damper on my wrestling schedule, I didn't do it. . . . I would rather be struggling to pay my bills, wrestling two or three times a month on weekends, a few times a week during practice. That's what makes me happy, you know? That's what it comes down to. There's very few things that make me feel like I do when I walk out that red curtain.

The rewards of performing drown out the numerous disincentives and impediments that participation entails. The rewards, along with a concomitant deep immersion in the scene, encourage wrestlers to sacrifice other social opportunities, including some better suited to provide long-term stability—perhaps even upward mobility.

Indie performers position themselves to receive live, unmediated validation and become someone whom people pay to see. They tell stories, fill seats, and make fans' hearts pound. Their pursuit grants recognition, connection, sense of purpose, and validation of self. What might appear as nihilistic or reckless endangerment is in fact a dangerous yet sensible vying for an enhanced life experience. They revel in this (at times Sisyphean) struggle, for it represents a means to defeat obscurity.

The costs of this pursuit cannot be underestimated. The performance is difficult, dangerous, and quite often painful. Every single performer is at one point or another debilitated by injuries—profound costs indeed, because a wrestler relies on his body far more than the average person. Personal struggles immediately emerge when the body breaks down; the connection between bodily performance and identity is so strong that it has the potential to cause calamity.

So when a performer climbs into the ring, at stake is his own body and his opponent's and their relationship to each other and to their fans. The crowd's response can either build or destroy a wrestler's sense of self, making the risks as big as or bigger than the risks taken by individuals who are paid for their dangerous labor—police officers, steelworkers, stunt men— let alone by middle-class folks performing community theater. In the intense brinksmanship of the live, interactive exchange, a young man could, if all goes poorly, elicit nothing but injuries, deafening silence, or worst of all, the catastrophic, ego-crushing chant "BOR-ing! BOR-ing!"

The stakes for identity are high because, come show time, wrestlers enter the ring and stand, half-naked, as totally exposed individuals completely at the crowd's mercy. Whereas a boxer's focus is on footwork and impending strikes, the successful pro wrestler's inner focus is on the relationship to his opponent and winning over the crowd. If the match goes well, the crowd is in the palm of *his* hand. If it goes poorly, he is in the palm of *their* hand.

If all goes well, he both safeguards his opponent and wins a roaring pop from the crowd. When the craft is honed, the story line creative, and the partnership with opponent fluid, the loud, immediate, and live recognition from fans and fellow performers flows. Indie wrestling offers an attractive, alternative world where a young man can leap for cheers and chants of "Holy shit!" while an opponent cares for him. Within this enclave of legitimation and potential adoration is a palpable affirmation of the pained self.

APPENDIX A

HOW IT BEGAN

In 2002, a student of mine walked in during my office hours. At the end of our long conversation about race, politics, and sociology, I asked for his e-mail and he handed me a business card which stated, *Tommy T—The Enforcer*. I asked what this title meant and he stated matter-of-factly, "Oh, I do pro wrestling promotions." I had more or less forgotten about this staple of the American cultural diet. Only then did I begin to rethink pro wrestling.

I recalled this exchange a few months later, when taking an ethnography seminar with Javier Auyero. I looked on the Internet for pro wrestling and, as it happened, there was a training school for aspiring pro wrestlers near my own university. I learned that on the following Sunday it would be staging a show at a community center about a thirty-minute drive away, so I went to it. This, it turns out, became the unofficial beginning of my fieldwork.

At the intermission a short guy in his early twenties with a goatee and a big smile approached me. Enthusiastically he said, "Hey man, how are you?" At first I was sure he was talking to the guy behind me, but he asked what I had been up to and mentioned that his name was Ryan, perhaps realizing that I was having trouble placing him. He kept talking—where was I living now, what had I been up to? I didn't even think to correct him because he seemed so glad to see me. I told him I needed to go to the bathroom. "It was great to see you!" he said, just before giving me a big hug and parting.

The bear hug resulting from a case of mistaken identity revealed several things. First, fans and wrestlers made up a rather tight-knit community. Contrary to the stereotype of pro wrestlers and their fans as tough degenerates "who beat their wives,"[1] I had witnessed a congenial and caring group. The boundary between performers and fans was unclear; many fans were connected to performers by acquaintance of some kind (friendship, family, work, etc.). So I experienced a shared community very *unlike* professional sports or professional theater, where the audience usually has very little means of tangible interaction.[2] Second, although I really didn't know anyone, I apparently looked familiar enough to be mistaken for one of them—reasonably resembling them in age, sex, race, and dress. In actuality, I was most likely the only person at the show (performer or fan) who knew absolutely no one. Third, if I pursued this project, I would be an outsider needing to break through a social group's boundaries—a group with its own rules, codes, and language, few of which I knew. I knew that, being relatively shy, I would have a lot of work to do to become a good ethnographer. While many of these tattooed, muscular young men gave no hint of warmth, my hunch was that I could crack the intimidating countenance with sincere curiosity.

I proceeded to attend the group's small Sunday night shows at their first training center, a converted auto body garage about thirty miles outside New York City. At these intimate Sunday night shows—consisting of a ring and row of chairs for no more than twenty-five spectators—I was an anonymous audience member only twice before all such small shows were banned by a New York State Athletic Commission regulation stipulating the requirements for spaces where such promotions took place. However, the two visits left me with a clear enough understanding that behind their braggadocio, several wrestlers were affable guys who would be open to talking with me. Also, this was not a part-time hobby or leisure activity; it was high-risk, dangerous *work*—and they took it seriously. So finally, having determined the general hierarchy, I knew I had to get the approval of Cuss.

When I returned, I felt compelled to say something about myself. I was too uncomfortable with being nothing more than an onlooker—everyone but me had a role or identity of some sort: wrestling student, trainer, veteran, former wrestler, brother to a wrestler, hardcore fan.[3] I didn't know anyone, I was standing around empty-handed, I wasn't paying to learn or watch, I wasn't trying to get in the ring, and I looked on with a different stance (unlike the eager young men, I was thirty years old and not vying for the same type of acceptance).[4]

As I left that night I shook Cuss's hand and somewhat nervously blurted out: "Thanks a lot for letting me check it out. I plan to come back. I want to wrestle but I am not really sure how that would work because of my knee injury. But maybe I can announce or ref or something. . . . And another part of me wants to write a book about it." He received this well, saying "no problem, come on by anytime." From there, the project took off.

DOCUMENTING

I went to the group's practices every week, sometimes twice a week, for about two and a half years, from 2003 through 2005. During this time I observed over twenty-five public wrestling events and attended over sixty three-hour-long practices, amounting to over 350 hours of research in the field. I used several forms of documentation, gathering data through notes, photographs, e-mails, and audio and video recordings.

Practices were in the evening from roughly six to ten. About halfway through my fieldwork, the school moved from the former auto body garage thirty miles outside

Manhattan to a gym at a community center farther from the city, a space where the group also held its monthly shows. When I could, I spent time with the wrestlers at local bars or eateries and communed after their shows and practices. Over fifteen times, I spoke with wrestlers in my car when I gave a wrestler a ride home or to a train station.

My participation, as usually happens in the course of ethnographic research, became more and more involved. My time was mainly spent in five spaces: the auto body shop–cum–training gym (for a year before it was vacated altogether); the ringside training space during practices; the behind-the-scenes space ("backstage") during practices; the performance space ("onstage") during shows, alongside the other spectators; and the backstage locker room space on show nights. Aside from interviews, the bulk of my data derives from conversations and observations that took place while I stood beside the ring or on the ground below it during practices.

Each space had a different look and feel. The locker room was tight and smelly, clogged with the detritus of teaching and child care. The ceilings were very low, and the walls were covered with epithets and maxims associated with the education of children. The training and performing space, in contrast, was a former middle-school gym and thus wide open. The data I acquired varied with the spaces. As one might expect, when guys are in the ring and have many eyes on them, they are very consciously performing (for either fans or fellow wrestlers); backstage, on the other hand, the level of trust and candor was higher.

My usual tactic was to speak into a tape recorder on my drive home from training sessions and shows. I always had a ride lasting anywhere from thirty to sixty minutes, so I used the time to reflect on details from the previous three to five hours that stuck in my mind. I then sat down the next morning and typed up as much as I could, straight from memory. Once I felt that my recollections had been exhausted, I turned on the tape to get more specific details and to add data I had forgotten but had tape-recorded on the drive home. A visit typically generated ten to fifteen single-spaced pages of notes.

I wrote little down while in the training space. Aside from a small, 3″ x 4″ notepad that I kept stuffed in my pocket and took out to jot down phone numbers, precise details and quotes that would be hard to replicate, my notes were reconstructed from memory. My notepad came out several times a night, but I seldom used it more than once. I was quick but not surreptitious. I did not want to call attention to my written documentation because I sought to avoid the question "Why does *that* comment or detail warrant putting pen to paper but not *this* one?"

I wove myself into the fabric of the group by talking with folks ringside, giving rides, running small errands (getting ice or fetching tapes from a car), timing drills, or helping with writing when asked.[5] I hung out in the locker room, at their practices, and behind the curtain. I went to their houses and their bars; I even went to Hooters.[6] Most importantly, I constantly asked questions and took an interest in all aspects of their lives and of the indie scene. I discovered the "range of unanticipated events" (Goffman 2002) that is possible only in a long-sustained, in-depth, multisite ethnographic study. I did my best to adhere to Jack Katz's advice regarding the "discipline of the negative case," meaning that when I was confronted with evidence contradicting a current explanation, I tried to "transform it into a confirming case by revising the definition of either the explaining or the explained phenomenon" (1982, 200).

Since injuries were common, they became opportunities to weave myself further into the group. When they occurred, I usually took the time to see how the person involved felt and whether there was anything I could do to help. Of course, this needed to be done without calling too much attention to the person, who was often doing his best to suppress any perception of suffering. I got ice, some Advil, or a chair, should it be needed. Once I ran down the ambulance and paramedics who responded to our 911 phone call but were having trouble locating us.

Since the research site was also a public performance venue every six weeks, I had the methodological advantage of videoing and photographing live matches inconspicuously.[7] I have videotapes and photos of shows from 2003 through 2006. I see no reason to believe that these recordings intruded on their performances (or altered behavior) on show nights. In addition, my partner helped by taking photographs and capturing many nuances of the live production. These include interactions with fans in the hallways and corridors, the individuals who posed for her, and the nuts-and-bolts personnel of a production: announcers, ticket sellers, and concessionaires.

Web message boards were another methodological tool. Rarely did I use these postings as primary data, but I did occasionally verify my own findings against conversations on message boards. Overall, very little of my data derived from these postings, but there were moments that I found explanatory or otherwise helpful. If message board users wrote about an event or moment that I was *not* present for, I did not use the information in this book or elsewhere.

Toward the end of my concentrated time in the field, videos of shows began to circulate via the group's website and YouTube. These clips allowed me to confirm certain story lines, characters, and matches after completing the more intensive fieldwork. They also let me keep up with events from a distance, something I appreciated when I could not attend as frequently. Generally speaking, I followed a grounded theory approach—the analysis was an iterative process where ideas were used to make sense of the data and data were used to change my ideas.

INTERVIEWS

All together, I conducted nineteen interviews: thirteen of these were one- to two-hour-long audio recordings made at diners, completely away from the group; three were done in a back room in the building where the shows and practice sessions were held; an additional three took place in the main gym space, with people milling all around, or at the WWE headquarters in Stamford, Connecticut. These were shorter, and though they were not audio-recorded, I did take notes that I used to reconstruct the conversation afterward.

The interviews were semistructured. By this I mean that I used a set of questions covering a number of basics—age, weight, height, wrestling experience, and childhood relationship to wrestling. However, I did not go sequentially, and respondents were welcome to wander into related subject areas if the material was appropriate or revealing (see appendix B). Seldom did I look at a sheet of questions or write things down during an interview. The point was to have an open discussion. When conversation stalled or the participant veered in an inappropriate direction (e.g., WWE lore from previous eras or gossip about a specific promoter in the region), I referred to a set question. Since I was recording the interviews, I wrote down only small reminders to myself about points to return to later on (e.g., a provocative detail might flash by when another point was being discussed—a detail needing further explanation).

When an interview took place at a local diner, I paid for the meal. Even though I always said beforehand that I would pay, only once at the end of the meal did a wrestler offer nothing. I read this gesture as reflecting how they viewed the interview; that is, not as work or a way to make cash. For the most part, they found the experience more enjoyable than they anticipated and *not* akin to being a "paid subject." Aside from buying tickets to the public shows, this was the only compensatory aspect of my research.

Once past the initial "what do you want?" suspicion that is an unfortunate derivative of many a young man's habitus, I felt as though I had, more or less, an open book. I started each interview with a brief explanation of what "my book" was generally to be about—a look at the indies and the wrestlers who perform in them. I then explained that I was recording the interview. Three-quarters of them *loved* to be listened to. With only two interviews did I feel any resistance or discomfort with the process. Participants spoke candidly of their body issues, relationships, wrestling challenges, and transgressions. I heard accounts of drug abuse, car accidents, crime, life in abusive households, yearned-for love from fathers, and childhood trauma. This material, perhaps more than anything else, propelled me through the project's doldrums and challenges. I wanted these honest accounts to be heard by a larger audience.

I believe my age (late twenties) was beneficial to me because I was given some unearned respect based purely on seniority. Moreover, I was within the range of recently shared experiences but old enough to have acquired some critical perspective about choices and experiences. While I had thought that being male would be more an obstacle than an advantage when I began the study—I based this on the generalized homophobia that taints male-to-male relationships more so than their female counterparts—I believe I was wrong. For the most part, these men had spent more time with men than women, and I believe most saw me as an ally of understanding who could relate to the dreams, pains, and frustrations of a young adult male.

With three exceptions, no wrestler in the group had been in an interview prior to mine. They were appreciative of the opportunity, for in a sense it was an hour and a half to two hours of uninterrupted recognition. Interviews became a catalyst, the breakthrough to the inner circle of teasing and berating. With one quiet, brooding, stoic type of member—who previously said very little to nothing to me—an endearing "What's up asshole?" replaced an uncommitted "How ya doin'?" or silent nod. After the interview, a wrestler who had otherwise been recalcitrant or smug might seek me out at practice to say hello and ask how I was. Additionally, as the "writer," interviews made research more comfortable because they were a visible form of *my* work.

When I began fieldwork I was pretty sure that I would participate in the wrestling. It seemed like an appetizing contrast with academia—an exciting outlet to revel in physicality and performance. In addition, I had once been a big fan of pro wrestling.

Growing up in the US suburbs in the early 1980s, I watched pro wrestling on Saturday mornings. Back then it was a morning program, and I would wake up and watch it while at my father's house (every other weekend). Like many boys, I was captivated for several years; I got sucked into the drama of Macho Man, Hulk Hogan, Sergeant Slaughter, and George the Animal Steel. I was a big mark for George the Animal Steel's maniacal gimmick of chewing up the turnbuckle after a victory. Although I never attended a live show at the old Spectrum arena, near where I grew up, I always wanted to.

Like most fans, I reveled in the physicality, emotion, and illicit nature of the performance. At my mother's house I wasn't really allowed to watch wrestling—my older sisters, who had more say in the household programming, took no interest— but this made it all the more enticing. Our mom really let us watch only the wholesome Cosby show, so I watched pro wrestling at my dad's house, because he did not care. It was vulgar, violent, and filled with a brazen attitude I could only dream of having.

As with many other fans, young ones especially, my interest eroded the more I realized how staged everything was. I cared less and less about each character. I confess that it took me a long time to *really* know that it was a staged fight. The one part of the programming that always baffled me was the sharing of the microphone by two supposed "enemies." It didn't make sense that two out-of-control adversaries would have the decency and poise to share something in this manner. Even at nine years old, I could not wrap my head around the idea that these two men would be raging mad, yelling in each other's face, and then be able to politely pass a microphone back and forth. The coordination broke the illusion of realness—much as when actors in a musical break into song in the midst of an otherwise convincing dialogue.

When I began my fieldwork about fifteen years later, I had long outgrown my fandom. I had not watched wrestling since I was a kid and saw it as most of the general public does—odd and amusing shtick. I did not closely follow the WWE, and so I knew about contemporary wrestling stars only through movies, advertising, and National Public Radio interviews.

All that notwithstanding, I was sucked into the drama at the very first indie show I attended. Just after intermission, a skinny young white man with long blond hair, wearing white jeans and no shirt, came out of nowhere and jumped into the ring.

He demanded "to have a word with the commissioner." Adamant and indignant, he sold it well. Two large security guards dressed in black sport coats (with Event Security printed on the back) jumped into the ring and attempted to get him out. The commissioner arrived after a minute or two, looking very annoyed. The guards restrained the teenager as someone else put the microphone in front of him. Now broadcasting to 150 people, he explained that he wanted a chance to wrestle and that the promoter did not return his phone calls. He appeared very upset and ready to hit the promoter. Then the promoter took the microphone placed in front of him and responded to the man's accusation, saying he should leave the ring and shut up (after cutting him down him with a comment about how this "loser guy had no friends"). The security guards finally wrangled him out of the ring while he continued to yell that the promoter was a jerk and should have given him a match. The manager, now alone in the ring with the microphone, yelled, "Well if you *really* want to fight, you better show up on November 15, you little faggot!" The outright homophobia caught me off guard, although it added to the believability. For a few minutes, I thought it was all real. This moment corroborated Goffman's point that you see more on the first day of research "than you'll ever see again. And you'll see things that you won't see again" (2002, 152). If I could be duped, I shared that core ingredient of fandom, the suspension of disbelief.

Despite no longer being a big fan, I could appreciate the appeal of being a wrestler. During my undergraduate years I took some drama classes and performed in a large-scale production. I wholeheartedly endorse combining theater, physicality, and playfulness, things, I am afraid, that many men do not (unless intoxicated, of course). I still have the occasional fantasy of getting in the ring in front of a crowd. I know the character I would adopt ("the Mad Professor"), and I have thought of several promo lines, too ("I will school you!").

I was confident that I could learn to execute the physical moves; I am athletic enough and not horrible at impersonations. Being physical with other men is nothing new to me, since I have competed regularly in many contact sports (including Olympic wrestling in grade school). I still participate in team sports whenever the opportunity arises, and I have lots of firsthand experience with competitive sports. Thanks to sports I have broken four different bones at various times. Needless to say, I share a deep appreciation for the strategy, physicality, discipline, pain, and camaraderie of sports. This orientation helps me appreciate the rush of endorphins, the battering of the body, the sweat, the trust, and the teamwork inherent in pro wrestling.

This particular praxis, I believe, is likely to have made me a harsher skeptic of the participants' athleticism—in terms of both exertion and the collective athleticism of pro wrestling performance. Only a few times while watching did I think to myself, "Damn, that move took strength!" More often, I thought, "Whoa! That was crazy?" The endurance and strength are essential qualities, but I focused more on the pain, dramaturgy, emotions, and bodily collusion. In my understanding, pro wrestling is a hybrid entertainment: sporting theater.

Although I expected to wrestle in some capacity (the wrestlers expected it, too),

I never ended up doing it. After just two visits to the trainings, I realized I did not want to take such risks with my own body. Since the second surgery on my right knee, I have been rather cautious with contact sports despite my love for them.[8] Prior to my injuries I was fairly akin to those young men who throw caution to the wind and partake in high-risk physicality. Because of this I can identify with wrestlers who do high spots and flips and the more extreme maneuvers because fifteen years ago, I might have been right there with them. Today, as a spectator with a screw in his knee, however, I cringe when I see two young wrestlers jump flip from a ladder while in an embrace. So these injuries, coupled with general aging (where perspectives on mortality and parenthood increasingly shade understandings of the body's preciousness), altered my relationship to my body. This significantly distinguishes me from nearly all the wrestlers.

BECOMING "THE BOOK WRITER"

Wrestlers expected a very different book than this. Most envisioned a glossy best seller sitting on the front table at Barnes and Noble, not an academic book. I learned of this disjunction when Patrick confronted me about some photos I had just taken of everybody striking the ring after a show. I was documenting all aspects of the production and pursuit, not just the in-ring action. Patrick saw it differently and rather aggressively inquired, "What's up with you taking photos of me taking down the ring?"

The day after Louie learned that I was going to write a book about the wrestlers, I entered the space and he announced loudly, "Hey, it's the book writer!" I initially scorned this title but later came to embrace it. It gave me a stable identity, a place-holder in the melee of characters and faces that drifted in and out of the scene. Once everyone knew me as "the book writer," folks mentioned ideas about what I should put in the book, what should be on the cover, and what the chapters should consist of. Guys suggested titles. Most commonly, people would say things along the lines of "Why don't you put *that* in your book?" Others might say, "This could be the cover of your book!" or "You should write a whole chapter on this!"

By and large, the wrestlers were very receptive, and I never sensed any change once I was styled the "book writer." Generally there was little curiosity from members (whether regulars or new or intermittent members I hadn't formally introduced myself to) about what I was doing there. When I was asked something about either myself or what I was doing, the question four out of five times was not "What specifically are you looking at?" but rather "Are you going to wrestle?" or "*When* are you going to wrestle?"[9]

The most evident form of *reactivity* that I had on the research was the provision of added recognition. I was another set of eyes and ears that witnessed, documented, and legitimized the collectivity. Wrestlers stated such demands as "You better get out there and see my match!" all the time. I contributed to the individual and collective recognition. For example, Patrick, a veteran with a great stake in the collective endeavor, suggested I note certain moments. One night, just before a show with a sizable attendance, he said, "How about that crowd!? . . . Take some photos for the book!"

Particularly in the early part of fieldwork, photographs were a tremendous means of access. Initially, I took shots because, in part, it was not easy to stand around night after night simply watching, empty-handed. I wanted to feel more involved; it was a collective production, and I wanted to pitch in in any way I could (other than with this book). So when I could, I did. I was happy to help them. Later on in the project, I took photos more for my own research purposes and for fun. Photos were almost always appreciated. When I didn't have a photo of someone who expected one, it occasionally cut the other way. But by and large, this task brought me further into the group's fold.[10]

My more educated status went in and out of salience even though I always downplayed it. Timmy regularly made the difference conspicuous, however. Having never finished high school, he was probably most threatened by it. Also, he had significant power within the group, but wrestling capital was its basis. Since I was no longer interested in training to be a wrestler, he held no influence or power over me. Our differences were highlighted in occasional asides, such as "What do you think of that, Doc?" (referring to the PhD). In general, however, Timmy was the exception in the group despite his higher status.

Even though I did not inhabit the same social location, I rarely sensed that I was being treated with kid gloves. I tried to interrogate my level of access from time to time, and when I did, I was reassured that if I was missing out on something, the act itself was not vital to my findings. I was aware that my presence did not stifle insensitive or "offensive" dialogue and gestures. I knew this, in part, because of the configuration of the space—often I was within hearing distance of the interactions, but wrestlers did not know I was even there.

Several times, in fact, matches were downright boring and hard to watch. Skits went on way too long; no chemistry or psychology was developed. Often the audience concurred. When *they* started chanting "Boring! . . . boring! . . . boring!" my experience was the same.[11]

RESEARCHING "BADASS" YOUNG MEN

Young men present a challenge in that they may seek distinction and recognition, yet they invest in being inexpressive, tough badasses. Naturally, I grew to care for the group members the more I got to know and understand them. Understanding was sometimes made difficult because these young men constantly put themselves at risk and I was witness to the self-inflicted harm. Even though they generally tried to avoid injury, it occurred all the time. From time to time I was angered by the performers' use of bodily damage to manipulate the audience's emotions. Irate, after one show in particular, I wrote the following in my notes:[12]

> I am angry. I felt as though they were taking advantage of our appreciation and going too far with the manipulation of the spectators' fandom. In a very cheap

way, they took that gimmick to an uncomfortable and unnecessary extreme which took advantage of our feelings for them. This was a huge high spot done two times, and based on the "acting" afterward, it could be construed only one way: full destruction (or paralysis). When Donny was carted away, why didn't he raise his hand or give clear indication that he was actually okay? Fans were absolutely confused, some were crying. By the end of the night I had made phone calls and looked into his well-being (before I spent time backstage). It made me even angrier to learn that he was thrilled with how concerned we all were.

The more I knew about them, the more I knew about family members who depended on them (or their paycheck). Their recklessness was cause for concern. Did they realize that this or that move could easily lead to paralysis? Sometimes I wanted to ask (or yell), "What are you doing? You won't be walking at all in a few years if you keep this up! How can you do this when you are the father of a young kid?" Yet as Goffman aptly states regarding the task of raising the consciousness of research subjects, an attempt to intervene would not necessarily be right, let alone successful. "I can only suggest that he who would combat false consciousness and awaken people to their true interests has much to do, because the sleep is very deep. And I do not intend to provide a lullaby, but merely to sneak in and watch the people snore" (Goffman 1974, 14).

Humor was another type of "badass" threat that I had to endlessly navigate. Subtle jokes and references are the backbone of much dialogue, and one needs to be fluent in this lingua franca to grasp the subtleties of group dynamics. So I needed to participate in the banter in order to be a part of the group. At the same time, I did not want to hurt anyone's feelings as either a researcher (needing to be open, accessible, and trusted) or a humanitarian. It was hard to know how much to participate in their put-downs and pranks because they were largely driven by performative dominance. I had great discomfort with mean jokes targeting a member who was present. I generally refrained from joining in—not wanting to contribute to the replication of dominance-based homophobic, size-ist, or sexist jokes—but I did chime in every so often. It would have been fraudulent to pretend that I did *not* have a sense of humor or that I was not above their bathroom humor. Sometimes I hated their jokes, sometimes I yawned, and every so often they were really funny. Depending on who said it, how it was said, and my particular mood, one joke could elicit different reactions. I recall laughing at a horrific pedophile joke that was absolutely depraved but also somewhat creative. Self-deprecating jokes usually went over well. Sometimes I thought of a poignant joke before anyone else but held back out of respect for the recipient of the put-down. I had never-ending ambivalence about joining the fray.

TYSON THE BOOK WRITER, TYSON THE WRESTLER

"It is doubtful whether one can become a good social reporter unless he has been able to look, in a reporting mood, at the social world in which he was reared" (Hughes 2002, 144). Being white meant that I generally blended in and benefited from racial privilege and the *lack* of difference. This commonality with most group members, one among several, minimized difference and blunted both real and perceived differences. Race was a regular theme in the story lines. When I took an acquaintance (who is black) to a show, I was concerned that something offensive might occur in the show. I didn't know him very well at this point, so I felt responsible. Nothing offended him.

I can relate to concerns with feeling not big enough or strong enough or attractive enough. I remember quite well my own acute adolescent and early adult concern with masculinity. Growing up as the youngest of four in an often tumultuous household, I appreciate their yearning for attention and recognition, as I too had to fight for focused attention and love. I have experienced the rush that comes after stepping off the stage—the exuberant feeling that can make hanging out with thespians after a rehearsal or performance so exhausting.

I typically had some stubble on my face and dressed very casually: running shoes or sneakers, T-shirt, blue jeans, a Dickies coat—so I more or less fit the mold of a suburban American white guy in his twenties. The moment I deviated from monochrome guy wear, it was noted (e.g., when I wore red socks, Timmy stopped his group commentary and said, "Nice socks!"). A few times people commented on my weight (even though it never varied more than five pounds throughout all the fieldwork) or haircut, "You look good, did you get a haircut?" In many ways, however, the appearance norms capture a tension within the group: expression, panache, and creativity—despite being valued and encouraged onstage—remain deviant.

In a way that I anticipated, I never felt entirely comfortable with the group: a hang-up related to the predatory nature of "participant" research. A longer immersion *might* have lessened the social distance between me and the group. Perhaps I'd have been better able to reduce the distance or come closer to resolving the "unending dialectic" that Hughes describes.

> The unending dialectic between the role of member (participant) and stranger (observer and reporter) is essential to the very concept of fieldwork. . . . But the dialectic is never fully resolved, for to do good social observation one has to be close to people living their lives and must be himself living his life and must also report. The problem of maintaining good balance between these roles lies at the very heart of sociology, and indeed of all social science. (2002, 144)

Yet the consistent discomfort could also stem from the fact that I was a "fink" (Goffman 2002). I never really was one of them. Also, I had a private life to live, and it became busier while doing fieldwork. Certain differences were too obstinate to overcome, and for better or worse, I am not the kind of "ethnographic cowboy" (Trimbur 2008) who prides himself on the perceived ability to transcend a connection to the marginalized. For me, it would have been a farce to enter this activity with the idea that I could adopt the habitus (and respective motivations) for participation. I always felt a social distance. At first I wanted to believe that I *could* become one with them, but things changed. I realized that this was not only OK; it was the only way. I was hyperconscious of the fact that at the end of the day, I was doing research for the sake of knowledge, not out of a committed desire for recognition, camaraderie, and solidarity. Doing the latter would have been inappropriate and uncomfortable. Had I entered the ring and become a performer, I think it would have been completely disingenuous, a form of ironic slumming, and would have made me feel self-conscious.[13]

I of course experience many of the same fundamental social needs—recognition, intimacy, camaraderie, and corporeal pleasures—but I tend to find them in other domains and by other methods. I don't know the names of all the current WWE wrestlers, just as few wrestlers are familiar with authors I appreciate. I avoid fast food when possible, wear a bike helmet when commuting to work, and worry about the cartilage in my knee, not the next concussion, if I am thinking about my own bodily harm at all. At times I felt these differences keenly, and wrestlers sometimes made light of them. I was called out for being a liberal a few months into my fieldwork when I accidentally forwarded an antiwar e-mail to two wrestlers. I immediately received an angry reply from Matt, seething at the arguments I implicitly endorsed. His fury startled me, but the more I spent time with the group, the more I came to see it as his way of saying, "I call bullshit, asshole!" In other words, the confrontational tone was different than the more formal, more heady ("civil"), academic tone that I had grown accustomed to within the halls of academia (where passions are squeezed through the formal discourse of studies, methodology, and theory).[14] Nevertheless, my reaction to his e-mail spoke to my concern for being called out as a lefty elitist and highlighted my concern with maintaining their trust of me, a preoccupation that remained during most of my fieldwork.[15]

APPENDIX B

RAGE WRESTLERS/PARTICIPANTS

NAME	AGE	RACE	EDUCATION	YEARS OF EXPERIENCE	RELATIONSHIP TO SCHOOL	DAY JOB
Andre	23	White	Associate degree	4	Referee (doesn't attend practices)	Customer service for regional furniture chain
Bobby	18	White	Unknown	>1	Student (very briefly)	Unknown
Chris	22	White	Some college	2.5	Referee	EMT (also student at vocational college)
Cobra	21	Latino	High school degree	4	Veteran; core group member	Customer service for local newspaper
Cuss	35	White	College degree	6+	Owner and trainer; core group member	Financial analyst at international bank
Damon	21	White	High school degree	<2	Student; occasional performer	Security guard
Dan	22	White	High school degree (enrolled in local college)	3+	Veteran; core group member	Clerk at local sports/play space
Donny	23	White	High school degree	<3	High-status student becoming veteran (becomes part-trainer); core group member	UPS warehouse worker

NAME	AGE	RACE	EDUCATION	YEARS OF EXPERIENCE	RELATIONSHIP TO SCHOOL	DAY JOB
Drew	20	White	Unknown	Unknown	Student (very briefly; maybe 3 times)	Arby's restaurant worker
Fishman	24	White	Associate degree	>4	Veteran; core group member	Mechanic for regional transit authority
Epic	25	Black	Unknown	>5	Veteran; core group member	Unknown
Johnny	21	White	High school degree	>3	Veteran (fades out after six months)	Door-to-door marketing
Josh	19	White	High school degree	<1	Student	Applebee's waiter
Junior	19	Middle Eastern descent	High school degree	<1	Student	Unknown
Al	19	White	No high school degree	<1	Student; core group member	Barback and busboy at restaurant
Matt	27	White	Local college degree	>4	Trainer and occasional performer	Middle school teacher in city school
Timmy	34	White	High school degree	10	Lead trainer; part-booker; scriptwriter; core group member	Sells/makes signs at local print shop
Mike M.	18	White	High school degree	<1	Student; core group member	Cashier and retail at garden/outdoor furniture shop
Pete	24	White	Some college	1	Student; just starting to perform; core group member	Filing clerk at local law firm
Brickman	27	White	College degree	1.5	Student; rapidly advances to veteran; core group member	High school teacher
"Slaughter"	35	White	Unknown	>7	Lead trainer; occasional performer. Core group member.	Unknown

NAME	AGE	RACE	EDUCATION	YEARS OF EXPERIENCE	RELATIONSHIP TO SCHOOL	DAY JOB
Tony "Lethal"	23	White (Croatian descent)	High school degree	>3	Regular who transitions to veteran; core group member	CVS drugstore clerk (and part-time work for party rental equipment company
Tyler	24	White (Italian American)	Working on associate degree	4–5	Booker; veteran; core group member	Enrolled part-time at local college; considering the police academy
Vince "Southern Bad Boy"	23	White	High school degree	>3	Veteran	Unknown
Patrick	25	White	College degree	3–4	Booker; veteran; performer; core group member	Middle school teacher of special education

NOTES

1. The WWE is a publicly traded US corporation with annual revenue exceeding $500 million. The company owns and produces over 300 live wrestling shows per year along with numerous entertainment products, which include television shows, video games, movies, action figures, books, smart phone applications, magazines, websites, DVDs, music, and calendars. The company airs programs in 30 languages in more than 145 countries (Schneiderman 2008; see also *Wall Street Journal* 2010).

2. It is not uncommon for shows to be staged in the same space that the wrestling school rents for training.

3. In a typical script sketched by the booker, one wrestler dominates for three to four minutes and then is crushed by the subordinate wrestler for a few minutes, at which point the originally dominant opponent regains control, maintains it, and wins the match. As wrestlers might say, babyface shines, heel cuts off baby-face, heel delivers heat, babyface has a hope spot, heel cuts him off, then a false finish, and finally babyface wins.

4. In the 1990s, these moral categories were muddled, even inverted in cases, and the WWE's "attitude era" was indicative of such a state of affairs. Story lines in the 1990s began to feature performers (e.g., Stone Cold Steve Austin and New World Order) whose rude defiance was celebrated and became the basis for fan support. Stone Cold Steve Austin was known for wearing a T-shirt with "Fuck fear, drink beer" on it. Nicholas Sammond suggests that the former "popular entertainment that spanned class lines, like vaudeville and variety television, has [now] come back as a representation of working-class rebellion specifically tied to youth culture: a fantasy of impropriety that adolescent boys are meant to use to thumb their noses at the imagined descendants of June Cleaver" (2005, 134).

5. See La Pradelle on the contrived nature of exchanges at French Farmers Markets, Grazian on the way urban nightlife transports the consumer, and Benzecry on

how opera transports the audience (2011). In Grazian's work, consumers find that it is in their best interest to suspend disbelief because it is "all the better to enjoy the excitement of urban glamour, no matter how contrived" (2008, 94). Michele de La Pradelle found in her work on French farmers' markets that shoppers and farmers collectively "produce the illusion that they are practicing a bygone type of social interaction. . . . [They create] a happy enclave in a world of tension, an island of asylum where whims and fancies may be indulged, in a universe of glum rationality" (2006, 241).

6. *New York Times* columnist Neil Genzlinger classifies indie pro wrestling as "most lowbrow" in his review of *Slap Happy* (2006).

7. Rage is a pseudonym, as are all the names of participants and school affiliates. The design and methodology of the study are described in detail in appendix A.

8. "Professional wrestling is at once like life and like a lot of other things, theater and academic included: real and fake, spontaneous and rehearsed, genuinely felt and staged for effect, prodigious and reductive, profoundly transgressive and essentially conservative" (Mazer 2005, 84). Likewise, Matthew Gutmann, in his study of male identities in Mexico City, traces different categories of masculinity that are constantly renegotiated; in male identities there are "ambiguity, confusion, and contradiction," all of which are characterized by inconsistency (1996).

9. Of course, even these more iconically masculine identities are never fully stable and are often fraught with contradictions. See Aaron Belkin's study of American military masculinity, *Bring Me Men*, for a great analysis of the gendered contradictions of soldiers in the US military (2012).

10. Several exemplary ethnographies of recent years trace how working-class and working-poor men cultivate identity, dignity, and meaning via occupational or cultural practices. Investigations illuminate the resourceful ways that such men find meaning and redemption in the often bleak US (and Mexican) postindustrial landscape. They include studies of bodybuilders (Alan Klein 1993), drug dealers (Philippe Bourgois 2003), Mexican men and fathers (Gutmann 1996), boxers (Loïc Wacquant 2004, Lucia Trimbur 2013), gang members (Sudhir Venkatesh 2008), urban pigeon flyers (Jerolmack 2013), Minutemen at the US border (Shapira 2013), and forest firefighter crews (Matthew Desmond 2007).

11. Sociology has contributed to an understanding of the ravages of the last thirty years of US penal policy. See Western 2006, Devah Pager 2003, Pettit and Western 2004, Wacquant 2004, and Goffman 2009.

CHAPTER 1. THE INDIES

1. The WWE was formerly known as the WWF (World Wrestling Federation), but after the company lost a lawsuit to the World Wildlife Fund in 2001, it changed its name to World Wrestling Entertainment. They claim to have 15 million weekly viewers filling arenas three times a week, fifty-two weeks a year. Fans consume more than a dozen pay-per-view programs, each of which net the WWE several hundred thousand buys. Wrestlemania, the annual marquee pay-per-view event,

had more than 1 million buys in 2008—and despite being known as a "male soap opera," one-quarter to one-third of its viewers are female. In addition to their nearly 300 live productions a year, WWE merchandises dozens of products. Fans swallow up WWE-produced and -licensed apparel, video games, magazines, movies, action figures, books, DVDs, music, video-on-demand subscriptions to wrestling "classics," and downloadable ringtones, updates, and videos for mobile phones. Between 1998 and 2008, the WWE increased its earnings outside North America from $3.5 million to $135 million. Donna Goldsmith, the WWE's chief operating officer stated, "The international sector now represents about 26 percent of our overall business, so it's hugely important for us" (*Wall Street Journal* 2010).

2. Wrestling is of course one of the very oldest of sports, if not *the* oldest. See Morton and O'Brien (1985), Ball (1990), and Beekman (2006) for thorough histories of pro wrestling. In the United States, pro wrestling began as a legitimate athletic activity in the mid to late 1800s, but by the early 1900s fixed matches were on the increase (Morton and O'Brien 1985). Although shady, and sometimes scandalous, professional wrestling continued as a legitimate sport; the first decades of the twentieth century "marked the last gasp of authentic, competitive professional wrestling in the United States" (Beekman 2006, 35). After World War I, promoters began to exert greater control over the business than individual wrestlers, whose autonomy receded (2006, 35).

3. Performances of various sorts may or may not have a live audience, but pro wrestling is inherently dependent on an *interactive* live audience. This is unlike traditional sports, where fans can be relatively inconsequential since the immediate objective of the competition, from the standpoint of the athletes, is winning. For example, because of persistent problems with violent fans, certain European professional football (soccer) matches are played in empty stadiums.

4. In his analysis of audience responses in the *Southwest Review*, Roger Gilbert suggests that a reason "applause can be deeply satisfying is that it confirms the deep-seated intuition that our own aesthetic responses are not simply perverse or idiosyncratic but find an answering chord in other minds. . . . We feel ourselves merging into a collective body, yet we also feel that the body is ours, that we stand at the source of the storm, that the roar we hear is an emanation of our own wills. Your own paltry claps return to your ears multiplied a thousandfold" (2001).

5. Norbert Elias and Eric Dunning argue that we yearn for outright appeals to emotions, like pro wrestling, because they have been policed out of modern civilization. "Social survival and success in these [contemporary] societies depend . . . on a reliable armour, not too strong and not too weak, of individual self-restraint. In such societies, there is only a comparatively limited scope for the show of strong feelings, of strong antipathies towards and dislike of other people, let alone of hot anger, wild hatred or the urge to hit someone over the head" (1986, 41). Sports constitute one of the spaces created for the production and expression of this affective display.

6. The one competitor of significance is Total Nonstop Action Wrestling (TNA), a privately owned promotion that televises events on the Spike cable channel. This competitor is by no means a passing phenomenon: many big name stars are on its roster, some (Hulk Hogan, Kurt Angle, and AJ Styles) are arguably bigger than those in the WWE. It is important to note that the WWE has not always been the most dominant. Until the late 1990s the company competed aggressively with many promotions and even struggled at times. This reflects how the business of pro wrestling evolved, with promotions maintaining regional strongholds. American Wrestling Alliance (AWA) was a major promotion from the middle part of the USA that featured at one point Verne Gagne, Jesse "the Body" Ventura, and Hulk Hogan. Gilbert's tended to dominate in the Florida region, Jim Crockett Promotions were from the North Carolina area, Texas World Class Wrestling was popular (managing to draw over 40,000 fans to a show in 1984) in Texas and the Southwest, and WWF was strong in the Northeast. World Championship Wrestling (WCW), a promotion broadcast by Ted Turner's TBS network, was highly successful and competed strongly with the WWF for many years.

7. Most major American sports leagues, including football, baseball, and basketball, have several hundred players under contract during any given season (when secondary rosters, such as the practice squads for the National Football League, are included, the number rises to over 2,000). Mainstream pro sports provide several outlets (e.g., Arena League, Canadian Football League, European basketball leagues) for athletes who do not make the top league. Coaching, management, and consulting positions within these second-tier organizations provide employment opportunities for former athletes who no longer compete. More dependable, longer-term contracts within such fields are possible because of these organizations' finances, size, and extensive reach—not to mention the role of Division I college sports. In many instances these are farm systems for the pro leagues; they have large budgets and an elaborate bureaucracy. Far fewer people compete for the coveted WWE slots than is the case with other major league rosters (due to the lack of institutionalized support from high school and collegiate sports), but several hundred indie wrestlers vie for WWE notice at any given time.

8. This distinction represents a type of "moral boundary" (Lamont 2000) in which the indies occupy a space between the big-money, high-profile WWE above and the more disparaged, albeit mystical, "backyard wrestling" below. Backyard wrestling, also a form of staged wrestling, is the province of teenagers (usually suburbanites), who set up primitive rings in their backyards and produce shows for friends and neighbors.

9. The best-known extreme wrestling federation is the Extreme Championship Wrestling (ECW) promotion. ECW is an example of how the distinction between the indies and the WWE is not always clear. Despite a smaller budget and far less recognition than WWE, ECW was televised nationally, produced action figures, and collaborated with the WWE in some capacity. Some might say that this pro-

motion was so well established, profitable, and long running that it was not an indie fed.

10. This also applies to other sports, of course. See Atyeo (1979) for a discussion of the blurry line between "entertainment" and "criminality" in certain violent sports. The interpretation of acts is fundamental to what we classify as a crime. For an excellent analysis of the social construction of crime and how the attribution of meaning is important to classification, see Nils Christie's *A Suitable Amount of Crime* (2004).

11. Few contemporary media depictions offer representations of middle-class black families, for example. For that matter, few offer any working-class representations that are not of buffoons (Butsche 2003). The racial stereotypes within wrestling programs are arguably less pernicious because they are patently absurd caricatures, which fans interpret as over-the-top stereotypes. No question, a scowling urban black thug character animated by hustling and "bling" is racist. But such story lines are not evidently more harmful than the limited everyday representations of blacks or Latinos that saturate mainstream media and local newscasts. Few mainstream programs offer a broad, nuanced array of Latino and African American characters or stories that accurately reflect the range of social classes, neighborhoods, family arrangements, and histories.

12. Despite the election of the first African American president and the demographic shift that is likely to make whites a numerical minority within fifty years, whites remain the dominant group (by almost all measures). That is, we are not living in a postracial society. While it may be less obvious (e.g., the outright condemnation of the "N-word" within all but a few spaces), racism continues to pervade many relationships, interactions, and social structures, be it via media, financial systems, interpersonal interactions, or academic curricula (to name a few). In the spaces I am most familiar with the subtle, everyday forms of institutionalized racism are far more common (and mostly tend to go uncontested). Yet these everyday injustices are as likely to occur in white upper-middle-class enclaves in "blue states" as in "red state" or working-class enclaves. The people involved may look and sound different, but I doubt whether they act any less perniciously than indie wrestlers do in their interactions.

13. In some cases, the booker is assisted by a creative team that assists with story ideas and advice. Patrick, Tyler, and Timmy were the primary writers at Rage, and Cuss, Slaughter, Danny, and Donny were occasionally involved. While the former "star" is not likely to be known outside pro wrestling culture, his wrestling has usually included some TV exposure. Television appearances are the benedictory medium through which wrestling status is measured.

14. Some promoters manage every aspect of the show, including match times and story lines. This is more likely if the promoter is a veteran or former star with credibility among the performers. Promoters lacking such a background thus rely on bookers' respect, expertise, and networks.

15. "Promotion" and "federation" are sometimes used interchangeably. Both equate to a group or organization that produces repeated pro wrestling events.

16. Determining a precise number is difficult. When doing a national count of the indies, there are overlapping performers, roving productions, and productions that change venues every few years (e.g., short-lived rental spaces suitable for shows). For example, although the Rage promotions typically took place in the same local community center gym space, in a few cases shows were held in a nearby town's veterans' hall or middle-school gymnasium. Moreover, there is an overlap with respect to the performers. Most wrestlers who are healthy (enough) perform in at least a few promotions within the region they live in. Some perform in a dozen or more; this entails extensive travel, especially if a performer lives in an area with few active promotions. As of late 2013, there appeared to be thirteen *active* indie promotions in the state of New York, six in New Jersey, and one in Connecticut. Four promotions were actively producing shows in the New York City metropolitan area.

17. The school relocated to a community center during the course of my fieldwork. The rent for the original space (the auto body garage described in the vignette that opens this chapter) was $1,600 a month; the liability insurance was a few hundred dollars a year. I never learned how much the senior trainers were paid. My guess is a few hundred dollars per month.

18. WWE wrestlers of course also face many hardships. "Wrestling is a non-regulated industry bereft of unions and benefits, with few job options. There is no off season. Most in WWE make $100,000 a year. Only a few earn more than $1 million. A vast majority of pro wrestlers make less than $50,000" (Swartz 2007).

19. The NFL's and NHL's concern for head trauma was prompted by the research of a professional wrestler named Chris Nowinski. Nowinski was a college-educated pro wrestler who retired early after suffering at least six concussions. His book, *Head Games: Football's Concussion Crisis* (2006), profiled several NFL players who exhibited symptoms of neurological damage after their playing careers ended. The book helped to make concussions an issue within first the NFL and now numerous other sports leagues.

20. One exception being MTV's *Tough Enough*, a reality TV program (2001–2003) that featured aspiring wrestlers undergoing intensive pro wrestling training.

21. In this way, novice wrestlers are like the new marijuana users sociologist Howard Becker found. Both groups find that their activities involve "sensations [that] are not automatically or necessarily pleasurable. The taste for such experience is a socially acquired one . . . the beginner will not continue use unless he learns to redefine the sensations as pleasurable" (1953, 239–240).

22. The 2013 Brookings Institution report on poverty in America's suburbs found a shrinking middle class and falling income for the typical household even before the 2008 financial collapse. The economic crises of the 2000s enlarged the number of people in poverty and broadened its geographic reach. Suburbia is now

home to the "fastest growing poor population in the country" (Berube and Knee-bone 2013).

23. This seemed to apply regardless of how close their relationship is/was to their father. As Osherson (1986) and Messner (1990) have found, boys' introductions to organized sports are often made by fathers who might otherwise be absent or emotionally distant, and this adds a powerful emotional charge to these early experiences. Some fathers watched with their young sons, while others might have only given their son an occasional wrestling magazine. This was enough to spark early intrigue even in cases where fathers were mostly absent. Hackett found in his conversations with indie wrestlers that many "touched on fathering, specifically on their wanting to correct the neglect, in some cases the abuse, that they had known as boys" (Hackett 2006, 95). In addition, fathers and male relatives often encourage fighting (and/or interest in violent entertainment) and reward sons for engaging in it (Messerschmidt 2000).

24. Wrestling is dangerous and difficult to learn. But oftentimes Cuss seemed to be teaching a larger life lesson, one unrelated to the development of wrestling skills. It was reminiscent of the men Michelle Lamont researched who speak of their "struggle to 'make it through' and keep the world together in the face of economic uncertainty, physical dangers, and the general unpredictability of life" (2000, 23). It is not unlike George Lakoff's characterization of the "strict father model" in American political discourse. This righteous ideology "assumes that the world is and always will be dangerous and difficult . . . the only way to [teach kids right from wrong] is through painful punishment—physical discipline that by adulthood will develop into internal discipline" (2004, 40).

25. Indie promotions periodically hire former big-name WWE stars to perform in a specific show. These wrestlers charge fees ranging from $200 to $1,000, depending on factors such as distance, stature, and personal connections. The Rage show lost rather than made money, Cuss explained, because "[the high school] didn't advertise it the way they should have . . . [we were] promised between 1,000 and 2,000 people, but it was like 650 people. . . . The high school [was] supposed to take care of that. When you see the crowd, a lot of them were our regular fans. And a lot of it was young kids. It was supposed to be a high school show. Where are all the high school kids? Something happened there."

26. I asked about which drugs, and he said the following: "Anything. Pot. We were doing pot every day. Every single day, every night, in between pizza deliveries, whenever. Pills, I guess. Painkillers and stuff. That was my favorite. Drinking beer and taking those." I asked if he meant at the same time, and he clarified, "Yeah. In wrestling, that's like a lethal combination. So many guys died from it. . . . That's already my favorite thing to do. This may not be the best profession for me, but I'm willing to risk it." I asked about which painkillers, and he explained, "Vicodin, Percocet, whatever was around, really. Then it was meth, coke, whatever."

27. Backyard wrestling, also a form of staged wrestling, is the province of teenagers (usually suburbanites) who set up primitive rings in their backyards and produce scrappy shows for friends, neighbors, or any other willing spectators.

28. Peter Freund speaks to how scripted acts and manicured bodies "act as 'natural' embodied 'proof' for our assumptions about different people.... Even if we accept these differences as 'intrinsic' and natural, this should not preclude recognizing the role that social construction plays in *amplifying* them" (1988, 855). This is echoed by Daniel Chambliss's findings from his research on competitive swimmers (1989). Excellence is less a derivative of natural talent than a "confluence of small skills or activities, each one learned or stumbled upon, which have been carefully drilled into habit and then are fitted together into a synthesized whole" (1989, 81).

CHAPTER 2. FIGHTING FOR A POP

1. In 2008, the leading presidential candidates addressed the pro wrestling community. It is common for WWE pro wrestlers to make international, government-sanctioned trips to entertain US troops serving abroad. Another indication of pro wrestling's significance was the 1998 election of Jesse Ventura, a former professional wrestler with almost no political experience, as the governor of the state of Minnesota.

2. "It is not a natural mode of sensibility, if there be any such. Indeed, the essence of Camp is its love of the unnatural: of artifice and exaggeration" (Sontag 1982, 105).

3. The criticism is sometimes appropriate, yet insiders can gain "credibility with [their] audiences by portraying its critics as prudish, 'politically correct,' and ignorant about the fluidity of identity or the difference between representation and reality" (Sammond 2005, 134).

4. Generally speaking, conventional theater actors are not subject to the same ridicule because they operate in a more refined cultural field. High school or collegiate wrestlers evade cynicism as they compete in "true" pugilism. While response varies by context, in most high schools wrestlers are esteemed. There is arguably some overlap in the disparaging stereotype of amateur actors, especially high school actors, as effeminate—a slight in a sexist society that devalues femininity.

5. A Bud Lite ad, in the company's popular "We salute you ..." series, sarcastically salutes the man who assembles costumes for pro wrestlers. Ads for Geico Insurance and Miller Lite ridicule widely inaccurate pro wrestling "punches." An ESPN spot shows "Stone Cold" Steve Austin being repeatedly nailed in the head with a metal chair while asleep ... yet the beating fails to wake him up. These ads use irony (see Smith 2005 for a full discussion of the use of irony in ads targeting men).

6. As Robert Rinehart suggests, "There is a growing sense that sport is not sport unless and until it becomes televised—that the very act of being televised validates and authenticates its claim to being sport" (2007, 504).

7. In his book on the indies, Thomas Hackett describes the community as "odd, lost souls" (2006, 2). As for the fans, he states, "These fans seemed to take a freaked pleasure in their own insignificance. . . . Their resistance to self-improvement represented a statement of profound identification, a personal avowal, like a monk's tonsure. . . . [One fan] brandished signs declaring himself a nerd, a geek, a freak, a dork, a slob. 'Fat, Ugly, and Stupid,' said one guy's T-shirt, just about summing it up" (2006, 15–16).

8. David Denby defines *snark* as "a teasing, rug-pulling form of insult that attempts to steal someone's mojo, erase her cool, annihilate her effectiveness, and it appeals to a knowing audience that shares the contempt of the snarker and therefore understands whatever references he makes" (2009, 4).

9. After two people crashed a White House dinner in 2009 and became instant celebrities, analysts contextualized the act as part of the "spellbinding power" of fame in American society. It is "the one thing that can trump wealth, talent, breeding and even elected office. Reality shows and social Web sites like Facebook long ago knocked down the barriers that kept ordinary people trapped in obscurity. . . . [But] one of the letdowns of fame nowadays is that precisely because it is so easily and widely bestowed, it grows ever more fleeting and faint" (Stanley 2009).

10. This is a reference to the WWE's former name WWF (World Wrestling Federation). In 2002, the company launched a cheeky "Get the F Out" marketing campaign and changed all references from "WWF" to "WWE."

11. One wrestler in the group (not Patrick) became the subject of a national news story when he was fired from his (well-paid and stable) teaching job because it was discovered that he missed work to perform in shows. See chapter 4.

12. In *Tally's Corner*, Liebow notes a similarly biologically rooted need. "The desire to be . . . noticed by the world he lives in is shared by each of the men on the street corner. Whether they articulate this desire . . . or not, one can see them position themselves to catch the attention of their fellows in much the same way as plants bend or stretch to catch the sunlight" (1967, 60).

13. According to Taylor, we as individuals are profoundly vulnerable to the ways in which others perceive and characterize us (1994). Richard Sennett addresses the varied understandings of the concept. "Fichte first cast recognition into real language, exploring how laws can be framed so that the needs of strangers, foreigners, and migrants are acknowledged in a constitution. Rousseau enlarged the discussion of recognition to include the street as well as the court, mutual acknowledgement a matter of social behavior as much as of legal right. In the writings of John Rawls, recognition means respecting the needs of those who are unequal; in the writings of Jürgen Habermas, recognition means respecting the views of those whose interests lead them to disagree" (Sennett 2003, 54).

14. As Matt the wrestler confided, he sees himself as a kid who sought this type of attention. He shared a story about doing something well in school (for a change). "[My teacher] kept me after class and I was like, 'Oh man what did I do now?' He

said, 'You know, I would never have expected that from you. You know, you're this boisterous, loud, too-cool-for-school kid.' And I mean, he must have seen through it all that I just wanted to be noticed."

15. Within academia alone, for example, one can attain recognition through research, through teaching, or through a respectable salary. It may emanate from colleagues, students, administrators, or from the public at large (see Bourdieu's *Homo Academicus*, 1984). In *The Money Shot*, Laura Grindstaff's fascinating book on TV talk shows, she notes the myriad ways we quench our need for recognition: "The desire to leave a mark is surely common to all classes and strata of society even if the specific avenues for fulfilling it are not. Professors write books; politicians author laws; athletes win medals; directors make films; artists make art; activists effect social change. Some ways of making one's mark on the world are clearly more prestigious and far-reaching than others." She found that starring in a TV talk show may be less prestigious and even unflattering, but "it does not much matter that the role is a negative or unflattering one, for the larger goal is simply to participate in the discourse and be a part of the scene" (Grindstaff 2002, 258–259).

16. Elisabeth Wood and Javier Auyero agree that the quest for collective recognition is a key dimension in joint struggle (Auyero 2003, Wood 2003). David Snow and Leon Anderson show how even the most indigent—the homeless—place concerns for self-respect, dignity, and recognition above more physiological survival requisites (1993). Philippe Bourgois's research reveals how street-level drug-dealing enterprise is in part a "search for respect" (2003).

17. "The making and sustaining of our identity, in the absence of a heroic effort to break out of ordinary existence, remains dialogical throughout our lives" (Taylor 1992, 34). Recognition is powerful because people experience a "response from the other which makes meaningful the feelings, intentions, and actions of the self. It allows the self to realize its agency and authorship in a tangible way" (Benjamin 1988, 12).

18. Halfway through my fieldwork, the training space, originally a converted garage located at the back of a strip mall, relocated to a community center that had previously been the site of a public school. Both of these spaces were located in working- to lower-middle-class suburbs.

19. Exceptions are doing "chain" (i.e., a sequenced technical move ordinarily used as a feeling-out process in the initial stages of a match) and occasional cardio drills. These drills function more to solidify the hierarchy of the group than as physical conditioning (see chapter 5). Rage, like most indie wrestling schools, can afford only one ring, and there is a heavy emphasis on in-ring techniques (as opposed to dramaturgy).

20. All of the wrestlers identify as heterosexual.

21. A *New York Times* article discussed mischievous suburban teenagers from these same neighborhoods who capture their stunts on video and post the footage

on the Internet. "Schoolyard scraps, spectacular skateboard spills, puppy-love quarrels, goofy antics like placing a slice of American cheese over the face of a snoring buddy, and bruising stunts like hurling one's body through a neighbor's wooden fence—these and other staples of suburban teenage life have taken on a new dimension as online cinéma vérité. . . . Such rites of ridiculousness are now routinely captured on video and posted on the Internet for worldwide perusal, and posterity. . . . 'Teens always do crazy stuff, but it's just that much more intense and fun when you can post it,' said Nathaniel Visneaskous, 18, of Deer Park. 'When you live in a boring town, what else is there to do?'" (Kilgannon 2007).

22. Lower-level pro wrestling promotion, not unlike the music industry, has always been in some kind of competitive relationship with larger media companies that maintain a greater share of the market. Because of this, pro wrestling fans have found resourceful ways to circulate footage of wrestlers and shows from promotions and events that were not broadcast over major networks. RF Video, e.g., videotaped events (in the '90s and early aughts) held by smaller, less popular, regional wrestling promotions and sold these through a catalog and website.

23. The highly accomplished Tina Fey articulates this yearning for documentation when she explains her 2008 *Saturday Night Live* performances in which she played the part of Sarah Palin. "I remember very distinctly walking off the stage after Latifah yelled 'Live from New York,' thinking that this was the most fun, exciting thing I would ever do. I remember thinking this was a 'permanent win.' No one would ever be able to take it away from me. *The proof existed permanently on tape that on this one occasion, I was funny*" (Fey 2011, 222; my emphasis).

24. Maniac, like a few others in the book, is mentioned only briefly because he is not part of the core group and I may have met him only once or twice.

25. Like other ethnographers, I was always granting a form of recognition as a participant-observer. I often heard comments like, "You better get out there and see my match!" Immediately upon my seeing the group after a show, they would ask what I thought of it. Likewise, I frequently handed out photographs I'd taken of them and usually praised their live performances. I expand on this role as a researcher in appendix A.

26. By and large, vets appreciate this relationship, too, because of the respect and adoration. Matt, a veteran of five years, told me what it's like being in the locker room on the night of a show: "I look around and I can't avoid the fact that I am someone they look up to . . . guys come up and say, 'Hey can you come watch my match?' And I like that, I like being there to help people. I'd rather be loved than hated."

27. Jack Katz, whose ethnographic insights inform much of this book, articulates the objective of ethnographic analyses. "Explanations should show how the phenomena we wish to explain become compelling to the subjects themselves. In the end we must explain conduct as the outcome of a kind of self-mystification, a bootstrapping of motivations that does the double work of, on the one hand, per-

ceiving obstacles and attractions in the environment and, on the other, obscuring the work of recognizing forces that ultimately gives them objective status" (Katz 2002, 86).

CHAPTER 3. PASSION WORK

1. The emphasis has been on what Hochschild describes as the three characteristics of jobs that involve emotional labor: "face-to-face or voice-to-voice contact with the public"; the requirement that workers "produce an emotional state in another person—gratitude or fear, for example"; and, lastly, that employers have "a degree of control over the emotional activities of employees" (1983, 147). See Smith (2008) for a further elaboration of the literature on emotional labor and how it relates to wrestlers.

2. The concept has been criticized, however, because the presumed emotions underlying the behavior can sometimes be unclear (Ashforth and Humphrey 1993).

3. There are a few cases of other emotional work performed jointly, such as two flight attendants serving passengers together (Hochschild 1983) or the staff at a psychodrama support group (Thoits 1996). With the exception of criminal interrogators (Rafaeli and Sutton 1991) and paralegals (Lively 2000), these are generally brief descriptions.

4. "Kayfabe" is from carnival (or "carnie") vernacular. Pro wrestling is considered one of the five subcultures that have adopted carnie argot (Russell and Murray 2004). Also, see Kerrick (1980) on the jargon of pro wrestling.

5. Hochschild defines feeling rules as a set of "socially shared, albeit often latent (not thought about unless probed at), rules" (1979, 563) that create "guidelines for the assessment of fits and misfits between feeling and situation" (566). Hochschild explains the different ways that emotional labor can be done: "by the self upon the self, by the self upon others, and by others upon oneself" (1979, 562).

6. As Hochschild noted, "failed acts of management still indicate what ideal formations guide the effort" (1979, 561). Local emotional edicts can be at odds with larger goals of the production. Veterans' insistence on backstage feeling rules that stress independence, stoicism, and homophobia can hinder their development as a performer because for the public performances, emotive expression is valued, and cooperation is a necessity. This reveals how the more immediate feeling rules—what Hochschild calls the "bottom side of ideology" (1979, 566)—might be counterproductive to the broader objective.

7. As Roland Barthes observed about pro wrestling, "everyone must not only see that the man suffers, but also and above all understand *why* he suffers" (Barthes 1957, 20; emphasis added). The contrast strategy resembles the "good cop, bad cop" concept of police interrogation, analyzed by Rafaeli and Sutton (1991). Fishman explained that good bookers are people who can find the dramatic tension between the right characters. "You have to find where obvious conflicts would

be and then make them bigger than they actually are." Moreover, "it's not just coming out with a good story line, it's coming out with a good story line for the right person."

8. A DDT is a move in which a wrestler falls down or backward to drive a held opponent's head into the mat. It stands for "death drop technique" or "demonic death trap," depending on whom you ask.

9. Veteran police detectives come to understand their job as "higher mental work" than work done by the rest of the police force (Stenross and Kleinman 1989). The management of emotions becomes an important resource; it highlights how members with higher status "influence and evaluate others in terms of their own standards of delicacy and poise" (Cahill 1999, 114).

10. I am referring to Erving Goffman's theory of social life as a form of dramaturgy in which our social actions are part of a larger play. A disruption occurs when the script (which we all agree on and generally adhere to) is thrown off or broken. These moments often provoke embarrassment in everyday life.

11. "Put you over" means to help your partner win the match by losing.

12. A prototype is the store clerk whose job duties include serving customers with a smile (regardless of the status of the clerk's actual feelings). In general, though, the scholarship on emotional labor has focused on the negative effects of emotion work within female-dominated occupations as the economy has transitioned to a more service- and information-based one.

13. Laura Hillenbrand details a wonderful example of this dynamic in *Unbroken* (2010). While being held as a prisoner of war in World War II, the US airman Louie Zamperini had relationships with certain Japanese guards who in effect risked their lives by having empathy for their captives. They were forced to feign hatred and domination while in fact feeling sympathy. In David Grazian's superb book on urban nightlife, *On the Make*, we see the nighttime pursuits of college students in the sexual marketplaces of central Philadelphia. Grazian shows us the intricate backstaging of men's behaviors that purport to be motivated by prospects of sex but, in fact, have various ritualistic and performative functions. The "girl hunt" takes the form of an "inherently homosocial activity for which one's male peers serve as the intended audience for competitive games of sexual reputation and peer status, public displays of situational dominance and rule transgression, and in-group rituals of solidarity and loyalty" (Grazian 2008, 138).

14. On a recent visit to a correctional facility, I was informed by an officer that inmates are more likely to pick a fight in the cafeteria than the open yard because they "don't want to let it go too far." Inmates know that guards will intervene more quickly in the mess hall, so the destruction to each other will not be as extensive.

15. "Until a few years ago, helmets were removed as both a sign of toughness and consideration to the unprotected knuckles of the combatants. When the leagues made helmet removal illegal, players learned to delicately remove each other's

helmets before the fight began—a concoction of courtesy and showmanship"
(Branch 2011).

CHAPTER 4. "IN REAL LIFE I'M A TOTAL HOMOPHOBE"

1. Throughout this book I refer to the wrestlers as men/males. There was, however, one female member, Tamara, whom I interviewed and spent considerable time with. Within the group Tamara usually accepted, even abetted, its tendency to background her. She never challenged the norms either verbally or nonverbally, and overall she upheld existing rules about gender (i.e., women as passive and men as dominant). Tamara was Fishman's on-again, off-again girlfriend, who occasionally wrestled but usually played the part of a valet. When she wrestled it was in support of a story line that maintained the gender status quo.
2. "Doing" here echoes the West and Zimmerman concept of "doing gender" (1987).
3. Because the field developed out of feminist and queer theory, the scholarship has generally benefited from the more expansive post-1970s understanding of gender, which takes race, class, and sexuality into account (i.e., intersectionality). "Masculinities" is made plural to reflect the varied social locations and differential access to resources that shape men's lived experiences. Despite the fact that over the last half century the feminist movement has successfully broadened opportunities and definitions for men and women, men continue to generally maneuver within a relatively rigid script. The range of behaviors and identities for American men, especially more subordinate groups of men, remains limited. We do not recognize and value acts of supportive, relational nurturance, for example, to the extent that we have paved the way for women to enter legislatures and boardrooms. See Paula England's work (2010) on the "stalled revolution" regarding why the demands of the women's movement have not been realized and on the range of social scripts for men and women.
4. Scholars term this the "social construction of gender." Erving Goffman, Judith Lorber, and West and Zimmerman, among other sociologists, did groundbreaking scholarship in this area. Judith Butler, the philosopher known for her gender performance theory, builds on the work of scholars like Simone de Beauvoir and Goffman. "Gender is, thus, a construction that regularly conceals its genesis; the tacit collective agreement to perform, produce, and sustain discrete and polar genders as cultural fictions is obscured by the credibility of those productions—and the punishments that attend not agreeing to believe in them; the construction 'compels' our belief in its necessity and naturalness" (Butler 1990, 178).
5. The entertainment is premised on a violent sport that Kreager found increases the likelihood of actual violence among its high school participants (2007). His research found that "football players and wrestlers, as opposed to baseball, basketball, tennis, and other athletes, are significantly more likely than nonathletic males to be involved in a serious fight."
6. No wrestler directly termed his participation an exercise in masculinity validation, and I never asked about masculinity. In my use of "masculine," I take heed

of Gutmann's careful attempts to avoid reifying the category "macho" in his study of Mexican men. He explains that the challenge "was not a matter of avoiding macho stereotypes, since this was impossible, but rather one of identifying the echo effect of official interpretations of Mexican men on these men themselves" (1996, 247). In addition, I am hesitant to generalize about particular motivations. Motivations not only change; they range from solidarity, escape from boredom, recognition, corporeal sensations, and even play. Peter Freund suggests that early childhood experiences with play are relevant because "social contexts of early play shape what sensations are experienced as pleasurable, and the desire to reproduce such patterns of sensation, in turn, will have an influence on our subsequent choice of play activities" (1988, 850).

7. See Pope et al. 2000. As John Gagnon noted in 1974 (almost forty years before today's full-scale service-based economy), men's work is not likely to be physically demanding but rather "involves the management of people and things in ways that are relatively remote from bicep size or the ability to lift weights" (1974, 144). Paul Willis suggests that this emphasis on the body is particularly acute for working-class men. "Their economic downfall having removed the luxuries of their own exercise of the 'male gaze,' maybe some unemployed working-class males will find it better to strive to be the object of the gaze, finding or making sexualized features of the male body to enhance 'allure' to economic and social ends" (2000, 95).

8. Jack Katz describes the "badass" in *Seductions of Crime* (1988). "Someone who is 'real bad' must be tough, not easily influenced, highly impressionable, or anxious about the opinions that others hold of him; in a phrase, he must not be morally malleable. He must take on an existential posture that in effect states, 'You see me, but I am not here for you; I see you, and maybe you are here for me'" (1988, 80). Despite this status's esteem (even within pro wrestling), a badass would in actuality be very poorly suited for pro wrestling given the need to be relational, malleable, and concerned with partners.

9. See Brannon and David for 1970s Western masculinity's core tenets, which remain remarkably salient today. The tenets they describe are "be a sturdy oak," "be a big wheel," "give 'em hell," and "no sissy stuff" (1976).

10. Pope et al., in *The Adonis Complex,* study the prevalence of men's dysmorphia; they find an increased concern among men with body image (2000). "Metrosexual" is a contrived term that marketers developed to better identify a heterosexual male demographic as potential buyers of grooming products. See Smith (2005) for a discussion of the use of irony to sell products to skeptical young male consumers in a postfeminist era.

11. *New York Times* reporter David Coleman referred to the trend of heterosexual men taking more interest in fashion and style as "gay vague." "Straight men are more at ease flaunting a degree of muscle tone seldom seen outside of a Men's Health cover shoot. And they are adopting looks—muscle shirts, fitted jeans, sandals and shoulder bags—that as recently as a year ago might have read as,

well, gay. . . . What's happening is that many men have migrated to a middle ground where the cues traditionally used to pigeonhole sexual orientation—hair, clothing, voice, body language—are more and more ambiguous" (2005).

12. As the scholar and poet Gregory Woods said, "wrestling . . . is the heterosexually acceptable form of homosexual foreplay" (1987, 94); quoted in Pronger's *Arena of Masculinity* (1990, 184). Pronger found that several gay pornography producers focus on the homoeroticization of wrestling.

13. Pat Patterson played a flamboyant, arguably gay, character in the late 1950s (he is now openly gay). In the early 2000s the WWE crafted story lines around two gay wrestlers named Billy and Chuck. The two became tag team partners who won several matches and eventually married in an on-air ceremony. Apparently they were heterosexual and only played being gay. (See also Chris Kanyon's story, "Wrestling Reality," about being a gay wrestler (2001)). In Donny's case, his minstrel-like character solidified gender ideology by reinforcing pernicious stereotypes of homosexuality. It was not a subversive revision of the gender order.

14. I heard outright expressions of sexual desire dozens of times over the course of my fieldwork. For example, Al walks in one evening with a new haircut and Donny, looking at him, shouts, "Nice haircut! Now I want to fuck you more!" Such moments were always stated with either a forceful tone of dominance or distanced irony. This was all before the appearance of the popular "no homo" disclaimer phrase used by American boys today. The two-word phrase precedes an expression of appreciation or affection for another man or even an observation that might be perceived as unorthodox to a heterosexual, normative ideal of masculinity.

15. Research by Robb Willer et al. found that when men feel their masculinity threatened, they respond with "masculine overcompensation"; essentially, men express more pronounced attitudes associated with homophobia, war, and dominant status in such circumstances (2013). They found that threatened men reported more homophobia attitudes, greater support for war, belief in male superiority, and greater dominance attitudes. They note the contradiction related to this insecurity. "Perhaps the most successful way for men to disguise their masculine insecurity would be to behave in the same ways as unthreatened men do" (2013, 1016). This in some ways explains the "cool" parody of the testosterone-jacked "bro" by other men. It is not uncommon among heady, college-educated men to lampoon the "bro" who overcompensates (i.e., acts in ways that show overcommitment to the masculine game). This comedic dominance, expressed as clever parody or irony, is usually a masculine performance in and of itself.

16. This suggests that participants maintain a "double relationship: disparaging the 'other,' including women and gays (external relations), and at the same time expelling femininity and homosexuality from within themselves (internal relations)" (Mac an Ghaill 1996a, 133).

17. Most comments felt like attempts to pigeonhole or inoculate any association with homoeroticism, to change the topic rather than invite greater dialog. A

quick joke to diffuse the tension, then move on; in other words, a (subconscious) attempt at noting the elephant in the room but with no interest in either removing or describing the elephant. Brian Pronger wonderfully describes this tension in his work on sports and masculinity: "Always lurking in masculine camaraderie is a fear that something could go amiss, that the ostensible orthodoxy of a man's world might turn out to be paradoxical. Hidden in the orthodox relations between men is the potential of the homoerotic paradox. For some that is frightening, for others it's exciting, and for still others it's both" (1990, 76). I did not push the issue too far as it might have risked access to the higher-status members.

18. This expansion of sports in the late nineteenth century occurred at a time of great consternation regarding masculinity. "Muscular Christianity" and the "cult of manliness" were cultural movements animated by the shifts prompted by the industrial revolution. As Western society became less rural, less dependent on physical labor, and more industrialized, middle- and upper-class men were encouraged to pursue activities that championed rigor, physicality, and competition.

19. As Allan Klein found with bodybuilders, "masculine construction" in pro wrestling "rests on an equation of manhood with muscle size, but not necessarily with muscle function.... We are looking at a segment of the population that craves the look of power, that contents itself with the feel of physical power in terms of pumping muscles" (1993, 250). This craving, nevertheless, increasingly extends to many groups of men because, as Pope et al. state, "muscles are one of the few areas in which men can still clearly distinguish themselves from women or feel more powerful than other men" (2000, 24).

20. As Connell states, "The bodily capacity to commit violence becomes, for many boys and young men, part of their sense of masculinity, and a willingness to put their bodies on the line in violence remains as a test of hegemonic masculinity" (Connell 2000, 218). I believe most popular American sports are organized around not just competition but the capacity for violence. Collision sports like ice hockey and football are by definition violent, but even noncontact sports like "America's pastime," baseball, are arguably violent. Pitches aimed at the batter's head are sometimes endorsed by coaches and players (for retaliation), and a runner from third base bolting for the catcher at home plate often causes an epic collision that is implicitly encouraged (see Waldstein 2012).

21. This chapter is informed by Brian Pronger's suggestion that "homophobia in sport is the fear of the inherent slippage between orthodoxy and paradoxy realized in sporting scenes.... If deeply submerged in the orthodox pleasure of athletics, disguised by the 'orthodoxy' of athletics, is the pleasure of the homoerotic paradox, then the masculine patriarchal significance of athletics will show itself as containing the seeds of its own paradoxical destruction" (Pronger 1990, 182).

22. "Valet" is a term for a person who escorts a wrestler to the ring and cheers alongside as he wrestles.

23. In earlier times, the physical build of a wrestler was one of the most important aspects of character; the flabby or ugly oafs usually represented the evil side of human nature, while the virile, muscular, agile wrestlers represented the heroic (Ball 1990). While this still holds true to some extent, there is now another reading to fleshy bodies: outright defiance ("I don't give a fuck about my body or looks!"). While arguably self-protective, this defiance can also be read as a hard, aggressive stance (though nonetheless an act of vanity). As Thomas Hackett points out in his book on the indies, even the wrestlers "who seemed to defy glamour, the hairy and hideous ones with missing teeth and razored foreheads, were committed to the art of extravagant vanity, inviting fans to bask in their radiance" (2006, 154).

24. In a sense, Patrick's approach resembles that of Gorgeous George, a wrestling star from the 1950s. As Hackett writes, George "started saying something rather postmodern about success in the age of celebrity. He was ironic. He was playful. He was campy. He was contradictory. He turned old conventions in on themselves. He treated achievement as a glorious goof" (2006, 45).

25. Preston Hill, a seventeen-year-old high school wrestler from Fresno, California, was charged with the crime of "using a wrestling move to sexually assault a teammate." According to the police report, "Preston used a maneuver informally known as a 'butt drag'—which involves grabbing the haunch of an opponent to gain leverage—to roughly and intimately assault a smaller, younger wrestler on his team in retaliation for a supposed affront." Hill, "an accomplished wrestler, [and] a leader of his high school team" is fighting the charges. If he is convicted he could face six months in jail (McKinley 2010). Along similar lines, heterosexual urban professionals (who can choose from wider social circles) now express concern regarding intimacy with other men. A *New York Times* article on "man dates"—outings in which two straight men spend an evening together—noted, "The concern about being perceived as gay is one of the major complications of socializing one on one. . . . Many men say that a successful man date requires a guy to demonstrate concern for his friend without ever letting on. 'The amount of preparation that the other guy is making is directly proportional to how awkward it is,' Mr. McArdle of Washington said" (Lee 2005).

CHAPTER 5. PAIN IN THE ACT

1. At this point in my research, I knew everyone but was not yet spending time backstage in the locker room during or after the shows (i.e., only beforehand). I had yet to establish backstage locker room access.

2. "Such objectivations serve as more or less enduring indices of the subjective processes of their producers, allowing their availability to extend beyond the face-to-face situation in which they can be directly apprehended" (Berger and Luckmann 1967, 34).

3. Drew Leder's work on the body explains how pain cannot be reduced to just sensory qualities; rather, it is also a "manner of being-in-the-world . . . [that] re-

organizes our lived space and time, our relations with others and with ourselves" (1990, 73).

4. For great illustrations of this, see Good et al. 1992, Frank 1995, Charmaz 1999, and Newmahr 2011. Studies of boxers, dancers, and piano players, for example, show how their social worlds may assuage or exacerbate the likelihood of painful injuries and shape the lived experience of pain (Wacquant 2004, Alford and Szanto 1996, Wainwright et al. 2005). The specific social worlds in which participants are embedded shape their bodily disposition toward (or against) pain, and this, in turn, becomes central to one's identity.

5. See Messner 1987, Nixon 1992, Young et al. 1994, White et al. 1995, and Howe 2004.

6. I estimate that if an indie wrestler were able to endure wrestling for an entire year, he would likely experience anywhere from five to ten *significant injuries* during that year. I define *significant injuries* as injuries that demand, at the very least, a few days of rest. I define *debilitating injuries* as those that prevent a participant from wrestling for at least a month. Examples of debilitating injuries include a broken arm, herniated disc, and broken collarbone. Significant injuries include a broken nose, torn rotator cuff, concussion, and sprained knee or ankle. Very few wrestlers get through a year of wrestling, month after month, without sustaining injury of one kind or another.

7. The ACL (anterior cruciate ligament) is one of the four main ligaments in the knee.

8. Randall Godfrey, a former linebacker for the San Diego Chargers, compared the pain in pro football to that in pro wrestling. "We wear pads. They don't. Football is hard, but it can't compare to the physical punishment these guys take in the ring" (Schiesel 2007).

9. In the United States, the 2005 Clean Sports Act mandated *legislation* regarding sports and public health. It did not pertain to professional wrestling, however, because of its entertainment (nonsport) status (2005).

10. The only exception is "event insurance," which covers the overall production and the doctor who checks participants before they take the stage at the public shows. As mandated by the state, the doctor checks blood pressure and pulse and briefly inspects the performers for any obvious physical signs that would preclude their wrestling that night.

11. Two alternating doctors attended the Rage shows and served in this capacity. Like military health, the role of the backstage doctor is oxymoronic, in that he must overlook the health risk the activity itself presents. The doctors are paid for the night's work, but each of them suggested that they do not provide this service for the money. They characterized their work as "helping out guys" who love doing what they do, and assisting in the event of a serious injury.

12. "Between 1985 and 2006, 89 [professional] wrestlers have died before the age of 50 . . . this abnormally high number of deaths of young, fit athletes should raise congressional alarms" (Barker 2007).

13. I suspect other years would show similar rates, although I do not have this information. The same article points out that, in contrast to Wrestlemania, none

of the forty-four starters from the Super Bowl who played in 1991 have passed away, and only two of forty-four boxers who held a championship belt that year are gone (Chase 2011).

14. Thus day jobs themselves can cause or exacerbate injuries. If you have a physically demanding job, wrestle in your spare time, and work your body at the gym in any time remaining, you obviously increase your susceptibility to work-based ailments. I frequently heard about work-induced injuries, such as a pinched nerve, but it is hard to discern causality when the body is being bruised and battered on an everyday basis.

15. In fact, even in the very physical contact sport of football, many injuries stem from muscle overuse, overexertion, or impact from an opponent who's not an allied partner.

16. In a Battle Royal multiple wrestlers duel at the same time. It is very difficult, if not impossible, to anticipate and choreograph each move in such a large-scale battle.

17. It is not the case that blame is never cast. I witnessed several instances where, once offstage or out of the ring, a wrestler confronted his opponent. The conversation was often initiated by revealing the mark or bruise. Fishman snapped at Cobra one night, "You weren't supposed to get back up!" as he revealed a dark red mark near his waist. Anger, confusion, guilt, sympathy, or even fear of retribution was possible although mediated by status, degree of injury, or adrenaline.

18. Evidence suggests that if these injuries regularly resulted in severe consequences (such as paralysis or death), pro wrestling (and NASCAR for that matter) would quickly lose its appeal. Research on pro wrestling has also found that fans do not enjoy real injury (Kotarba 2004, 112).

19. Michael Messner further contextualizes the "pain principle," stating that the "pain principle is describing the social process of the masculinization of the male body through sport" (2003, 210).

20. In many respects this also applies to the boxers in Wacquant's study (2004): "No, nooo, boxers don't like pain! Who the hell likes to get hit in the face? I mean, (*dejectedly*) you gotta be nuts, nobody does!" However, in this study, "most grew up having to fight on the street sometimes on a daily basis" (2004, 26). Nonetheless, Wacquant notes that the "educational, employment, and economic status of professional boxers is . . . quite a bit higher than that of the average ghetto resident" (44).

21. Pain and injury are also "makers" of longevity and success for the aging. As the body deteriorates, respect and superiority are earned through years of suffering, not a healthy body.

22. There is growing evidence of football's impact on neurological disorders like chronic traumatic encephalopathy. This may suggest a turning point against the ready acceptance of injury and pain. Interestingly, much credit goes to Chris Nowinski, a former professional wrestler, for bringing to light the long-term neurological disorders that can come from violent sports like football and pro wrestling.

23. I follow Howe's research to distinguish between pain and injury. "Injury can be understood as a breakdown in the structure of the body, a breakdown that may affect its function. Pain is the marker of an injury and is an unpleasant sensory and emotional experience associated with actual or potential tissue [or skeletal] damage" (2004, 74). Acute pain is typically characterized by a "short, sharp sensation" located at the point where the injury occurs and lasts for a limited period; whereas, chronic pain, in contrast, "is often associated with a pathological process that causes continuous pain . . . sometimes [for] years after injury."

24. Donny's declaration is not entirely true because saying no would be very difficult in this environment. In fact, I heard it only twice during all of my fieldwork, and on one of those occasions it was uttered by a visitor, an outsider to the group.

25. This is in contrast to the everyday understanding of "pain management," defined as attempts to reduce or control pain and suffering through medication, stress reduction, exercise, etc.

26. "The abuse of an assortment of pills, including pain medication, has become one of the perceived necessary evils that many pro wrestlers feel they cannot do without in order to cope with the demands of the often tumultuous pro wrestling lifestyle. The death of Lance Cade [was] described by the medical examiner in San Antonio as an accidental ingestion of multiple drugs leading to an enlarged heart. . . . Cade's death was the most notable of multiple wrestlers who passed in 2010 including Luna (Gertrude) Vachon, who died of a similarly fatal cocktail of drugs" (Nasty 2010).

27. This is dubious advice, for while emergency medical care costs are initially obscured, they later catch up to you. (The emergency rooms of all US hospitals are required by law to help patients in need.)

28. The first time I witnessed a significant injury, I ran outside looking for assistance as wrestlers milled around the perimeter of the ring continuing their tomfoolery of adolescent jokes and fake punches. Tyler lay on the mat after an awkward neck twist that happened while wrestling with Fishman. Three wrestlers huddled around Tyler as I ran looking for Cuss. Cuss was nowhere to be found, and after five minutes that felt like a half hour, I spotted him casually walking toward the garage practice space. I raced up to him to tell him that Tyler was hurt, expecting him to snap into action. He calmly asked, "Where is he?" then took a few sips from his thirty-two-ounce Pepsi while maintaining a slow pace into the gym. Aside from Chris, the ref (who is an EMT), I felt as though I was the most concerned person in the entire gym. When I felt anxious, however, I never let on, and in retrospect (aside from getting ice and notifying Cuss), I acted in accordance with the local rules, barely altering the overriding tenor of the scene.

29. In certain respects, my adherence to their ethos came easily after many years on teams at sports camps and at an athletics-oriented all-boys school, where simply flinching or showing fear was cause for shaming. Having participated in activities that carried similar degrees of risk—during which, at one time or another, I broke ribs, feet, fingers, and nose and tore cartilage and ligaments—I could

appreciate the risk and the pain. But my experiences with risky activities were now long in the past; I was eight years older than the average wrestler, and my experiences never occurred with the same frequency, duration, or relational aspect. In fact, it is possible that by not participating in the wrestling, I experienced greater angst. Looking on from the sidelines animates a certain helplessness, as you dread the slightly out-of-place head; whereas when you yourself are in the ring—or on the court or field—you experience yourself as having control over your own fate, as being the master of your own destiny.

30. Consider the 2011 Broadway production of the *Spider-Man* musical. Despite the media attention on the injuries, medical costs, and harm to the actors throughout the many months of rehearsals, apparently only four people in all were injured. Still, this is a high number for a Broadway production (*New York Times* 2011). See also "Union Officials Say Accidents during Spider-Man Broadway Play Indicative of Chronic Safety Problem," http://blogs.bna.com/laborlaw/fulltext.aspx?id=4294969689&blogid=4294969397.

31. Perry Saturn is a former big-name star known for being rough with opponents.

32. One equivalent might be baseball catchers who must stand in place and look for an incoming baseball as a runner from third base comes barreling toward them. The journalist David Waldstein describes how this vulnerability, coupled with Pete Rose's approach, permanently altered Ray Fosse's career. "Rose's shoulder was planted into Fosse before the ball even arrived. For a catcher, the late throw leads to a frightening situation because there is no time to brace for an oncoming human battering ram who, chances are, is rather large and has momentum" (Waldstein 2012).

33. "Spot" is synonymous with a move or series of moves.

34. This is reminiscent of Bruce Springsteen's song "The Wrestler": ". . . bet I can make you smile when the blood, it hits the floor. Tell me, friend, can you ask for anything more? . . . These things that have comforted me, I drive away. This place that is my home I cannot stay. My only faith's in the broken bones and bruises I display" (Springsteen 2008).

CONCLUSION

1. See Messner, Faludi, Kimmel, and R. W. Connell for "crises" or "problem" frames regarding masculinity. Contemporary cultural critics like Christina Somers, Ann Coulter, and William Bennett point to the "softening" or feminizing of men and boys, even though this anxiety is an age-old one. See Gail Bederman's *Manliness and Civilization* (1995) for a discussion of how late-nineteenth-century US culture was shrouded in anxiety and doubt about manhood and masculinity. According to Bederman, understandings of American masculinity became aligned with white supremacy as the contrasting ideals of the intellect and the aggressive body were adjudicated by the larger discourse of "civilization."

2. See the works of Sandra Lee Bartky, Erving Goffman, Arlie Hochschild, Simone de Beauvoir, and Iris Marion Young.

3. This supports Lynne Segal's contention regarding the paradoxical, relational basis of masculinity. "The closer we come to uncovering some form of *exemplary* masculinity, a masculinity that is solid all the way through, the greater the evidence that masculinity is structured through contradiction: the more it asserts itself, the more it calls itself into question. . . . No one can be masculine through and through without constantly, and in the end rather obviously, doing violence to many of the most basic human attributes: the capacity for sensitivity to oneself and others, the expression of fear, the admission of weakness, the wisdom of co-operation, the satisfaction in servicing, the pleasures of passivity, the need to be needed—all quintessentially 'feminine.' So while the 'feminine' may appear to be dispatched in the insouciant bravado of masculine endeavor, itself as easily understood as a form of masochism or obedience to some more powerful authority or ideal, it will always return to haunt the tough guys most desperately in search of manhood" (Segal 1993, 635).

4. I do not mean to suggest that these social movements have ended and had their demands met. This is far from the case. I merely mean the social acceptance that has occurred after nearly forty years of organizing and awareness.

5. Almost twenty years ago, R. W. Connell presented the following quandary regarding the future of working-class men: "Large numbers of youth are now growing up without the expectation of stable employment around which familiar models of working class masculinity were organized. Instead they face intermittent employment and economic marginality. . . . In such conditions, what happens to the making of masculinity?" (Connell 1995, 94). Working-class white men, according to Fine and her colleagues, "no longer have a clear-cut material sphere in which they can assert lived power" (Fine et al. 2004, 139). Whether it is due to lower wages or to working in a feminized field alongside women or to the rise of a service-based economy in which men's physical strength is manifestly superfluous, today's workplace is less likely to provide a secure anchor for men's sense of manhood. The great decline in manufacturing and unionization, greater automation, and women's expanded labor-force participation have contributed to the erosion of resources and spaces previously considered uncontested spheres of masculine production. See Western and Rosenfeld (2011) for a discussion of how decreased unionization contributed to a rise in wage inequality.

6. Susan Faludi suggests that masculinity has become a type of "ornamental culture," a culture that is "constructed around celebrity and image, glamour and entertainment, marketing and consumerism . . . [which tells men] that masculinity is something to drape over the body, not draw from inner resources; that it is personal not societal; that manhood is displayed, not demonstrated" (1999, 35). Faludi's concept resembles R. W. Connell's "protest masculinity"—men with exaggerated claims of potency who present "a tense, freaky façade, making a claim to power where there are no real resources for power" (1995, 109). Likewise, Alan Klein found that with bodybuilders "the bodily fortress protected the vulnerability inside" (1993).

1. This was the comment from an acquaintance when I first explained this study.
2. Consider today's disparity in most US professional sports. Fans are increasingly people of middle to upper income, while the athletes come from mostly working-class or working-poor backgrounds. Moreover, there is seldom the chance for fans to interact with professional athletes aside from very contrived and prescribed events that are tightly managed by various agents and "handlers."
3. One disabled fan, a man named Louie, attended every practice and show. Then a twenty-one-year-old guy with cerebral palsy, he sat ringside in his motorized wheelchair. I don't think I ever attended when he was not present.
4. Depending on any particular night's exercises, trainers, and collective mood, an outsider might blend into the fray of mingling and carousing or he might really stand out. At times, as few as ten people attended; at other times, the crowd was more like twenty-five to thirty.
5. In a truly ironic moment, one of the wrestlers asked for my help with writing an analysis of pro wrestling for a sociology class he was taking at a local college. It was a unique moment of data verification: the wrestler wrote a richly detailed ten-page paper analyzing the scene, and I helped edit the paper.
6. One advisor (correctly) implored—very publicly at a Starbucks, I might add— "Go to Hooters!" after I mentioned skipping a group trip to the restaurant the previous night. This call to action provoked looks from other patrons despite being good methodological advice.
7. Some consequences with regard to "reactivity" (Katz 1982) are elaborated upon later in this appendix and elsewhere in the book. See, in particular, the field note referring to Donny's chastising me for leaving a show early.
8. In 2000, I was devastated when I tore the ACL (anterior cruciate ligament) in my knee while playing ultimate Frisbee. This was my first real brush with learning how fallible the body is. Fortunately, I had successful surgery, and I've rebounded enough to continue competing as a distance runner (I ran at the NCAA Division 1 level in college).
9. I tried at times to verify my effect on data collection. Before entering the space for the night, I would sometimes stand outside the garage or training space and listen closely. It was always very loud, so things could easily be heard. Also, before officially introducing myself, I was anonymous at the shows. Lastly, I would watch videos of public shows (shot by someone else) before and after I entered the field or if I happened to miss a show. As Jack Katz avers in his triumphant support for the analytic (induction) method of qualitative research, "From a sociological perspective on the relation between researcher and reader, the analytic method confers on readers unique powers to make their own judgments on reliability from independent encounters with data" (1982, 217).
10. Since I became known for taking decent photographs and sharing them with the wrestlers, there were a handful of moments where participants took offense

because I did *not* have a photo of them to share. Patrick in particular gave me a lot of grief for not having enough photos of him. My girlfriend, Justine, was able to capture the wrestlers in many great poses and expressions that I myself could not capture. In fact, after formally introducing myself to Cuss at the practices, he mentioned to me that he had already noticed Justine's presence at the shows. So she was known before I was. Her brother Mark also attended and took some photographs (a few of which are featured herein).

11. There were many days when fieldwork was the last thing I wanted to do. Some days, I detested driving for an hour to work for seven to eight hours in a hot, muggy gym or locker room that reeked of cheap body spray, trying to remember details of conversations while feigning mild interest in clichéd dick jokes.

12. This same event is described more fully in the field note at the beginning of chapter 5.

13. Generation X author Doug Coupland defines *summing* as the "act of visiting locations such as diners, smokestacks, industrial sites, rural villages—locations where time appears to have been frozen many years back—so as to experience relief when one returns back to 'the present'" (1991, 11).

14. In this terrain, a personal beef with someone gets deflected into an argument about the adversary's atheoretical viewpoint or shortcomings as a scholar—often in a public setting like some poor candidate's job talk!

15. The pro-war wrestler and I later joked about it—the next week he stated to me as he left for the night, "Stay away from the voting booth!"

REFERENCES

Adams, Charles S. 2001. "Myth and Ritual in Professional Wrestling." In *From Season to Season: Sports as American Religion*, edited by L. Price Joseph. Macon, GA: Mercer University Press.

Alexander, Michelle. 2010. *The New Jim Crow*. New York: New Press.

Alford, R. R., and A. Szanto. 1996. "Orpheus Wounded: The Experience of Pain in the Professional Worlds of the Piano." *Theory and Society* 25(1): 1–44.

Alter, Joseph S. *The Wrestler's Body: Identity and Ideology in North India*. Berkeley: University of California Press, 1992.

Ashforth, Blake E., and Ronald H. Humphrey. 1993. "Emotional Labor in Service Roles: The Influence of Identity." *Academy of Management Review* 18(1): 88–115.

Atyeo, D. 1979. *Blood and Guts: Violence in Sports*. New York: Paddington.

Auyero, Javier. 2003. *Contentious Lives: Two Argentine Women, Two Protests, and the Quest for Recognition*. Durham, NC: Duke University Press.

Ball, M. R. 1990. *Professional Wrestling as Ritual Drama in American Popular Culture*. Lewiston, NY: Edwin Mellon.

Barker, J. 2007. "Congressman Urges Hearing on Steroids." *Baltimore Sun*, July 10.

Barthes, Roland. [1957] 1972. *Mythologies*. New York: Hill and Wang.

Bartky, Sandra Lee. 1988. "Foucault, Femininity, and the Modernization of Patriarchal Power." In *Feminism and Foucault: Reflections on Resistance*, edited by Irene Diamond and Lee Quinby, 61–86. Boston: Northeastern Press.

Beauvoir, Simone de. 1953. *Le deuxième sexe*. New York: Random House Digital.

Becker, Howard S. 1953. "Becoming a Marijuana User." *American Journal of Sociology* 59(3): 235–242.

Beekman, Scott M. 2006. *Ringside: A History of Professional Wrestling in America*. Westport, CT: Praeger.

Belkin, Aaron. 2012. *Bring Me Men: Military Masculinity and the Benign Façade of American Empire, 1898–2001*. New York: Columbia University Press.

Bellas, Marcia L. 1999. "Emotional Labor in Academia: The Case of Professors." *Annals of the American Academy of Political and Social Sciences* 561: 96–110.

Benjamin, Jessica. 1988. *The Bonds of Love: Psychoanalysis, Feminism, and the Problem of Domination*. New York: Pantheon Books.

Benzecry, Claudio E. 2011. *The Opera Fanatic: Ethnography of an Obsession*. Chicago: University of Chicago Press.

Berger, John. 1972. *Ways of Seeing*. New York: Penguin.

Berger, Peter L., and Thomas Luckmann. 1967. *The Social Construction of Reality: A Treatise in the Sociology of Knowledge*. New York: Anchor Books.

Berube, Alan, and Elizabeth Kneebone. 2013. "Confronting Suburban Poverty in America." Brookings Institutions Press, www.brookings.edu/blogs/the-avenue/posts/2013/05/22-suburban-poverty-kneebone-berube?utm_source=Twitter andutm_medium=Socialandutm_campaign=BrookingsInst, accessed May 22, 2013.

Blank, Rebecca M. 2011. *Changing Inequality*. Berkeley: University of California Press.

Bonilla-Silva, Eduardo. 2010. *Racism without Racists: Color-blind Racism and the Persistence of Racial Inequality in the United States*. New York: Rowman and Littlefield.

Branch, John. 2011. "Derek Boogaard: A Boy Learns to Brawl." *New York Times*, December 3, p. SP1.

Bordo, Susan. 1999. *The Male Body: A New Look at Men in Public and in Private*. New York: Farrar, Straus Giroux.

Bourdieu, Pierre. 1984. *Homo Academicus*. Stanford, CA: Stanford University Press.

———. 1990. *In Other Words: Essays toward a Reflexive Sociology*. Stanford, CA: Stanford University Press.

———. 1991. "Sport and Social Class." In *Rethinking Popular Culture: Contemporary Perspectives in Cultural Studies*, edited by Chandra Mukerji and Michael Schudson. Berkeley: University of California Press.

———. 2000. *Pascalian Meditations*. Stanford, CA: Stanford University Press.

Bourgois, Philippe. 2003. *In Search of Respect: Selling Crack in El Barrio*. New York: Cambridge University Press.

Brannon, Robert, and David, Deborah S. 1976. *The Forty-Nine Percent Majority: The Male Sex Role*. New York: Random House.

Brod, Harry. 1994. "Some Thoughts on Some Histories of Some Masculinities: Jews and Other Others." In *Theorizing Masculinities*, edited by Harry Brod and Michael Kaufman, 82–96. Thousand Oaks, CA: Sage.

Burstyn, Varda. 1999. *The Rites of Men: Manhood, Politics, and the Cultural of Sport*. Toronto: University of Toronto Press.

Butler, Judith. 1990. *Gender Trouble: Feminism and the Subversion of Identity*. New York: Routledge.

Butsch, Richard. 2003. "Ralph, Fred, Archie, and Homer: Why Television Keeps

Re-creating the White Male Working-Class Buffoon." In *Gender, Race, and Class in Media: A Text-Reader*, edited by G. Dines and J. M. Humez, 575–585. Thousand Oaks, CA: Sage.

Buytendijk, F. J. 1974. *Prolegomena to an Anthropological Physiology*. Pittsburgh: Duquesne University Press.

Cahill, Spencer E. 1999. "Emotional Capital and Professional Socialization: The Case of Mortuary Science Students (and Me)." *Social Psychology Quarterly* 62(2): 101–116.

Canaan, Joyce E. 1996. "'One Thing Leads to Another': Drinking, Fighting and Working-Class Masculinities." In *Understanding Masculinities: Social Relations and Cultural Arenas*, edited by Máirtín Mac an Ghaill. Buckingham, UK: Open University Press.

Catano, James V. 2001. *Ragged Dicks: Masculinity, Steel, and the Rhetoric of the Self-Made Man*. Carbondale: Southern Illinois University Press.

Chambliss, Daniel F. 1989. "The Mundanity of Excellence: An Ethnographic Report on Stratification and Olympic Swimmers." *Sociological Theory* 7(1): 70–86.

Charmaz, K. 1999. "The Body, Identity, and Self: Adapting to Impairment." In *Health, Illness, and Healing: Society, Social Context, and Self*, edited by K. Charmaz and D. A. Paterniti. Los Angeles: Roxbury.

Chase, Chris. 2011. "Over 25 Percent of the Performers from Wrestlemania VII Have Died." *Yahoo Sports Blog*, May 23.

Christie, Nils. 2004. *A Suitable Amount of Crime*. New York: Routledge Press.

Coakley, Jay. 1989. *Sport in Society: Issues and Controversies*, 4th ed. St. Louis: Times Mirror Press.

Collins, Randall. 2008. *Violence: A Micro-Sociological Theory*. Princeton, NJ: Princeton University Press.

Collinson, David L., and Jeff Hearn. 1996. "'Men' at 'Work': Multiple Masculinities / Multiple Workplaces." In *Understanding Masculinities: Social Relations and Cultural Arenas*, edited by Máirtín Mac an Ghaill. Buckingham, UK: Open University Press.

Colman, David. 2005. "Gay or Straight? Hard to Tell." *New York Times*, June 19.

Connell, R. W. 1987. *Gender and Power*. Palo Alto, CA: Stanford University Press.

———. 1991. "Live Fast and Die Young: The Construction of Masculinity among Young Working-Class Men on the Margin of the Labour Market." *Australian and New Zealand Journal of Sociology* 27(2).

———. 1995. *Masculinities*. Cambridge, UK: Polity Press.

Connell, R. W. 2000. *The Men and the Boys*. Berkeley: University of California Press.

Coupland, Douglas. 1991. *Generation X*. New York: St. Martin's Press.

Curry, Timothy J. 1991. "Fraternal Bonding in the Locker Room: A Profeminist Analysis of Talk about Competition and Women." *Sociology of Sport* 8(2): 119–135.

Debord, Guy. [1967] 1994. *The Society of the Spectacle*. New York: Zone Books.

Deford, Frank. 1976. "Religion in Sport." *Sports Illustrated*. April 19. pp. 88–104.

Denby, David. 2009. *Snark*. New York: Simon and Schuster.

DeVault, Marjorie L. 1991. *Feeding the Family: The Social Organization of Caring as Gendered Work*. Chicago: University of Chicago Press.

———. 1999. "Comfort and Struggle: Emotion Work in Family Life." *Annals of the American Academy of Political and Social Sciences* 561: 52–63.

Donnelly, P. 2004. "Sport and Risk Culture." In *Sporting Bodies, Damaged Selves: Sociological Studies of Sports-Related Injury*, edited by K. Young, 29–57. New York: Elsevier.

DuRant, Robert H., Heather Champion, and Mark Wolfson. 2006. "The Relationship between Watching Professional Wrestling on Television and Engaging in Date Fighting among High School Students." *Pediatrics* 118(2): e265–e272.

Durkheim, Emile. [1912] 1995. *The Elementary Forms of Religious Life*. Karen E. Fields, trans. New York: Free Press.

Dyer, Richard. 1977. "Entertainment and Utopia." *Movie* 24 (spring). Reprinted in *The Cultural Studies Reader*, edited by Simon During. New York: Routledge, 1993.

Edwards, Tim. 2006. *Cultures of Masculinity*. New York: Routledge.

Eitzen, D. Stanley. 1975. "Athletics in the Status System of Male Adolescents: A Replication of Coleman's *The Adolescent Society*." *Adolescence* 10: 268–276.

———. 1999. "American Sport at Century's End." *Vital Speeches of the Day* 65 (Jan. 1): 189–191.

Elias, Norbert, and Eric Dunning. 1986. *The Quest for Excitement: Sport and Leisure in the Civilizing Process*. New York: Basil Blackwell.

Erickson, Karla. 2004. "To Invest or Detach? Coping Strategies and Workplace Culture in Service Work." *Symbolic Interaction* 27(4): 549–572.

Erickson, Rebecca J., and Christian Ritter. 2001. "Emotional Labor, Burnout, and Inauthenticity: Does Gender Matter?" *Social Psychology Quarterly* 64(2): 146–163.

Faludi, Susan. 1999. *Stiffed: The Betrayal of Modern Man*. New York: William Morrow.

Fey, Tina. 2011. *Bossypants*. New York: Little, Brown.

Fine, Gary Alan. 1987. *With the Boys: Little League Baseball and Preadolescent Culture*. Chicago: University of Chicago Press.

———. 1998. *Morel Tales*. Cambridge, MA: Harvard University Press.

Fine, Michelle, Lois Weis, Judi Addelston, and Julia Marusza. 1997. "(In)Secure Times: Constructing White Working-Class Masculinities in the Late 20th Century." *Gender and Society* 11:1 (Feb.): 52–68.

Fine, Michelle, Lois Weis, Amira Proweller, and Craig Centrie. 2004. "Excavating a 'Moment in History': Privilege and Loss inside White Working Class Masculinity." In *Off White: Readings on Power, Privilege, and Resistance*, 2nd ed., edited by Michelle Fine, Lois Weis, Linda Powell Pruitt, and April Burns. London: Taylor and Francis / Routledge.

Francis, Linda E. 1997. "Ideology and Interpersonal Emotion Management: Redefining Identity in Support Groups." *Social Psychology Quarterly* 60(2): 153–171.

Frank, Arthur W. 1995. *The Wounded Storyteller: Body, Illness, and Ethics.* Chicago: University of Chicago Press.

Frankenberg, R., ed. 1997. *Displacing Whiteness: Essays in Social and Cultural Criticism.* Durham, NC: Duke University Press.

Freund, P. 1988. "Bringing Society into the Body: Understanding Socialized Human Nature." *Theory and Society* 17(6): 839–864.

Frey, J. 1991. "Social Risk and the Meaning of Sport." *Sociology of Sport* 8: 136–145.

Gagnon, John H. 1974. "Physical Strength, Once of Significance." In *Men and Masculinity*, edited by Joseph H. Pleck and Jack Sawyer. Englewood Cliffs, NJ: Prentice Hall.

Geertz, Clifford. 1973. *The Interpretation of Cultures: Selected Essays.* Vol. 5019. New York: Basic Books.

Genzlinger, Neil. 2006. "That's Gotta Hurt." Review of *Slaphappy: Pride, Prejudice, and Professional Wrestling*, by Thomas Hackett. *New York Times*, April 2.

Gilbert, Roger. 2001. "Understanding Ovation" (abridged version of "Joyful Noise: Reflections on Applause"). *Harper's*, October (303/1817): 15–18.

Gilligan, James. 1996. *Violence: Reflections on a National Epidemic.* New York: Vintage Books.

Glaser B., and A. Strauss. 1967. *The Discovery of Grounded Theory: Strategies for Qualitative Research.* Chicago: Aldine Press.

Godwyn, Mary. 2006. "Using Emotional Labor to Create and Maintain Relationships in Service Interaction." *Symbolic Interaction* 29(4): 487–506.

Goffman, Alice. 2009. "On the Run: Wanted Men in a Philadelphia Ghetto." *American Sociological Review* 74: 339–357.

Goffman, Erving. 1959. *The Presentation of Self in Everyday Life.* New York: Anchor Books.

———. 1963. *Stigma: Notes on the Management of Spoiled Identity.* Englewood Cliffs, NJ: Prentice Hall.

———. 1967. *Interaction Ritual: Essays on Face to Face Behavior.* New York: Pantheon Books.

———. 1971. *Relations in Public.* New York: Basic Books

———. 1974. *Frame Analysis.* New York: Harper and Row.

———. 2002. "On Fieldwork." In *Qualitative Research Methods*, edited by Darin Weinberg. Malden, MA: Blackwell.

Goldstein, Jeffrey H. 1998. *Why We Watch: The Attractions of Violent Entertainment.* New York: Oxford University Press.

Good, M. D., P. E. Brodwin, J. G. Byron, and A. Kleinman. 1994. *Pain as Human Experience: An Anthropological Perspective.* Berkeley: University of California Press.

Gramzow, Richard H. 2002. "Threats to Masculinity Pits Straight Men against

Gay." *Reuters Health*, February 7, 2002. Paper presented to the Society for Personality and Social Psychology Annual Meeting.

Grazian, David. 2008. *On the Make: The Hustle of Urban Nightlife*. Chicago: University of Chicago Press.

Green, Kyle. 2011. "It Hurts So It Is Real: Sensing the Seduction of Mixed Martial Arts." *Social and Cultural Geography* 12(04): 377–396.

Gresson, Aaron David, III. 1997. "Professional Wrestling and Youth Culture: Teasing, Taunting, and the Containment of Civility." In *KinderCulture: The Corporate Construction of Childhood*, edited by Shirley R. Steinberg and Joe L. Kinchloe, 165–179. Boulder, CO: Westview Press.

Grindstaff, Laura. 2002. *The Money Shot: Trash, Class, and the Making of TV Talk Shows*. Chicago: University of Chicago Press.

Gutmann, Matthew C. 1996. *The Meanings of Macho: Being a Man in Mexico City*. Berkeley: University of California Press.

Guttmann, Allen. 2000. "The Development of Modern Sports." In *Handbook of Sport Studies*, edited by Jay Coakley and Eric Dunning. London: Sage.

Hackett, Thomas. 2006. *Slaphappy: Pride, Prejudice, and Professional Wrestling*. New York: Ecco Press.

Haenfler, Ross. 2004. "Manhood in Contradiction: The Two Faces of Straight Edge." *Men and Masculinities* 7(1): 77–99.

Halle, David. 1984. *America's Working Man: Work, Home Politics among Blue-Collar Property Owners*. Chicago: University of Chicago Press.

Hammersley, Martyn, and Paul Atkinson. 2007. *Ethnography: Principles in Practice*. New York: Routledge.

Hardin, Marie, and Brent Hardin. 2001. "Wrestling with Stereotypes: Depictions of the Mentally Ill/Disabled in the World Wrestling Federation." *Sociology of Sport Online* 3(1), http://physed.otago.ac.nz/sosol/v3i1a1.htm, accessed January 19, 2014.

Harlow, Roxanna. 2003. "'Race Doesn't Matter, but . . .': The Effect of Race on Professors' Experiences and Emotion Management in the Undergraduate College Classroom." *Social Psychology Quarterly* 66(4): 348–363.

Haywood, Chris, and Mairtin Mac an Ghaill. 1996. "'What about the Boys?' Regendered Local Labour Markets and the Recomposition of Working-Class Masculinities." *British Journal of Education and Work* 9(1):19–30.

Hearn, Jeff, and Collinson, David L. 1994. "Theorizing Unities and Differences between Men and between Masculinities." In *Theorizing Masculinities*, edited by Harry Brod and Michael Kaufman. London: Sage.

Henricks, Thomas. 1974. "Professional Wrestling as Moral Order." *Sociological Inquiry* 44(3): 177–188.

Hillenbrand, Laura. 2010. *Unbroken*. New York: Random House.

Hochschild, Arlie. 1979. "Emotion Work, Feeling Rules, and Social Structure." *American Journal of Sociology* 85: 551–575.

————. 1983. *The Managed Heart: The Commercialization of Feeling*. Berkeley: University of California Press.

————. 2003. *The Commercialization of Intimate Life*. Berkeley: University of California Press.

Honneth, Axel. 1995. *The Struggle for Recognition*. Cambridge, UK: Polity Press.

Howe, P. David. 2004. *Sport, Professionalism, and Pain: Ethnographies of Injury and Risk*. New York: Routledge.

Hughes, Everett C. 2002. "The Place of Field Work in Social Science." In *Qualitative Research Methods*, edited by Darin Weinberg. Malden, MA: Blackwell.

International Association for the Study of Pain. 1979. Pain 6, 249–252. Seattle: IASP Publications.

Jenkins, Henry. 1997. "'Never Trust a Snake!' WWF Wrestling as Masculine Melodrama." In *Out of Bounds: Sports, Media, and the Politics of Identity*, edited by Aaron Baker and Todd Boyd, 48–78. Bloomington: Indiana University Press.

Jenkins, Henry, IV. 2005. "Afterword Part II: Growing Up and Growing More Risque." In *Steel Chair to the Head: The Pleasure and Pain of Professional Wrestling*, edited by Nicholas Sammond, 317–342. Durham, NC: Duke University Press.

Jerolmack, Colin. 2013. *The Global Pigeon*. Chicago: University of Chicago Press.

Johnson, Kirk. 1998. "Professional Wrestling Cuts Good Guys from the Script." *New York Times*, March 30, pp. A1, C17.

Jones, Juston. 2007. "Running Wrestling's Empire." *New York Times*, August 18, http://www.nytimes.com/2007/08/18/business/18interview-web.html?page wanted=print, accessed January 20, 2014.

Kang, Miliann. 2003. "The Managed Hand: The Commercialization of Bodies and Emotions in Korean Immigrant–Owned Nail Salons." *Gender and Society* 17(6): 820–839.

Kanyon, Chris. 2011. *Wrestling Reality: The Life and Mind of Chris Kanyon, Wrestling's Gay Superstar*. Toronto: ECW Press.

Katz, Jack. 1982. *Poor People's Lawyers in Transition*. New Brunswick, NJ: Rutgers University Press.

————. 1988. *Seductions of Crime*. New York: Basic Books.

————. 2002. "From How to Why: On Luminous Description and Causal Inference in Ethnography (part 2)." *Ethnography* 3(1): 63–90 [1466–1381].

Katz, Jackson, and Sut Jhally. 2000. "Manhood on the Mat: The Problem Is Not That Pro Wrestling Makes Boys Violent. The Real Lesson of the Wildly Popular Pseudo-Sport Is More Insidious." *Boston Globe*, February 13, Focus section, p. E1.

Kaufman, Michael. 1996. "The Construction of Masculinity and the Triad of Men's Violence." In *Gender Violence: Interdisciplinary Perspectives*, edited by Jessica Schiffman and Laura L. O'Toole. New York: New York University Press.

Keck, William. 2000. "With Gov. Ventura, Call It 'The Young and the Wrestling.'" *Los Angeles Times*, July 10.

Kerrick, George E. 1980. "The Jargon of Professional Wrestling." *American Speech* 55(2): 142–145.

Kilgannon, Corey. 2007. "Teenagers Misbehaving, for All Online to Watch." *New York Times*, February 13.

Kimmel, Michael. 1994. "Masculinity as Homophobia: Fear, Shame and Silence in the Construction of Gender Identity." In *Theorizing Masculinities*, edited by Harry Brod and Michael Kaufman, 119–141. Thousand Oaks, CA: Sage.

———. 1996. *Manhood in America: A Cultural History*. New York: Free Press.

———. 2000. "The Gendered Workplace." Chapter 8 in *The Gendered Society*. New York: Oxford University Press.

Kimmel, Michael S., and Michael Messner, eds. 1998. *Men's Lives*, 4th ed. New York: Macmillan.

Klein, Alan M. 1993. *Little Big Men: Bodybuilding Subculture and Gender Construction*. Albany: State University of New York Press.

Kleinman, Arthur 1988. *The Illness Narratives: Suffering Healing, and the Human Condition*. New York: Basic Books.

———. 2007. "Opening Remarks: Pain and Experience." In *Pain and Its Transformations: The Interface of Biology and Culture*, edited by Kay Kaufman Shelemay. Boston: Harvard University Press.

Kotarba, J. A. 2004. "Professional Athletes' Injuries: From Existential to Organisational Analyses." In *Sporting Bodies, Damaged Selves: Sociological Studies of Sports-Related Injury*, edited by K. Young, 99–116. New York: Elsevier.

Kreager, Derek A. 2007. "Unnecessary Roughness? School Sports, Peer Networks, and Male Adolescent Violence." *American Sociological Review* 72: 705–724.

Lakoff, George. 2004. *Don't Think of an Elephant: Know Your Values and Frame the Debate*. White River Junction, VT: Chelsea Green.

Lamont, Michelle. 2000. *The Dignity of Working Men: Morality and the Boundaries of Race, Class, and Immigration*. Boston: Harvard University Press.

La Pradelle, Michele de. 2006. *Market Day in Provence*. Chicago: University of Chicago Press.

Leder, Drew. 1990. *The Absent Body*. Chicago: University of Chicago Press.

Lee, Jennifer. 2005. "The Man Date." *New York Times*, April 10.

Leidner, Robin. 1991. "Serving Hamburgers and Selling Insurance: Gender, Work, and Identity in Interactive Service Jobs." *Gender and Society* 5: 154–177.

———. 1993. *Fast Food, Fast Talk: Service Work and the Routinization of Everyday Life*. Berkeley: University of California Press.

Levi, Heather. 2008. *The World of Lucha Libre: Secrets, Revelations, and Mexican National Identity*. Durham, NC: Duke University Press.

Liebow, Elliot. 1967. *Tally's Corner: A Study of Negro Streetcorner Men*. New York: Rowman and Littlefield.

Lively, Kathryn J. 2000. "Reciprocal Emotion Management." *Work and Occupations* 27 (1): 32–63.

Lock, Margaret. 1993. "Cultivating the Body: Anthropology and Epistemologies of Bodily Practice and Knowledge." *Annual Review of Anthropology* 22: 133–155.

Lois, Jennifer. 2006. "Role Strain, Emotion Management, and Burnout: Homeschooling Mothers' Adjustment to the Teacher Role." *Symbolic Interaction* 29(4): 507–530.

Lutz, Phillip. 2003. "Lobbying to Keep Economic Identity." *New York Times*, July 20.

Lyman, S. M., and M. B. Scott. 1970. *A Sociology of the Absurd*. New York: Appleton-Century.

Lyng, Stephen. 1990. "Edgework: A Social Psychological Analysis of Voluntary Risk Taking." *American Journal of Sociology* 95(4): 851–886.

Mac an Ghaill, M. 1996a. "Irish Masculinities and Sexualities." In *Sexualizing the Social: Power and the Organization of Sexuality*, edited by England L. Adkins and V. Merchant, 122–144. London: Macmillan.

———. 1996b. *Understanding Masculinities: Social Relations and Cultural Areas*. Buckingham, UK: Open University Press.

MacInnes, John. 1996. "Analysing Men." *Gender, Work and Organization* 3(1): 51–63.

Maguire, Brendan. 2000. "Defining Deviancy Down: A Research Note regarding Professional Wrestling." *Deviant Behavior* 21: 551–565.

Malcom, N. L. 2006. "'Shaking It Off' and 'Toughing It Out': Socialization to Pain and Injury in Girls' Softball." *Journal of Contemporary Ethnography* 35(5): 495–525.

Markell, Patchen. 2003. *Bound by Recognition*. Princeton, NJ: Princeton University Press.

Martin, Joanne, Kathleen Knopoff, and Christine Beckman. 1998. "An Alternative to Bureaucratic Impersonality and Emotional Labor: Bounded Emotionality at the Body Shop." *Administrative Science Quarterly* 43(2): 429–469.

Martin, Susan Ehrlich. 1999. "Police Force or Police Service? Gender and Emotional Labor." *Annals of the American Academy of Political and Social Sciences* 561: 111–126.

Mazer, Sharon. 1998. *Professional Wrestling: Sport and Spectacle*. Jackson: University Press of Mississippi.

———. 2005. "'Real' Wrestling/'Real' Life." In *Steel Chair to the Head: The Pleasure and Pain of Professional Wrestling*, edited by Nicholas Sammond, 66–87. Durham, NC: Duke University Press.

McDowell, Linda. 2003. *Redundant Masculinities?: Employment Change and White Working Class Youth*. Malden MA: Blackwell.

McKinley, Jesse. 2010. "Wrestler Sees Legal Move; Prosecutor Sees Assault." *New York Times*, December 18.

Mears, A., and W. Finlay. 2005. "Not Just a Paper Doll: How Models Manage Bodily Capital and Why They Perform Emotional Labor." *Journal of Contemporary Ethnography* 34(3): 317–343.

Meltzer, Dave A. 2008. Personal communication, May 9 (e-mail).

Messerschmidt, James W. 2000. *Nine Lives: Adolescent Masculinities, the Body, and Violence*. Boulder, CO: Westview Press.

Messner, Michael. 1987. "The Meaning of Success: The Athletic Experience and the Development of Male Identity." In *The Making of Masculinities: The New Men's Studies*, edited by H. Brod, 193–210. Boston: Allen and Unwin.

———. 1990. "Boyhood, Organized Sports, and the Construction of Masculinities." *Journal of Contemporary Ethnography* 18(4): 416–444.

———. 2002. "Becoming 100 Percent Straight." In *Sexuality and Gender*, edited by Christine L. Williams and Arlene Stein. Malden MA: Blackwell.

———. 2002. *Taking the Field: Woman, Men and Sports*. Minneapolis: University of Minnesota Press.

———. 2003. "Men Studying Masculinity: Some Epistemological Issues in Sport Sociology." In *Sport: Critical Concepts in Sociology*, edited by Eric Dunning and Dominic Malcolm, 200–221. New York: Routledge.

Messner, Michael A., Michele Dunbar, and Darnell Hunt. 2000. "The Televised Sports Manhood Formula." *Journal of Sport and Social Issues* 24: 380–394.

Mondak, Jeffrey J. 1989. "The Politics of Professional Wrestling." *Journal of Popular Culture* 23(2): 139–149.

Morris, David. 1991. *The Culture of Pain*. Berkeley: University of California Press.

Morton, Gerald W., and George M. O'Brien. 1985. *Wrestling to Rasslin': Ancient Sport to American Spectacle*. Bowling Green, MI: Bowling Green State University Popular Press.

Mueller, Walt. 1999. "My Week in Professional Wrestling." *cpu Newsletter* (winter).

Nasty, Big. 2010. "wwe/tna Top Stories of 2010, no. 7: Lance Cade Dies of Heart Failure at Age 29." *Bleacher Report*, December 27, http://bleacherreport.com /articles/554408-wwetna-top-stories-of-2010-no-7-lance-cade-dies-of-heart -failure-at-age-29, accessed January 20, 2014.

Newmahr, Staci. 2011. *Playing on the Edge: Sadomasochism, Risk, and Intimacy*. Bloomington: Indiana University Press.

Newsweek. 2000. "Why America's Hooked On Wrestling." *Newsweek International*, http://www.newsweek.com/why-americas-hooked-wrestling-162367, accessed January 21, 2014.

New York State Athletic Commission website. 2005. www.dos.state.ny.us/athletic/.

New York Times. 2008. "World Wrestling Entertainment's Earnings Rise 29%." May 7.

Nixon, H. L. 1992. "A Social Network Analyses of Influences on Athletes to Play with Pain and Injury." *Journal of Sport and Social Issues* 16(2): 127–135.

———. 1996. "The Relationship of Friendship Networks, Sport Experiences, and Gender to Express Pain Thresholds." *Sociology of Sport* 13: 78–86.

Nowinski, Christopher. 2006. *Head Games: Football's Concussion Crisis from the nfl to Youth Leagues*. East Bridgewater, MA: Drummond.

Oliver, Kelly. 2001. *Witnessing: Beyond Recognition*. Minneapolis: University of Minnesota Press.

Osherson, S. 1986. *Finding Our Fathers: How a Man's Life Is Shaped by His Relationship with His Father*. New York: Fawcett Columbine.

Osterweis, Marian, Arthur Kleinman, and David Mechanic. 1987. *Pain and Disability: Clinical, Behavioral, and Public Policy Perspectives*. Washington, DC: National Academy Press.

Pascoe, C. J. 2005. "'Dude, You're a Fag': Adolescent Masculinity and the Fag Discourse." *Sexualities* 8: 329–346.

Pager, Devah. 20003. "The Mark of a Criminal Record." *American Journal of Sociology* 108(5): 937–975.

Pettit, Becky, and Bruce Western. 2004. "Mass Imprisonment and the Life Course: Race and Class Inequality in US Incarceration." *American Sociological Review* 69(2): 151–169.

Pierce, Jennifer. 1995. *Gender Trials: Emotional Lives in Contemporary Law Firms*. Berkeley: University of California Press.

Pope, Harrison G., Katharine A. Phillips, and Roberto Olivardia. 2000. *The Adonis Complex: The Secret Crisis of Male Body Obsession*. New York: Free Press.

Price, Joseph L. 2001. *From Season to Season: Sports as American Religion*. Macon, GA: Mercer University Press.

Pronger, Brian. 1990. *The Arena of Masculinity: Sports, Homosexuality, and the Meaning of Sex*. New York: St. Martin's Press.

Rafaeli, Anat, and Robert I. Sutton. 1991. "Emotional Contrast Strategies as a Means of Social Influence: Lessons from Criminal Interrogators and Bill Collectors." *Academy of Management Journal* 34(4): 749–775.

Reardon, Patrick. 1999. "Wrestle Maniacs." *Chicago Tribune*, April 1, sec. 2, pp. 1, 4.

Rickard, John. 1999. "'The Spectacle of Excess': The Emergence of Modern Professional Wrestling in the United States and Australia." *Journal of Popular Culture* 33(1): 129–137.

Rinehart, Robert E. 2007. "Arriving Sport: Alternatives to Formal Sports." In *Handbook of Sport Studies*, edited by Jay Coakley and Eric Dunning, 504–519. London: Sage.

Robinson, Sally. 2000. *Marked Men: White Masculinity in Crisis*. New York: Columbia University Press.

Rosellini, Lynn. 1999. "Lords of the Ring." *US News and World Report*, May 17.

Rueter, Ted. 2000. "Kids Grapple with Wrestling Violence." *USA Today*, March 30.

Russell, Carol L., and Thomas E. Murray. 2004. "The Life and Death of Carnie." *American Speech*. 79(4): 400–416.

Rutherford, J. 1992. *Men's Silences: Predicaments in Masculinity*. Boston: Routledge and Kegan Paul.

Sabo, Don. 1985. "Sport, Patriarchy and Male Identity: New Questions about Men and Sport." *Arena Review* 9(2): 1–30.

———. 1994. "Pigskin, Patriarchy, and Pain." In *Sex, Violence, and Power in Sports*, edited by Michael Messner and Don Sabo. Langhorne, PA: Crossing Press.

Sage, George. 2000. "Political Economy and Sport." In *Handbook of Sport Studies*, edited by Jay Coakley and Eric Dunning. London: Sage.

Sammond, Nicholas. 2005. *Steel Chair to the Head: The Pleasure and Pain of Professional Wrestling*. Durham, NC: Duke University Press.

———. 2005. "Squaring the Family Circle: WWF Smackdown Assaults the Social Body." In *Steel Chair to the Head: The Pleasure and Pain of Professional Wrestling*, edited by Nicholas Sammond, 132–166. Durham, NC: Duke University Press.

Saraceno, Jon. 2007. "Wrestling: Too Many Sequels to This Tragedy." *USA Today*, July 2.

Scarry, Elaine. 1987. *The Body in Pain: The Making and Unmaking of the World*. New York: Oxford University Press.

Scheper-Hughes, N., and M. Lock. 1987. "The Mindful Body: A Prolegomenon to Future Work in Medical Anthropology." *Medical Anthropology Quarterly* 1(1): 6–41.

Schiesel, Seth. 2007. "Flashy Wrestling Shows Grab the World by the Neck and Flex." *New York Times*, April 4.

Schneiderman, R. M. "Better Days, and Even the Candidates, Are Coming to W.W.E." *New York Times*, April 28.

Schrock, Douglas, and Michael Schwalbe. 2009. "Men, Masculinity, and Manhood Acts." *Annual Review of Sociology* 35: 277–295.

Schutz, Alfred. 1976. "Don Quixote and the Problem of Reality." In *Collected Papers*. Vol. 2, *Studies in Social Theory*, edited by Arvid Bodersen.

Schwarz, Alan. 2009. "Now, Pressure Is for Players Not to Play after a Concussion." *New York Times*, November 17.

Schweingruber, David, and Nancy Berns. 2005. "Shaping the Selves of Young Salespeople through Emotion Management." *Journal of Contemporary Ethnography* 34(6): 679–706.

Segal, Lyn. 1993. "Changing Men: Masculinities in Context." *Theory and Society* 22: 625–641.

Sennett, Richard. 2003. *Respect in a World of Inequality*. New York: Norton.

Shapira, Harel. 2013. *Waiting for José: The Minutemen's Pursuit of America*. Princeton, NJ: Princeton University Press.

Smith, R. Tyson. 2004. "Professional Wrestling." In *Men and Masculinities: A Social, Cultural, and Historical Encyclopedia*, edited by Michael Kimmel and Amy Aronson. Oxford, MA: ABC Clio.

———. 2005. "Pumping Irony: The Construction of Masculinity in a Post-feminist Advertising Campaign." *Advertising and Society Review* 6(3), http://muse.jhu.edu/journals/asr/v006/6.3smith.html, accessed January 20, 2014.

———. 2008. "Pain in the Act: The Meanings of Pain Among Professional Wrestlers." *Qualitative Sociology* 31(2): 129–148.

———. 2008. "Passion Work: The Joint Production of Emotional Labor in Professional Wrestling." *Social Psychology Quarterly* 71(2): 157–176.

Smith, Tyson, and Michael Kimmel. 2005. "The Hidden Discourse of Masculinity in Gender Discrimination Law." *Signs* 30(3): 1827–1849.

Snow, David A., and L. Anderson. 1993. *Down on Their Luck: A Study of Homeless Street People.* Berkeley: University of California Press.

Snow, David A., Calvin Morrill, and Leon Anderson. 2003. "Elaborating Analytic Ethnography: Linking Fieldwork and Theory." *Ethnography* 4(2): 181–200.

Sontag, Susan. 1982. *A Susan Sontag Reader.* New York: Farrar, Straus, Giroux.

Springsteen, Bruce. 2008. "The Wrestler." On "The Wrestler" Soundtrack. CD. Columbia Records.

Stallybrass, Peter, and Allon White. 1986. "Bourgeois Hysteria and the Carnivalesque." In *The Politics and Poetics of Transgression.* London: Methuen. Reprinted in *The Cultural Studies Reader,* edited by Simon During. New York: Routledge, 1993.

Stanislavsky, Konstantin. 1967. *On the Art of the Stage.* London: Faber and Faber.

Stanley, Alessandra. 2009. "For Some, a Search for Celebrity Is Worth Any Risk." *New York Times.* November 27.

Steinberg, Ronnie J., and Deborah M. Figart. 1999. "Emotional Labor since the Managed Heart." *Annals of the American Academy of Political and Social Science* 561: 8–26.

Stenross, Barbara, and Sherryl Kleinman. 1989. "The Highs and Lows of Emotional Labor: Detectives' Encounters with Criminals and Victims." *Journal of Contemporary Ethnography* 36: 245–268.

Strugatch, Warren. 2003. "Long Island at Work: Jobless Rate Masks Fundamental Shift." *New York Times,* January 5.

Sutton, Robert. 1991. "Maintaining Norms about Expressed Emotion: The Case of Bill Collectors." *Administrative Science Quarterly* 36: 245–268.

Swain, Scott. 1989. "Covert Intimacy: Closeness in Men's Friendships." In *Gender in Intimate Relationships,* edited by Barbara Risman and Pepper Schwartz, 71–85. New York: Wadsworth.

Swartz, Jon. 2007. "Doping Still an Issue in Wrestling." *USA Today,* November 19, www.usatoday.com/sports/2007-11-18-drugs-wrestling-cover_N.htm.

Taylor, Charles. 1994. "The Politics of Recognition." In *Multiculturalism: Examining the Politics of Recognition,* edited by Amy Gutmann. Princeton, NJ: Princeton University Press.

Thoits, Peggy A. 1996. "Managing the Emotions of Others." *Symbolic Interaction* 19(2): 85–109.

Tilly, C. 1999. *Durable Inequality.* Berkeley: California University Press.

———. 2006. *Identity, Boundaries, and Social Ties.* Boulder, CO: Paradigm Press.

Trimbur, Lucia. 2013. *Come Out Swinging: The Changing World of Boxing in Gleason's Gym.* Princeton, NJ: Princeton University Press.

———. 2008. Personal communication with author. December 15.

Trujillo, Nick, et al. 2000. "A Night with the Narcissist and the Nasty Boys: Interpreting the World Wrestling Federation." Communication Studies 298. *Qualitative Inquiry* 6: 4.

Turowetz, Allan, and M. Rosenberg. 1977. "Exaggerating Everyday Life: The Case of Professional Wrestling." In *Identities in Canadian Society*. edited by J. Haas and B. Shaffer, 87–100. Englewood Cliffs, NJ: Prentice Hall.

Updike, John. 1968. *Couples*. New York: Ballantine.

Vannini, Phillip. 2006. "Dead Poets' Society: Teaching, Publish-or-Perish, and Professors' Experiences of Authenticity." *Symbolic Interaction* 29(2): 235–257.

Venkatesh, Sudhir. 2008. *Gang Leader for a Day*. New York: Penguin.

Wacquant, Loïc. 1992. "The Social Logic of Boxing in Black Chicago: Toward a Sociology of Pugilism." *Sociology of Sport* 9: 221–254.

———. 1998. "A Fleshpeddler at Work: Power, Pain, and Profit in the Prizefighting Economy." *Theory and Society* 27(1): 1–42.

———. 2004. *Body and Soul: Notebooks of an Apprentice Boxer*. New York: Oxford University Press.

Wainwright, S. P., C. Williams, and B. S. Turner. 2005. "Fractured Identities: Injury and the Balletic Body." *Health* 9(1): 49–66.

Waldstein, David. 2012. "The Dirtiest Part of a Catcher's Job." *New York Times*, September 28.

Waxmonsky, Jim, and Eugene V. Beresin. 2001. "Taking Professional Wrestling to the Mat: A Look at the Appeal and Potential Effects of Professional Wrestling on Children." *Academic Psychiatry* 25(2).

Weber, Bruce. 2005. "Don't Let Your Head Flop, and Flip the Other Guy." *New York Times*, March 15.

Weis, L. 1990. *Working Class without Work: High School Students in a Deindustrializing Economy*. New York: Routledge.

Weis, L., A. Proweller, and C. Centrie. 1996. "Re-examining a Moment in History: Loss of Privledge Inside White Working Class Masculinity in the 1990s." In *Men's Lives*, edited by Michael Kimmel and Michael S. Messner. Needham Heights, MA: Allyn and Bacon, 2001.

West, Candace, and Don H. Zimmerman. 1987. "Doing Gender." *Gender and Society* 1: 125–151.

Western, Bruce. 2006. *Punishment and Inequality in America*. Albany, NY: Russell Sage Foundation.

Western, Bruce, and Jake Rosenfeld. 2011. "Unions, Norms, and the Rise in U.S. Wage Inequality." *American Sociological Review* 76: 513.

White, Philip, Kevin Young, and William McTeer. 1995. "Sport, Masculinity, and the Injured Body." In *Men's Health and Illness: Gender, Power, and the Body*, edited by D. Sabo and F. Gordon. London: Sage.

Willer, Robb, Christable L. Rogalin, Bridget Conlon, and Michael T. Wojnowicz. 2013. "Overdoing Gender: A Test of the Masculine Overcompensation Thesis." *American Journal of Sociology* 118(4): 980–1022.

Williams, Christine L. 1992. "The Glass Escalator: Hidden Advantages for Men in the 'Female' Professions." *Social Problems* 39(3): 253–267.

Willis, Paul. 2000. *The Ethnographic Imagination*. Malden, MA: Polity Press.

Wood, Elisabeth Jean. 2003. *Insurgent Collective Action and Civil War in El Salvador*. New York: Cambridge University Press.

Woods, Gregory. 1987. *Articulate Flesh: Male Homoeroticism and Modern Poetry*. New Haven, CT: Yale University Press.

Worcester Telegram Gazette. 2000. "Fathers Advised to Teach Sons about Emotions." March 13.

Young, Kevin, and Philip White. 2000. "Researching Sports Injury," In *Masculinities, Gender Relations and Sport*, edited by Jim McKay, Michael Messner, Don Sabo, 108–126. Thousand Oaks, CA: Sage.

Young, Kevin, Philip White, and William McTeer. 1994. "Body Talk: Male Athletes Reflect on Sport, Injury and Pain." *Sociology of Sport* 11: 175–194.

Young, Iris Marion. 1990. *Throwing like a Girl and Other Essays in Feminist Philosophy and Social Theory*. Bloomington: Indiana University Press.

Zborowski, M. 1969. *People in Pain*. San Francisco: Jossey-Bass.

Index

Note: page numbers in italics refer to illustrations; those followed by "n" indicate endnotes.

bodies (*continued*)
　　intimacy and, 99; show business skill
　　vs., 111–12. *See also* injury; pain; physi-
　　cality
body image: Donny and, 28–29; masculin-
　　ity and, 98–99, 151; size, 24, 29
bookers, 13, 90–91
Bordo, Susan, 96, 148
Bourdieu, Pierre, 41, 42
Bourgois, Philippe, 180n16
boxers, 153, 189n4, 190n14, 190n20
The Brick, 55
Brickman: characteristics of, 35; injury
　　and, 129–30; preperformance prepa-
　　rations, 90, 91; profile, 168; trapdoor
　　gimmick, 115–16
Broadway productions, 136, 192n30
bumps, 64–65, 78
Burstyn, Varda, 106
Butler, Judith, 184n4

Cade, Lance, 191n26
camp, 38
Chambliss, Daniel, 178n28
charisma, in kayfabe, 69
Chris, 98, 130, 167, 191n28
Clean Sports Act, 189n9
Cobra: blame and, 190n17; profile, 167;
　　talents of, 35, 60–61, 91
Coleman, David, 185n11
compensation theory, 94–95, 186n15
Connell, R. W., 147, 151, 187n20, 193nn5–6
coworker opinions, 39–40
criminality and entertainment, 11, 175n10
cultural capital, 44–45
culture, ornamental, 151, 193n6
Cuss: author's introduction to, 156; doctor
　　visits, 135; on entry into wrestling, 15; on
　　fear, 127; on high-school show, 177n25;
　　on joint labor vs. physicality, 78; on
　　medical care, 133; mother and, 18; pain
　　and injury and, 128, 130, 131, 191n28;
　　paternalism and, 111; preperformance
　　preparations, 90; profile, 24–27, 167; in

training session, 63–64; women, degra-
　　dation of, 110

Damon, 142, 167
Dan: on exchange during match, 73; on
　　immersion, 42; on injuries and life
　　effects, 17–18, 135; preperformance
　　preparations, 91; profile, 167
day jobs: finances and, 15, 41, 124; health
　　care and, 134; identity and, 20, 151; inju-
　　ries and, 3, 190n14; of specific wrestlers,
　　167–69; teaching as common job, 46;
　　value of wrestling vs., 43, 134
DDT (death drop technique or demonic
　　death trap), 183n8
death, premature, 123–24, 189n12
demographics of wrestlers, 19
Denby, David, 179n8
dislocations, 135
disruptions, 80, 82–86
doctors, 123, 135, 189nn10–11
documentation, role of, 53–58
dominance. *See* hierarchy
Dominic, 110
Donny, 28; body consciousness and, 98;
　　on coworker opinions, 39; family and,
　　16; gay wrestler character, 29–30,
　　100–101, 186n13; girlfriend and, 46;
　　on gym workouts, 44; homophobia
　　and, 105; on immersion, 1, 43, 47; on
　　light touch, 72; on manhood, 108;
　　matches, 56, 58; old-school experience,
　　139–40; pain and injury and, 125, 131;
　　on picture taking, 57; preperformance
　　preparations, 90; profile, 27–30, 167;
　　on recognition, 58–59; on sacrifices,
　　46–47; sexual banter, 186n14; sexualized
　　behavior and, 103; on social life, 52–53;
　　in training session, 65; trapdoor gim-
　　mick, 115–19, 164
dreams, adjustment of, 15–16
dreams as inspiration, 75
Drozdov, Darren, 16
drugs, 31, 124, 134, 177n26, 191n26

La Pradelle, Michelle de, 171n5
Leder, Drew, 142, 188n3
left side, working, 77
Liebow, Elliot, 179n12
life expectancy, 123–24, 189n12
light touch, 71–72, 102–3
loose and light body technique, 71–72
Lorber, Judith, 184n4
Louie (fan), 25, 48–49, 110, 162
Luckmann, Thomas, 188n2

makeup, 60–61, 91
male gaze, 96, 185n7
The Managed Heart (Hochschild), 67
marijuana appreciation compared to wrestling, 176n21
masculinity: appearance, outfits, and accoutrements, 96–97; "badass" and, 96; body consciousness and, 98–99; compensation theory, 94–95, 186n15; as crisis, 147; critiques and commentary on wrestling and, 93–95; double-bind of, 148; generalizations about, 185n6; hegemonic, 147; homosocial solidarity, bodily duress, and, 107–9; identity and, 4, 150–52, 172n9; inversion and reinterpretation, 106–7; locker room preperformance rituals and, 89–93; ornamental culture and, 151, 193n6; pain and, 121, 145, 190n19; paradoxes and contradictions in, 147–50; as performance, 149–50; professionalism of show business and, 111–13; protest masculinity, 151, 193n6; sexual dominance and, 109–10; sexualization, homoeroticism, and homophobia, 99–105, 150, 187n17; social construction of, 93, 184n4; sport and, 4, 105–6, 187n17, 187n19; tradition, paternalism, and, 110–11; violence and, 93–94, 106, 148–49, 187n20; in Western culture, 96, 145, 185n9
Matt: autographs and, 49–50; on childhood, 179n14; on day jobs, 46; email interaction with, 166; father and, 59;

injury self-treatment and, 134–35; on locker room atmosphere, 181n26; paternalism and, 110–11; preperformance preparations, 90, 91; profile, 168; shoots and, 139; in WWE incubator league, 140
Mayhem, 134
Mazer, Sharon, 95, 172n8
McDowell, Linda, 95
Meltzer, Dave, 14
mental devotion, 47
merchandise, 51
Messner, Michael, 71, 93–94, 190n19
Mike M.: father and, 16; injury and, 130; on lying about wrestling, 40; on pain, 107–8; profile, 30–32, 168; on recognition from veterans, 58; tapes, obsession with, 54; on Timmy, 22–23; in training session, 63
minstrel characters, 29–30, 35, 186n13
mistakes and incompetence, 141–42
The Money Shot (Grindstaff), 180n15
Morris, David, 120, 129
muscles, 187n19

narrative and story: in 1990s, 171n4; connective, 2; fakery and, 2–3; heels and babyfaces in, 75; justice motif, 124; sequencing and building, 75–76; typical script, 171n3; writers, 175n13
neurological disorders, 190n22
Nick (emcee), 91
Nixon, H. L., 121
"no," saying, 131, 191n24
Nowinski, Chris, 176n19, 190n22

objectivation of pain, 119–20, 188n2
Oliver, Kelly, 42
onstage: emotional labor and, 68 69; masculinity and, 149; pain and, 132; as sphere, 5. *See also specific topics, such as* recognition
opera compared to wrestling, 2
ornamental culture, 151, 193n6
outfits, 97

violence (*continued*)

linity and, 93–94, 106, 148–49, 187n20; messages regarding, 148–49; wrestling vs. real threats of, 152

Wacquant, Loïc, 190n20
Waldstein, David, 192n32
West, Candace, 184n2, 184n4
Willer, Robb, 186n15
Willis, Paul, 20, 185n7
women, degradation of, 110
Wood, Elisabeth, 180n16
Woods, Gregory, 186n12
working-class status: caricatures of, 94; Connell on quandary of, 193n5; embodiment and, 20, 95, 185n7; ethnographies of, 172n10; masculinity and, 95, 145; popular entertainment and, 171n4; poverty and insecurity, 150–51, 176n22; racist assumptions about, 11; suburban background and, 19–20; variation and, 35; wrestler profiles and, 20–21, 35
World Championship Wrestling (wcw), 174n6
World Wrestling Entertainment Cor-

poration (wwe): about, 171n1, 172n1; "attitude era" of, 171n4; cameos from former stars of, 109; competitors of, 174n6; crowd manipulation in, 56; dominance of, 10; dream of reaching, 15–16; earnings in, 176n18; gay wrestler narratives, 186n13; incubator league, 140; indie disaffiliation with, 10–11, 174n8; indie wrestling compared to, 9; injury and, 126; popularity of, 1; scripting in, 79
Wrestlemania, 124
The Wrestler (film), 14
"The Wrestler" (song), 192n34
wrestler profiles: Al, 32–35, *33*; childhood fandom, 19–20; Cuss, 24–27; demographics, 19; Donny, 27–30, *28*; Mike, 30–32; socioeconomic status and, 20–21, 35; table of, 167–69; Timmy, 21–24, *22*; variation in, 35
Wrestling for Gay Guys (Black), *101*

Zamperini, Louie, 183n13
Zborowski, M., 129
Zimmerman, Don H., 184n2, 184n4